International Business Strategy

B H *contemporary* BUSINESS SERIES

Series Editor: Professor Andrew Lock
Manchester Metropolitan University

The Contemporary Business Series is designed with the needs of business studies undergraduates and MBA students in mind, and each title is written in a straightforward, student friendly style. Though all of the books in the series reflect the individuality of their authors, you will find that you can count on certain key features in each text which maintain high standards of structure and approach:

- excellent coverage of core and option subject
- UK/international examples or case studies throughout
- full references and further reading suggestions
- written in direct, easily accessible style, for ease of use by full, part-time and self-study students

Books in the series

Accounting for Business (2nd edition)
Peter Atrill, David Harvey and Edward McLaney

Cases in International Business Strategy
Werner Ketelhöhn and Jan Kubes

Human Resource Management: A Strategic Approach to Employment
Chris Hendry

Information Resources Management
John R. Beaumont and Ewan Sutherland

International Business Strategy
Werner Ketelhöhn

Management Accounting for Financial Decisions
Keith Ward, Sri Srikanthan and Richard Neal

The Management and Marketing of Services
Peter Mudie and Angela Cottam

Organisational Behaviour in International Management
Terence Jackson

Quantitative Approaches to Management
Robert Ball

International Business Strategy

Werner Ketelhöhn

Butterworth-Heinemann Ltd
Linacre House, Jordan Hill, Oxford OX2 8DP

A member of the Reed Elsevier plc group

OXFORD LONDON BOSTON
MUNICH NEW DELHI SINGAPORE SYDNEY
TOKYO TORONTO WELLINGTON

First published 1993
Reprinted 1994, 1995

British Library Cataloguing in Publication Data

Ketelhöhn, Werner
International Business Strategy. –
(Contemporary Business Series)
I. Title II. Series
658.4

ISBN 0 7506 0645 2

Set by Hope Services (Abingdon) Ltd
Printed and bound in Great Britain by Thomson Litho, East Kilbride

Contents

Preface

Business strategy is dependent upon the forward-looking beliefs and values of management and more specifically, by the belief that the future can be determined by executive decision-making. Strategists firmly believe that the future can be shaped.

In practice, however, the first obstacles to strategic choice are the fatalistic beliefs and values found in some management teams. Team members may place undue emphasis on assumptions such as: everything is preordained; forecasting is usually inaccurate; of course, our formula is the right one; with this method we will outsmart our competitors; to succeed all we need do is imitate the market leaders, etc.

If such attitudes predominate, the future of the company will be determined more by external forces than by the decisions of the management team. To exercise a positive influence on the company's future, the management team must develop its own sense of direction – its own strategic intent.

To develop this sense of direction, a model for the understanding of the economic activity in the industry at hand must be used. Here we would recommend, besides the ideas presented in this book, those ideas that make the most sense to *you*. Complicated explanations of business are of no use to strategic decision-makers, and, in practice, would be substituted by those concepts, ideas and simple models that proved to be the most helpful.

We do not recommend using impractical concepts, or models from elastomechanics, Boolean algebra or even militaristic metaphors or myths with mysterious connections with the Japanese and Germans. Our recommendation is simple: use only the business ideology that helps you to understand what is going on in your economy, industry and business; that business ideology that helps you to set your own strategic direction and influences your strategic decision-making.

If your current business ideology fails you in a particular situation, don't take refuge in some mystical Far Eastern philosophy or military tradition. Seek help in the business frameworks explained in this book; they have a good track record in understanding business with the purpose of problem-solving.

We're not arguing that ideas, models and experiences in other human activities are of no use in creating appropriate analogies for business. We believe that our duty as students is to get out there and learn how real business people understand their businesses, and then – based on their constructs – try to make some generalizations that can be used in other businesses.

This book is based upon the value of learning from real businesses. The business ideology presented in Part One was derived from ideas formed through the observation of Benetton, IMS, NWZ and SEMCO. This approach to learning also contributed to Part Two in the form of the search for similarities and differences between ABB Robotics, IBM and Uponor Oy.

The beliefs, values, and attitudes about the future and the superstitions about successful foreign competitors – generally the Japanese and Germans –

are at the centre of developed and underdeveloped[1] minds. Whereas the former strongly believe in controlling the future and consider it in terms of business ideologies; the latter either seek refuge in fate or worse still, use meta-economic models and reasoning to cover up for their lack of understanding of business and management. In essence, there are no developed or underdeveloped countries; there are only people with beliefs, values and attitudes that are developed or underdeveloped.

For instance, an underdeveloped, fatalistic attitude exists where people believe that only fools work, and that workers are, and always will be, exploited by the ruling classes. They believe that their future is somehow preordained. Obviously, such attitudes are useless for strategic thinking.

Strategic thinking demands a proactive attitude and a deeply held conviction that the future is built with managerial decisions based on appropriate business ideologies and not with mysterious meta-economic myths.

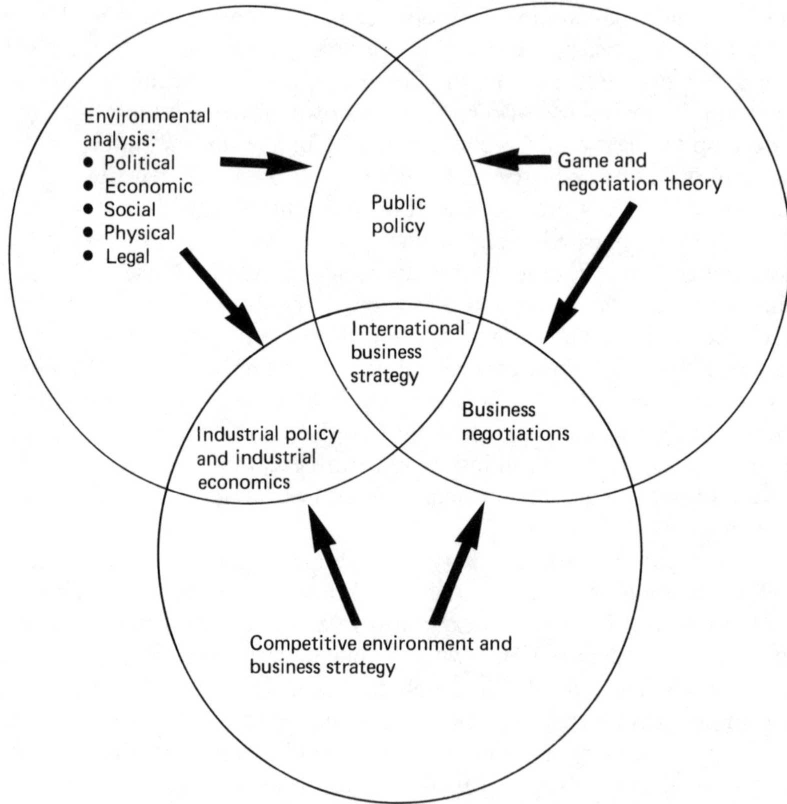

One view of international business strategy

The above figure illustrates the three groups of disciplines in which our conception of international business strategy has its roots. The circle on the left groups the disciplines providing conceptual frameworks that help practising

[1] This is a relative concept, people are developed or underdeveloped depending to whom they are being compared.

managers to understand the country environment in which their business units operates. We discovered the need to understand environmental forces while living through several years of Central American social revolt. From this experience we offer the frameworks that proved useful for understanding a business environment.

The circle on the right groups the theoretical foundations with which the allocation of resources in a society can be examined. We researched in detail case studies on business negotiations – point observations of reality. Finally, the third circle at the bottom of the graph groups concepts and frameworks useful for understanding the competitive environment.

I have been engaged in research and business strategy consultancy since 1974, formerly in Latin America and latterly in Europe, and have gained numerous insights on how to understand an industry. In my view, international business strategy is the overlap of the three circles, and I present in this book a summary of my experience in these fields. I recognize that this definition is as arbitrary as any other, but I present it to show where my experience originates, and why I'm interested in such diverse problems.

I would like to acknowledge the contributions of many students of the management problem, whose ideas I present and use here. Without those thinkers this book would not have been written. I realize that these ideas may have emerged simultaneously in different places, and that by giving credit to one author, or none, I may fail to acknowledge someone's contribution. For this I apologize in advance and ask for understanding. I am especially grateful to the hundreds of MBA students and executives who have corrected my ideas and ensured that I have kept only those that passed their rigorous, utilitarian tests.

Finally, I apologize to our female readers for the use of male gender throughout the book. I made this choice for reasons of style, and advise them to read *She* whenever it says *He*.

Werner Ketelhöhn

Introduction

International Business Strategy draws its justification from the fact that books on international business generally concentrate on financial markets, macroeconomics, foreign trade, currency fluctuations, marketing problems, international law or political risk, but seldom examine the impact of events, trends, and environmental pressures occurring in foreign markets on the strategic posture of business units. The purpose of this book is to provide a set of ideas and organizing concepts for use when thinking about the strategic posture of business units operating in international markets. It is hoped that these will be useful to practising managers, strategy consultants and business schools' professors in the solution of strategic adjustment problems.

The strategic posture of a corporation is composed of its shared vision, specific objectives, strategic decisions and business policies. The key message is that there is no such thing as a purely deliberate – nor randomly generated – strategic posture in corporations engaged in global competition: a business unit's strategic posture results from adapting corporate strategic postures to a market's environmental pressures. In short, global corporate strategic postures are sensitive to market-specific environmental events, human resources, leadership style and subsidiary culture.

Since no one knows enough to work out every detail of a strategic posture in a market in advance, nor how to correctly forecast all environmental pressures, business unit managers must constantly adjust the strategic posture of their firm to the pressures of the environment in which they operate. Business unit managers must construct a strategic posture that incorporates all market-specific demands and pressures while maintaining those key elements of the corporate strategic posture that characterize their firm. This process of strategic adaptation is essentially a synthetic proposition: the business unit manager identifies key events, trends and pressures in his environment and examines their impact on the strategic posture and operations of his company.

This book reflects the fact that international business cannot be reduced to foreign trade, currency speculation, accounting or politics, but that at some point in an international manager's career he has to live, work and successfully lead a business unit within a foreign environment, where economics, politics and other events interact with the strategic posture and operations of the firm. Therefore, this book not only offers the missing unified framework for the country manager's job but also complements publications in all other categories, particularly those dealing with managing subsidiaries in foreign markets.

International Business Strategy starts by examining the theoretical frameworks developed from both research and consulting experience in the triad countries. Part One – 'Competitive and Cooperative Business Strategy' – presents the author's easy-to-use framework for strategic analysis.

The essential forces affecting the international corporation and alternative organizational forms are examined and discussed in Part Two – 'International Business Strategy'. For instance, the well-accepted notion that corporations have to nourish and protect champions within their organizations is challenged.

The identification of environmental events, trends and pressures – with their significance to the strategic posture of a company – are discussed in Part Three – 'Understanding Environmental Pressures'. Here, simple models demonstrating how to understand the economy and political forces in a country are presented.

Finally, in Part Four – 'Doing Business in Turbulent Environments' – we discuss the changes originating in inflationary forces and violently changing environments.

In essence, this book takes the international business strategy debate a step further: it deals with those strategic problems that every business unit manager, business school educator, and business consultant confronts in his international, executive, teaching and/or consulting career.

Part One

Competitive and Cooperative Business Strategy

In this part we present our framework for the understanding of management and business strategy. This framework or business ideology combines Michael Porter's ideas with those originating in systems analysis, which have been developed by academics and consultants. We have found this model very useful when trying to understand an industry.

An ideology is a set of interrelated beliefs,[1] values[2] and attitudes[3] that form the basis upon which we construct our frameworks and models to pass judgements, generate alternatives, make choices and express preferences. An ideology provides us with the means to understand the world: it provides our 'weltanschauung'.

What we propose is a 'geschaeftsanschauung' – business perspective – that is consistent in explaining most events in the business world, no matter what industry we examine. For business strategy we present a robust ideology, capable of explaining an industry in a way that is consistent with the understanding of other industries.

All frameworks are created to simplify complexity in a way that helps the thinking processes of decision-makers. The goal is to understand reality, and then to shape it. Useful models have three properties: first, they increase our understanding of complexity; second, they are used for proactive decision-making; and third, they produce simple, feasible, acceptable and implementable decisions.

We believe that our business ideology is able to incorporate the changes occurring in technological, physical, political, economical and social environments into the analysis. Our ideology is dynamic, it changes to explain new events in the environment, and does so in a way consistent with all previous explanations of similar phenomena.

Consider the Benetton's rags-to-riches story, which provides fantastic opportunities to learn about strategy and management. Over the past thirty years, self-made billionaire Luciano Benetton has created, without formal education or business degrees, the world's best example of a successful network company. By the mid-1970s, when Benetton's agent-retail concept was already fully developed, Luciano, his brothers and sister, still lacked formal training in finance and business strategy, let alone in agency and network theory. However, they created a network of entrepreneurs in ignorance of the many game-theoretic lucubrations discussed by outstanding mathematicians. This success demonstrates that there are no right or wrong business ideologies; rather, we would argue that managers should use the ideas that help them the most in understanding their businesses.

Before I present this part, I would like to recognize the contributions of Kenneth

[1] Beliefs are the basic relationships that we assume exist between two things, e.g. work produces prosperity and freedom as opposed to work is God's curse on mankind. Our belief and value systems determine our understanding of ourselves and our surrounding world.

[2] Values are concerned with what is right or wrong, with what should and should not be done, e.g. people should work as opposed to people should avoid work.

[3] Attitudes are assumptions based on our beliefs and values, e.g. people in the southern hemisphere will never reach Japanese productivity, as opposed to people's productivity depends on their beliefs, values and attitudes.

Andrews, Roland Christensen, Xavier Gilbert, Ray Goldberg, Jan Kubes, Michael Porter, Paul Strebel, and many other students of management, towards the ideas explained in this part. However, I am responsible totally for conceptual misinterpretations that may have occurred.

The strategy concept

Our concept of strategy is dynamic. Dynamic, because it evolves as the environmental conditions evolve. According to Aldo Palmeri, chief strategist of the Benetton family for ten years, 'the nature of a network organization changes in different environments: what works well in Italy may not do so in Japan, and vice versa; that is why we must adapt our organization to the local conditions and culture'. Thus the concept of strategy must be adaptable to different cultures and industries.

Our concept of strategy is really 'a strategic management process' that adapts the corporation's basic posture to the different environments in which it is present. These processes can be summarized within the 'Strategic posture' presented in the illustration below, which is defined as the set of management processes that specify the following components:

1 A vision for the business.
2 Its specific objectives.
3 The corresponding strategic decisions.
4 The business policies that ensure that the myriad of small daily decisions are complementary.

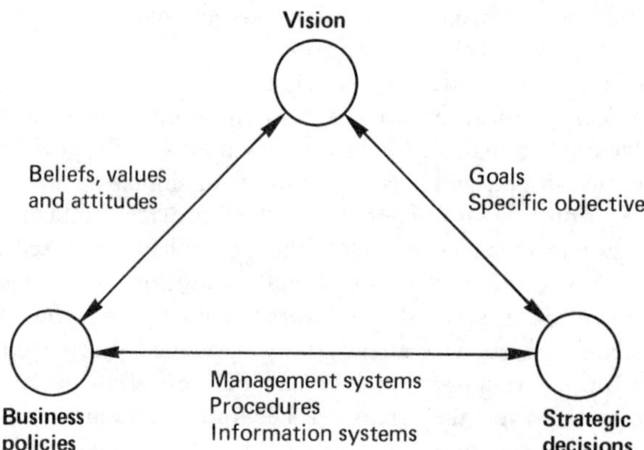

Strategic posture

The 'vision' of the business is defined for an environment by its socioeconomic mission in that society, in terms of the needs of consumers and other interest groups,[4] in that country or in its country of origin.

For instance, IBM's vision to emphasize systems integration in the 1990s originated in an earlier outlook for the computer industry. Based on this vision, top managers set

[4] An interest group is an individual or group of individuals who influence, directly or indirectly, the behaviour of an organization.

in motion a series of organizational changes designed to create the organization capable of competing in the solution business of the 1990s.

Choosing a vision is like choosing the destination for a journey. The point on a map results from past visions, present environmental conditions and scenarios of possible futures. The vision results from a complex blend of people's desires, company capabilities and environmental opportunities.

The vision generates a set of clear and achievable specific objectives, the mission, which guides 'strategic decision-making'. These are important investment decisions taken to accomplish strategic objectives. Strategic decisions make use of considerable corporate resources, have long-term consequences and are extremely difficult to reverse. Strategic investments put the business one step closer to fulfilling its mission in the marketplace.

The vision is also dynamic and flexible because it evolves over the years as it is adapted for changing environmental conditions; thus it is fair to say that the mission of a business is fulfilled each time a set of specific objectives is achieved, but that the vision of the business is an ever escaping goal.

Finally, 'business policies' are the set of formal and informal rules that guide the thousands of small decisions taken by corporate executives managing a wide variety of issues. These policies guide daily operative decisions so that they are consistent with the overall strategic direction of the business; they can be used to concentrate operative decision-making on a chosen strategy. Business policies coordinate operative decision-making by providing a guide that produces complementary decisions in the different parts of the corporation.

Nestlé, for example, modified its strategic posture in baby foods in the 1980s because of intense pressure originating from radical groups in developed countries. Motivated by this pressure, Nestlé's specific commercialization policies for baby food in developing countries were modified.

Clearly, since the strategic posture is dynamic: it changes through time and environments, it is very important to understand the processes that generate its different components. By controlling these processes one controls the shape of the future strategic posture. For instance, a shared vision, an institutional vision, of the business and its goals, guides the diverse business activities of the long line through space and time of executives, employees and projects.

The development of a shared vision is not based on large analyses nor does it require star consultants. A shared vision evolves over time by accumulating experience on technologies, industries and markets, in which, and with which, the company competes. This shared vision emerges from the interactions of executives, employees and workers; and from the processes set in motion by management and pressure groups.

Our concept of Strategy comprises of processes that generate strategic postures in the various countries in which a corporation competes.

1 The enterprise system

1.1 The business web

Most people have difficulties defining the industry in which their company competes because it is not clear to them what business their companies are in. Reviewing what the business literature says does not help either, because most authors avoid defining explicitly an industry. In this chapter we take a courageous step forward and propose that an industry is composed by whatever businesses we consider to be important for understanding the dynamics of competition and cooperation for our business. We propose that differences in these definitions have their roots in different understandings of an industry, and that managers must learn to live with these differences.

Consider – for instance – the following description of the computer industry offered by Richard Florida and Martin Kenney in 'Silicon Valley and Route 128 Won't Save Us' (*California Management Review*, autumn 1990).

> The computer industry is divided into at least ten separate segments, with only a handful of companies like IBM, DEC and Hewlett-Packard, important players in more than one. The mainframe segment remains dominated by IBM, and to a lesser extent by the remaining members of the BUNCH (Burroughs, Univac (now Unisys), NCR, Control Data and Honeywell (now out of business); two Japanese players, Fujitsu and Hitachi, have also joined this sector, as well as plug-compatible manufacturers like Amdahl. DEC, Data General, IBM and HP are the major producers of minicomputers. Fault-tolerant computers are made by Tandem, Stratus, and Tolerant Systems. Sun Microsystems and Hewlett-Packard are the largest producers of engineering workstations. Apple, IBM and Compaq dominate the personal computer segment. Laptops are made by Compaq, Grid Systems, and Zenith, including Agis, Go Corporation, Information Appliance, and Poqet Computer, which is 38 per cent owned by Fujitsu.
>
> The supercomputer segment is populated by more than twenty-five companies, which compete in a variety of areas. Recently, Cray Research has been challenged by Supercomputers Systems, a company founded by a former Cray computer scientist, Steven Chen, and forty-five defecting Cray employees. The supercomputer segment has divided into a series of mini-segments. . . .

Most industry experts follow a common sequence of ideas and concepts when they describe their industry. First, they refer to companies in the industry by grouping them according to the types of products they sell and the markets they serve. This defines the boundaries of the industry. Second, they classify the different companies in similar competitive segments, which we will call 'business nodes'. For instance, the computer industry was quickly described with ten different business nodes: mainframes, minicomputers, fault-tolerant computers, workstations, personal computers, laptops, notebooks, and several nodes of supercomputers. Third, experts then describe the activities performed by the companies in a business node. It is clear that the understanding of an industry and its activities depends upon the businesses included in its description and the way these businesses are grouped to define business nodes.

By describing business nodes – and the activities in them – industry experts seem to recognize that existing economic disequilibria provide the hard evidence needed for industry description. An economic disequilibrium exists in those places where demand is greater than supply, or vice versa, for current and perceived future prices. Thus entrepreneurs operating in these business nodes seek to satisfy customer needs by selling and buying the products and services in demand, from each other.

There are many reasons why experts prefer to talk about business nodes first in order to understand an industry. The most important is that their understanding of the industry is made explicit through the companies that are included in their analysis. A second reason is that 'corporate activities' do not face the rigours of the marketplace and may have been created by 'corporate overhead'. Over the years, Parkinson's laws[1] create a lack of motivation, increased costs and a 'management' that creates activities not needed to deliver value but instead to preserve management's existence. Thus, by grouping similar competitors in business nodes before we study a company's activities, we can analyse value-adding and unnecessary activities (those created by Parkinson's laws) in that industry sector. We add value just by discovering which activities are not needed. For instance, consider the activities of corporate champions that are nurtured intentionally to fight corporate overhead; these activities are, in a way, created to justify the very existence of corporate overhead.

We must be careful when we think about industry activities. Assuming technological rigidity in a business node is wrong. We should never assume that competitors use the same technology for sourcing, processing, delivering and supporting when there are several dynamic alternatives, nor ignore the possibility that companies following different strategies may perform different value adding activities, or the same activities differently. When it comes to the value being added by activities, we find it much easier to discuss the activities performed by companies following specific strategies. Comparisons between the way competitors perform their value-adding activities provide us with facts and generate insights for competitive and cooperative decision-making.

1.2 Business nodes

Thus an economy can be conceived as a set of interconnected nodes in which economic activity takes place (see Figure 1.1). Entrepreneurs localize economic

[1] In the late 1950s, British economist Cyril Northcote Parkinson proposed the following laws for collective behaviour in big organizations:

1 Every employee needs at least two assistants.
2 The number of employees grows geometrically through time, regardless of the work needed to deliver value.
3 All employees are effectively busy managing each other.
4 Work keeps expanding to fill the time available.

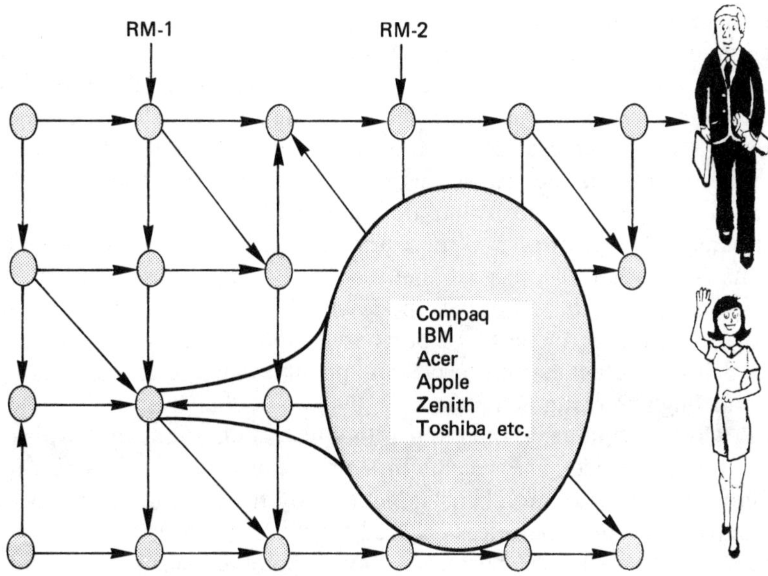

Figure 1.1 Laptop computer business node

disequilibria – nodes – and proceed to buy raw materials, components and other inputs; hire some people and install businesses that supply the goods and services in demand. Consequently they have a double role: first, finding or creating disequilibria and second, restoring economic equilibrium by satisfying demand.

Consider the business node containing laptop computers. In addition to the companies already mentioned, it also contains Toshiba, IBM, Acer and Apple, all competing for a share of the pie. But these companies are basically assemblers of the components manufactured by many other companies that are located in neighbouring business nodes, such as semiconductor suppliers, disk drive suppliers, monitor manufacturers, keyboard suppliers and so on. Each one of these nodes, in turn contains companies competing for a piece of the pie. Thus, each node contains a group of businesses exploiting the value to be added by selling a specific product/service that pays off.

Definition 1: *The value added by a business is the difference between the price paid for purchased inputs and the price at which the product/services are sold.*
Axiom 1: *Each product has a value added, it is the difference between the cost of purchased inputs and its selling price.*

The total value added in a node can be calculated by the difference between the inputs purchased by all competitors in the node and their corresponding selling prices. Notice that overhead costs, labour costs, financial costs, etc. have not been included in the definition; only the difference between purchased inputs and selling price because the value added measures the premium that the customer is willing to pay; value added does not relate to difficulty of production, costs, or any other measure of value.

Two more things need to be noted: first, the value added will differ between competitors in a node because of different selling prices and purchasing costs; and second, where value added is low, it is generally hard to make money because there is little money to deal with in the first place.

Clearly, some people will exploit the value added better than others. Thus the company with the lowest cost in a price category sets a competitive benchmark – its cost – that all other competitors face. In this sense, the activities of companies competing in a business node should be compared on a full-cost basis, that is, including the costs of purchased inputs. Comparing only processing and delivery activities may leave out possible value-gains or cost-savings achieved through sourcing activities.

This is why consultants, Hanna and Lundquist,[2] talk about the surplus available in a business node. The surplus in a price category of a business node is the difference between the total costs, incurred by the lowest cost competitor in that price category, and the prices charged for its product/services.

As shown in Table 1.1, all businesses have a potential surplus: it is the profit before taxes[3] of the lowest cost producer in their price category. The lowest cost (75 per cent of sales) producer of the three competitors in this business node, sets its profit margin (25 per cent of sales) as a competitive benchmark. The different margins of the other two competitors in the business node show that not everyone is harvesting the available surplus of 25 per cent. Since for every successful micro-computer company, for instance, there were many failures, one can easily conclude that not everyone is capable of making money in places with economic disequilibria. Competitors in different price categories of a node have different potential surpluses.

Table 1.1 Surplus available in a business node

Company	*Sales*	*Cost as % sales*	*Profit as % sales*	*Surplus as % sales*
A	100	80	20	25
B	100	75	25	25
C	100	78	22	25
Total			67	75

Definition 2: *A business exists only where entrepreneurs perceive profitable value to be added in the long run.*

A business is sustainable if in the long run the value added is enough to pay for the costs of the value-adding activities and also to leave some profit for the investors. Thus competitors in a node have two degrees of freedom to increase their profits from a product/service: either they decrease their total costs or

[2] Hanna, Alistair M. and Lundquist, Jerrold T., 'Creative strategies', *The McKinsey Quarterly*, 1990, No. 3.

[3] As percentage of sales.

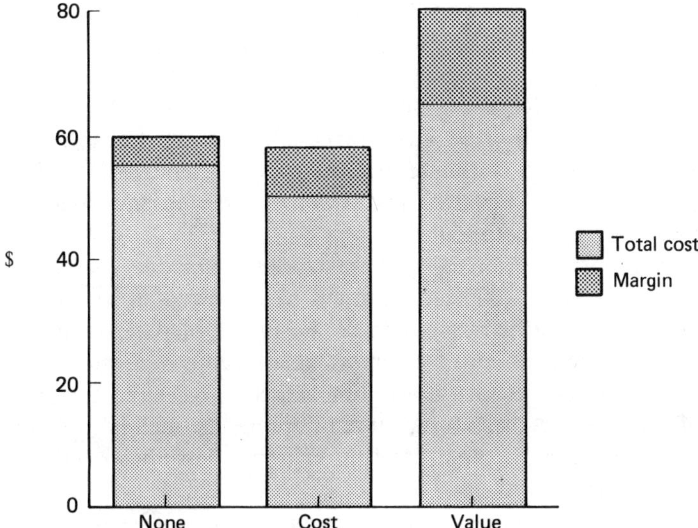

Figure 1.2 Strategic drives
Adapted from the ideas of Michael Porter[4]

increase their prices (see Figure 1.2). Businesses prosper if they do these things well, otherwise they fail because their potential surplus is lost to some neighbouring business-node or a competitor.

Michael Porter showed us his five forces and other ideas to analyse the structural economic conditions in a business node. His framework has helped us understand the changes in the number of competitors in a node and the alternative ways to compete profitably. He brings into consideration the questions to be asked when considering entering to compete in a business node:

1 Is it easy or difficult and why?
2 What are the structural economic reasons explaining the existence of the companies in a node?
3 What is their value added, their surplus, their margins?
4 How many competitors can the market sustain?
5 What is the minimum size necessary to achieve economies of scale? And so on.

(We will not discuss Michael Porter's framework in this book, we assume familiarity with his ideas.)

1.3 Strategic decision-making

Traditional strategic analysis has asked: how much is the profit margin in this business node and how can we capture it? Of course, what really matters is not

[4] Porter, Michael E., 'On competitive strategy', *Harvard Business School Video Series*, 1988.

the potential profit margin or value added that we control in a business node, but the returns that we are able to make by working within the captured value added.[5]

Return on equity (ROE), a static point of view, tells us a lot about past business attractiveness. For businesses located in different countries, an alternative measure of return is the return on capital employed (ROCE).[6] ROCE eliminates the effects of different tax laws and banking environments. How do we examine strategic investment decisions?

The most important financial concepts for strategic decisions deal with capital investment decisions.[7] The discounted cash flow of a business is the best measure of the present attractiveness of the future of that business. Instead of looking at past returns of a business, management must find sustainable returns on investment in future economic disequilibria: the future value to be added will be found at these future disequilibria. The idea is to identify and get ready to harvest future profits; but future profits depend on future technology and market dynamics.

The difficulties of finding the net present value (NPV) of strategic investments, let alone the NPV of a business, are: first, finding where disequilibria will occur; second, estimating future demand; third, studying existing technology; fourth, investing in the right technology to harvest future profits; and fifth, innovating products with newly available technology.

Why not simply add up the capital investment budgets of all departments to obtain the strategy of the firm by default? If these investments have positive NPVs for acceptable discount rates, shouldn't the resulting strategy be acceptable? The answer is no. Using this approach a company loses focus, and in the long run, it ends up with over-extended, or even without, capabilities, i.e. a random-walk strategy. A company should not invest in all projects originating in investment budgets: strategic investments should capitalize on company capabilities, those things at which the company does a competent job. If the latter advice is followed, eventually specialization occurs and these capabilities turn into distinctive competencies. Excellence in these capabilities is reached through the cultivation and protection of a selected set of basic company skills. But to do this we need a clear vision of what skills to cultivate.

To illustrate the complexity of these strategic decisions let us consider forecasting price-volume relationships for a potential product.[8] At a given price it pays the company to increase its production until its marginal contribution disappears. If the surplus is attractive, a number of competitors may also enter the market, and over time the increased supply may lower the price, a clear drive towards economic equilibrium.

When the supply exceeds demand the price may fall below the average unit cost of the lowest cost producer; it is here when all producers feel the crunch

[5] Myers, Stewart C., 'Finance theory and financial strategy', *Interfaces*, vol. 14, Jan.–Feb. 1984, pp. 126-37.

[6] The return before taxes and interests on long-term debt, divided by equity plus long-term debt.

[7] Ketelhöhn, Werner R. and Marin, Jose N., 'Decisiones Estrategicas: Un Enfoque Mulitdimensional', *Libro Libre*, 1991, San Jose, Costa Rica.

[8] Bilas, Richard A., *Microeconomic Theory: A Graphical Analysis*, McGraw-Hill, 1967.

and the most inefficient may leave the market. If so, supply diminishes and prices may increase again. In real life things are not so simple, companies don't enter and leave markets so swiftly. (Porter also showed us the barriers to entry and exit from a business node.)

However, when companies intend to compete in a business node that approaches conditions of economic equilibrium, they have only two ways to maintain high prices: first, they may attempt to create differentiated products by increasing quality, services or choosing to serve specially created market segments; and second, they may attempt to cooperate with their competitors and agree to sell the products/services at cartel prices. Otherwise, they are forced to lower their costs, either through efficiency drives, new technology or by pressuring their suppliers. Thus, there are only five situations in which companies in a business node near to equilibrium will not compete on price:

1 If they can't source the required inputs.
2 If they can't produce an identical product.
3 If they can't lower their costs.
4 If they can't deliver to special market segments.
5 If they agree to form a price cartel.

Strategists revise the feasibility and sustainability of projects justified with price–volume projections that don't meet one of the above five criteria. But demand will depend on what competitors choose to do, and therefore, price–volume projections have to take into account dynamic, rather than static, microeconomic relations.

Consider Apple Computer, which for years concentrated on milking its Macintosh line of micro-computers, and refused to lower its prices to the PC-clone levels. In 1990, however, Microsoft's release of Windows 3.0 forced them to offer low-priced Macintoshes. By December 1990, despite a backlog of tens of thousands unfulfilled orders for their new computers, some observers argued that Macintosh had lost the battle of the standards to the PC-clones; that most of the new software would be developed for MS-Windows, which in November 1990 sold thousands of copies. With capital investment analysis we could prove these arguments right or wrong if we only knew how many Macintoshes will be sold at the new low price.

Thus, today's strategic investment decisions in products, markets and technologies determine future sales, costs and ultimately, cash flows. So, although in theory the best strategy corresponds to the alternative producing the highest NPV, in practice it is nearly impossible to conceive all future business dynamics, let alone to obtain reliable numbers for calculating NPVs for the whole corporation.

1.4 Vision: a strategic intent

Finding future economic disequilibria, that is, business nodes in which to compete, is equivalent to defining business units. This job is better performed by entrepreneurs, because big corporations, like governments distorting an economy's incentive systems, also tend to distort their managers' ability to find and exploit these disequilibria. Therefore, *defining business units properly – part of a corporation's organizational strategy – is the most important strategic decision in a corporation.* It follows that getting reliable cash flow projections for these business units, under alternative strategic scenarios, is an important step in strategic thinking.

However, experienced business people avoid substituting sound industry and company understanding with quantified variables that may be wild guesses for future company value. Strategic thinking is much more than a simple numbers game. To perform the complex, strategic capital investment analysis for a business unit, most successful business people refuse to follow a wishful number game and prefer to first set a strategic direction based on experience and some rationale in order to consider feasible future scenarios.

This is why strategic analysis starts with questions like: Where do we come from?; Where are we?; Where do we want to go?; How can we get there? To answer these questions the proactive reasoning goes something like this:

1 Following some logical framework the environmental variables affecting future sales and costs of the business are examined.
2 The above analysis leads to the selection of a strategic intent: a general direction (vision) and specific objectives (mission).
3 To accomplish the specific objectives a number of strategic investments are identified.
4 Finally, capital investment techniques are used to determine the payoffs and attractiveness of these investment projects.

This approach uses investment analysis to check the financial attractiveness of the chosen strategic investment decisions; the projects must increase the total value of the business unit. Strategists reason that the net present value of the business unit is maximized if the investment projects are identified by selecting a strategic direction first, and then analysing the projects needed to accomplish the selected objective.

Consider Cray Computer's refusal,[9] in the mid-1980s, to develop 'super-minicomputers' for the commercial market. Despite the extremely profitable projections found in their project analysis, top management rejected the move arguing that it would dilute the strengths of the company and divert them from their present 'supercomputer' niche; a clear statement of strategic intent about the chosen direction.

The SKIL Corporation,[10] another American company, rejected manufacturing portable power tools for mass merchandisers and discount stores, arguing that this would undermine their support to their distribution channels. Again, a strategic argument overriding profitable business and a 33 per cent jump in size.

[9] Porter, Michael E., 'On competitive strategy', *Harvard Business School Video Series*, 1988.
[10] Ibid.

In both cases investment analysis could have been used – in theory – to show that these 'strategic decisions' were right (if the total NPV of Cray or SKIL were greater without the additional business than with it) or wrong (if the contrary was true). Despite the fact that the estimated returns on the new investments were extremely attractive, both companies decided not to get involved in the 'new' business. They did so without looking at explicit estimates of the NPV of the potential 'new' company; they were guided by their shared vision of what they wanted to be.

Both examples show that shaping the future of a business is still more a matter of strategic will or strategic intent to guide strategic decisions than a matter of forecasting for investment analysis. How do we know that the vision, goals or intent are all right? Could they not produce wrong decisions? Clearly yes! Obviously, experience, judgement and common sense are at the core of business strategy. In essence, experienced business people believe in positive NPVs of a business only if they can explain the strategy qualitatively.

1.5 The enterprise system

Four clearly distinct generic business activities help us think about strategy in a business node: sourcing, processing, delivery and support activities. For better understanding of these ideas let us propose two definitions illustrated in Figure 1.3:

> **Definition 3:** *Downstream businesses are the set of all customers, and customers of customers, of the competitors established in a particular business node.*

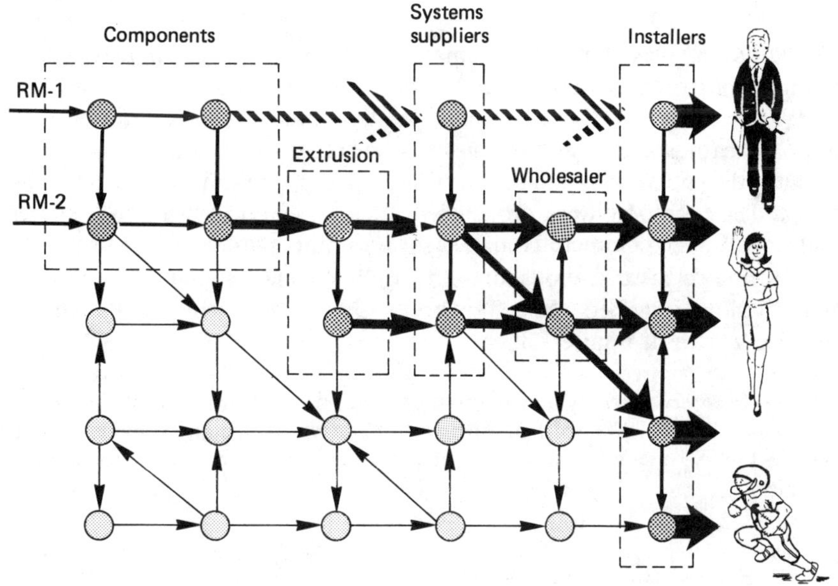

Figure 1.3 The enterprise system of Uponor Oy's Hot Water Systems Division

Definition 4: *Upstream businesses are the set of all suppliers, and suppliers of suppliers, of the competitors established in a particular business node.*

Three things need to be noted in these definitions: first, that they are relative to a business node (businesses are located both upstream of their customer set and downstream of their supplier set); second, that downstream business activities are more concerned with the delivery and consumption of a business node's product/services, whereas upstream business activities are more concerned with the sourcing of a business node's inputs; third, that Michael Porter's five forces model for competitive analysis can easily be applied to individual business nodes.

Porter's model is simple, easy to understand and is used worldwide because it produces robust and consistent results. We believe, however, that the understanding of an industry can be increased if we include more than just three types of business nodes in the study of an industry (suppliers, competitors and customers). As illustrated by our business web, things are more interdependent, therefore our model represents this complexity without losing simplicity and usefulness. What we propose is a model that includes all businesses that serve the final consumer, the *enterprise system.*

Definition 5: *An industry's enterprise system is the sequence of existing businesses between the supplier of raw materials (physical or other) and the final consumer of the product or service.*
Axiom 2: *An element in an enterprise system exists if, and only if, it contains at least one business exploiting an economic disequilibrium.*

The first applications of systems analysis in the study of an industry appear in the work of Davis and Goldberg[11] in the late 1950s.

Consider Uponor Oy, a conglomerate of about 60 operating companies which sold US$800 million in 1990. Uponor specialized in the development and manufacture of plastic pipes systems for a wide range of industrial sectors, including construction, municipal engineering, agriculture and forestry. The Hot Water Systems (HWS) division manufactured cross-linked polyethylene pipes for heating and tap-water systems. A range of products was marketed through independent companies or subsidiaries as semi-finished or as complete systems. The best sales were obtained by Velta and Polytherm, both successful brand names in the German complete-systems market.

In a strategic review workshop, fifty of the business unit managers in the HWS division described their industry with the six elements shown in the enterprise system of Figure 1.3:

> The *raw material suppliers* they referred to were mainly pellet suppliers like Neste. This view clearly eliminated from their considerations the suppliers of raw materials used in the manufacture of the components – a conscious choice for industry definition.

[11] Davis, John H. and Goldberg, Ray A., *A Concept of Agribusiness*, Division of Research, Harvard Graduate School of Business Administration, Boston, Mass, 1957). Goldberg's later work dealt mainly with agribusiness systems on a global scale (long before global became an important buzz word).

The *component suppliers* included in their discussions were classified in several business nodes: manifolds, connectors, panels, steel meshes, foils, insulation, controls, regulators, boilers and radiator manufacturers. A total of ten different types of business nodes.

The *pipe manufacturers* were considered to be important enough to warrant their inclusion as one element in the enterprise system.

The *systems suppliers* – Velta, Polytherm, etc. – were started by entrepreneurs who, having identified a market need (economic disequilibrium) decided to satisfy it with complete kits for underfloor hot water heating. As the market reacted favourably to such systems, brand name loyalties developed and several competitors entered the market because the barriers to entry were low.

Several *specialist wholesalers* populate the European building market. They deal with all construction materials, including hot water systems.

Finally, *independent installers* were considered important because of their influence in buying decisions.

The first thing to be noted in a model of an enterprise system is that the elements of the model are symbols, often including several business nodes. For example, in the fashion industry – cut, make and trim subcontractors may include several tiers of subcontractors, which in turn may work for different assemblers of final products: sweaters, shirts, coats and so on. Similarly, automobile engine assemblers may use the same subcontractors as other engine assemblers.

An element of the enterprise system is just a grouping of related business nodes, for instance, manufacturers of car components include many different types of business nodes: electronics, bearings, plastic parts, etc. It is clear that including a particular business node in an element depends upon our understanding of the industry. In fact, the definition of the enterprise system of an industry is a matter of our personal understanding of what is going on.

The second thing to be noted is that the business nodes, included in an element of the enterprise system, may be exploiting radically different economic disequilibria, for example, producing electronic, mechanical or plastic components for cars. However, in any element of the enterprise system, competitors are in a continuous search to improve products, processes and services. The company that concerns itself with choosing the right technologies, processes, products and markets, probably learns the fastest.

The selection of the businesses to include in an enterprise system is a matter of judgement. The 'best' representation is the one that better facilitates our understanding of the industry (i.e. our definition of the industry). It is important to realize that under the definitions and axioms presented above, managers will define different enterprise systems for the same 'industry' – none of which is 'wrong'. There are no right or wrong enterprise systems, only different ways to understand the current situation and the potential future disequilibria in the 'industry'. The best model is the one that helps *us* more.

We realize that proposing that an industry is whatever you understand it to be does not provide the tranquillizing certainty found in 'knowledge' or 'formulas'; but uncertainty is what business is all about, and an industry's definition should be flexible: it should change through time, space and the business people that work in it.

1.6 The value added chain

A business looking for competitive advantage can use this systemic view of industry definition to identify where in the system the value added can be exploited most profitably. Since the elements of the enterprise system are defined by actual competitors, we look at the value added by them as illustrated by the value added chain[12] shown in figure 1.4.

> **Definition 6:** *The value added chain in an enterprise system presents the way the full retail price is distributed among the different elements in the system.*
> **Axiom 3:** *In each element of the enterprise system the value added equals the difference between the price paid for purchased inputs and the price at which the product/services are sold to the next element.*

The best place to capture value added may occur in some downstream or upstream element of the system, and may be best achieved by redefining products, markets, technologies, or something else, so that a bigger share of the value to be added by the entire industry is controlled.

For Uponor's hot water systems division, for instance, the value added chain was estimated to be in 1989:

Table 1.2 Estimated value added chain for Uponor's hot water systems division

	%
Raw material suppliers	8
Component suppliers	18
Pipe extruders	10
Systems suppliers	16
Wholesalers	13
Installers	35
Consumers	100

Clearly, forward or backward integration is not the only means to control value added. Joseph L. Bower points to some of the following six implications:

1 If the retail price is driven down by competition, then the value added in all elements of the system is reduced. For example, when Timex's retailing strategy of using mass merchandisers to retail their watches lowered consumer prices, some Swiss watch manufacturers were left with no value to add.
2 The relative importance and number of intermediate competitors determines how the remaining values added is shared. For instance, Intel, in the micro

[12] A definition of value added chain proposed by Bower, Joseph L. Simple, *Economic Tools for Strategic Analysis*, 9/373-094, publishing division Harvard Business School, 1972, Boston, MA 02163.

computer industry, enjoys a near monopoly on processor chips and as a result is sometimes able to claim about 10 per cent of a machine's retail price.

3 Businesses competing in an element of the system may add different values because their technology, costs and delivered value differ. For instance, General Motors in the US produced small cars at much higher costs than in those US plants belonging to their joint venture with Toyota.

4 The enterprise system used by high volume-low cost(price) competitors may differ from the system used by high price(quality)-low volume competitors. Clearly, the enterprise systems used by Rolex and Swatch are different because their strategies are different. Rolex retails through jewellery stores whereas Swatch sells just about everywhere.

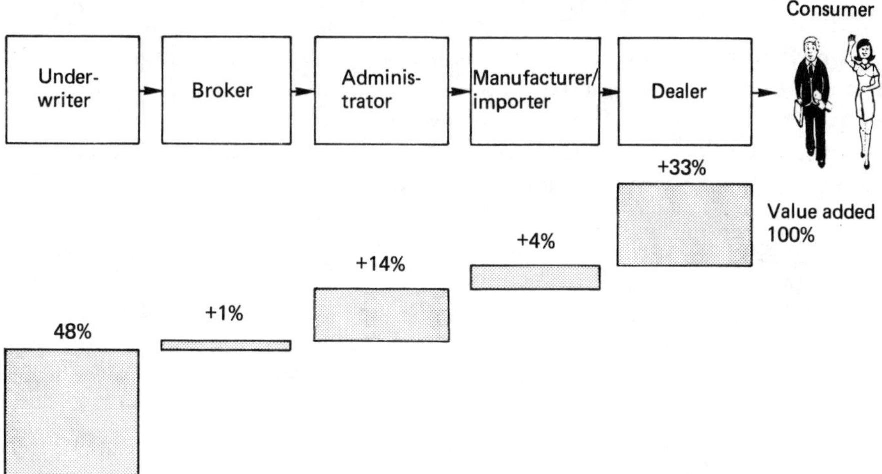

Figure 1.4 The value added chain of the extended car warranty industry in the UK

5 The value added by companies following different strategies may also differ in each element of the enterprise system. Again, the value added by Rolex, for example, differs from that added by Swatch in the common elements of their enterprise systems.

6 Finally, even when value added is low, return on investment can be very high and conversely, when the value added is highest, return on investment can be the lowest. For instance, retail commands about 50 per cent of the value added in many enterprise systems; yet it does not necessarily yield the highest returns on investment.

When the value added in an element of the enterprise system ceases to be attractive, the system eliminates the companies in that element. Clearly, in elements with large value added there is a lot of money available to produce profits, and thus they tend to be important elements of the enterprise system. In these cases the role of the competitors in that element may be crucial, because big profits tend to attract eager and intense competition which, in turn, lowers everybody's profits and re-establishes economic equilibrium. This is why big profits generally come with big business risk.

Hanna and Lundquist[13] evaluate product options by considering three additional notions: the surplus chain, the complements chain and the substitutes chain. They define the surplus chain, for a price category, as the sequence of economic surpluses available to the lowest cost competitors in each element of the enterprise system.

By studying the surplus chain they devise alternative ways to capture surplus from other elements of the enterprise system. Integration strategies play an important role in the capture of this available surplus.

When the surplus is negative the money has been absorbed by overhead, employee salaries, unions or financial costs. In these cases it is either impossible to make money with the available value added and technology, or else all players in the element are value destroyers. In the former case industry restructuring will take place in the short run, since long-run profitability cannot be sustained; in the latter case internal measures call for turnaround management. In many cases the best alternative sources of additional surplus lie within the company; it is a matter of mismanagement.

Sometimes price competition transfers the surplus in the chain to the end consumer. When all of an industry's surplus goes to end consumers, consultants devise strategies that seek to pull it back to one of the elements of the enterprise system. This may be caused by mismanagement or by competitors practising forward pricing. In the latter it is a strategy: they transfer surplus to the end consumer on purpose because they seek to stimulate demand, gain market share, eliminate weak competitors and ultimately, capture this surplus back when the volumes are much larger and they have advanced in the learning curve to lower their costs.

Hanna and Lundquist look for alternative sources of profit in the enterprise system of complementary products/services. For example, they considered all the expenses that consumers incur in the use and maintenance of Walkman-type products throughout their useful life: batteries, cassettes, and repairs. By reviewing who was taking most of the profits in these industries they generated alternative strategies such as: offering alternative cassettes; integrating into cassettes; integrating towards software in the cassettes; alliances with battery manufacturers to supply batteries with owned brand names; and so on. In this way, they suggest, product development can give access to profits that have been traditionally controlled in other enterprise systems.

Their first step in a complements analysis is to construct a pie chart that illustrates the costs, in a time frame, of owning and operating a product. In an example, they point out that United Technologies developed a fuel control device that saved as much as 2 per cent of the fuel costs – some $8 million – during the lifetime of a Boeing 747. They argue that the pricing of such devices should ensure that airlines share these savings, or 'the surplus', captured from oil companies – with United Technologies.

They further investigate the product/services that customers perceive as substitutes of those under consideration. They explain that Yamaha's electronic

[13] Hanna, Alistair M. and Lundquist, Jerrold T., 'Creative strategies', *The McKinsey Quarterly*, 1990, No. 3.

piano – for instance – provides the complementary benefit of giving music lessons by simply inserting a diskette and turning on a switch. As it plays music we now have a substitute for cassette players. The profits in the consumer electronic music industry – in which Yamaha participates with synthesizers and components – are accessed with this piano on which we can also listen to recordings we play in other electronic devices, as well as recording our family pianist.

In their view, the market for pianos appeared saturated, while the market for electronic music hardware continued to grow. Obviously, a barrier to purchasing a piano was the need to spend long hours learning how to play before hearing a result. They point out that by allowing people to play without expensive and time-consuming lessons, Yamaha eliminated an important barrier to purchase.

Assignment questions

1 What is a business node?
2 What is a business web?
3 Define value added in a business node. How can we use it? Give an example.
4 Why do we need strategy? Can we do without it?
5 What is the most important strategic decision in a corporation? Why?
6 What defines a strategic posture? Give an example.
7 What is an enterprise system? How does it help us?
8 What is the value added chain? What is it used for?
9 What are the complements and substitutes chains? Why are they important?

2
Generic strategies

2.1 A microcomputer saga[1]

Consider IBM's release, over a decade ago, of their personal computer (PC), which transformed our learning and working habits. By 1990, 85 per cent of the PCs sold, in the more than US$100 billion PC-industry, were IBM-compatible machines. Although IBM was still the largest PC assembler (in 1990 it sold about US$9 billion in PC-related products, out of Big Blue's US$67 billion sales), its market share had eroded because of many smaller and profitable competitors.

Two strategic subcontracting decisions led to an easy-to-copy computer with open architecture. Rather than manufacturing all its own computer components and developing its own software, IBM used Intel's microprocessors and Microsoft's DOS operating system.

The agreements allowed Intel and Microsoft to sell these same products to other companies. Subsequently, hundreds of IBM-clone makers rushed to harvest profits in the fast growing PC market. By 1991, the situation was such that out of about 800 microcomputer assemblers, two were entering the market each week, while another two were leaving it. In 1991, IBM, the creator of the standard-PC, struggled to make a profit in a mature industry sector, whereas Microsoft and Intel enjoyed the profits generated by their core products: DOS and microprocecessors.

Core products – as explained by Prahalad and Hamel[2] – are the components at the centre of an end-product's functionality. For instance, motors in cars or compressors in refrigerators are core products. Cars and refrigerators would be the end-products.

Core businesses cultivate the core technologies that can build world dominance in the design, development, manufacture and delivery of core products. To sustain dominance in chosen core technologies the core businesses of a corporation should maximize their world manufacturing share in core products.

In an interview with *Mac World* Magazine, Steve Jobs – Apple's founder – referred to Microsoft's DOS as the 'small orifice' through which all hardware and software companies had to go if they wanted to compete in the PC-clone market. Effectively, the hundreds of companies assembling PC-clones in 1991 had to use a logic chip from Intel's 80n86 genre. Downstream, even more companies were making software to run in millions of PC-clones, and every one of them had to use MS-DOS. Steven Job's 'small orifice' is our 'core product'.

But why would IBM subcontract such profitable core products in the first

[1] Ketelhöhn, Werner, Boscheck, Ralph, *et al.*, Compaq Computer Corporation, IMD Case Copyright 1991 by International Institute for Management Development, Lausanne, Switzerland.

[2] Prahalad, C.K. and Hemel, Gary, 'The core competence of the corporation', *Harvard Business Review*, May–June 1990.

place? Considering that Big Blue has competencies in both software development and chip technology, it is a valid question to ask. One answer is that, at the time it was imperative to establish an industry standard – to see what kind of market would develop – and subcontracting, coupled with open architecture, could attract – as it did – clone investors to IBM's machine and ensure an IBM-standard. Apple, instead, chose to keep its technology proprietary, deciding to work in a niche market, first with their Apple II, and then with their Macintosh computers.

IBM's and Apple's strategies were generically different. While the former sought to establish a standard product for the industry, with which to pursue premium prices and high volumes; the latter looked for a niche market segment in which to add value at high prices and relatively lower volumes. As a result, by 1991, the microcomputer industry was dominated upstream by Intel, selling about US$3 billion in 80n86 microprocessors; and downstream by Microsoft with DOS and many other software packages.

Intel's 80n86 genre of processors and Motorola's 68000 genre are known as CISC chips: Complex Instructions Set Computers. A new architecture RISC, for Reduced Instruction Set Computers, was made available by IBM, Sun and others. This opened the door for independence from Intel and Motorola, as Sun Microsystems and Digital Equipment Corporation also offered RISC products to the open market.

In logic chips manufacturing, once about $1 billion have been invested, most other costs become negligible when compared with fixed costs. And when most costs are fixed, the name of the game is volume. This high up-front investment, necessary to achieve minimum efficient size, constituted a barrier to entry in logic and memory chips.

In 1991, with more than 7000 employees and over a billion dollars in annual sales, Microsoft was bigger and more profitable than any other software company. Bill Gates, Microsoft's Chairman, had the vision of positioning Microsoft as the dominant force in multimedia for the twenty-first century. This explains why Microsoft was purchasing electronic rights to books, artwork and videos with potential in multimedia products.

Seeking to gain independence from Microsoft's DOS, IBM became a licensee of Nextstep software, Steven Jobs' operating system for Next computers. IBM also worked together with Microsoft on OS/2, a potential successor to DOS in the 1990s. Since the sales of the first release of OS/2 were disappointing, Microsoft released, in mid-1990, Windows 3.0, a program that enhances DOS machines by giving them some Macintosh features.

Windows was an immediate and surprising hit, it gave millions of old DOS machines a second life. As a result, all other software companies had to pass through a second 'small orifice': Windows. Apple, with only 7 per cent of the global PC market, was hurt badly by Microsoft's success with Windows 3.0. Microsoft hurt Apple by making DOS machines look like Macs, and IBM by destroying its plans for OS/2. Worse still, Apple saw its niche market strategy destroyed by the millions of installed DOS machines which could suddenly function as a Mac; and IBM had to watch the erosion of the value added by OS/2 and PS/2. Both companies' PC strategies were suddenly obsolete, because an outsider – Microsoft – sold a product that upgraded an immense base of installed DOS machines.

With sales of US$6.5 billion, Apple was – in 1991 – one of the largest microcomputer companies in the world, ahead of Compaq and NEC. Over 50 per cent of Apple's sales originated outside the US and the company supported about 40 different languages in its 'Operating System'. In addition it was implementing a new product strategy for the fast growing laptop market segment.

Historically, Apple marketed top of the line products at premium prices. It had been able to maintain high margins because its proprietary technology kept others from cloning its computers. However, because 85 per cent of personal computers ran IBM-compatible software, most software companies increasingly focused their product development on these computers, starting a vicious cycle: the more software, the more DOS-computers would be sold, and the more DOS-machines were sold, the more software was developed for them. As a result, Apple's world market share declined from 7.6 per cent to 6.9 per cent. So in October 1990, Apple reversed a 6-year-old policy of charging high prices for its Macintosh personal computers and axed prices by about 40 per cent. Apple introduced its low price line of Macintosh computers: the Classic, LC and the IIsi.

Six months later, though quarterly unit sales had nearly doubled, (the Classic was selling 100,000 units per month) the company was not doing well. In March 1991, worldwide sales were up 19 per cent on the same month in the previous year, yet Apple managed only a slight increase to 8.3 per cent of market share. The situation had remained much the same, software houses could still not see a big enough market for which to develop new products. Instead, the market demanded Windows 3.0 compatible software, for millions of DOS-machines.

IBM responded with aggressive pricing and a new set of alliances like the one signed with Micrografx to help improve OS/2's performance. But the struggle for industry dominance with core products continued. IBM planned to make a return on its core technological competence by licensing its RISC processors to Motorola; and attracting Apple, the major quality PC-assembler, to its RISC chip. At the time Apple was considering RISC chips from Motorola, Hewlett-Packard and Acorn. In this way both computer assemblers could make sure that there would be several suppliers for this core product.

By 1991, Apple had decided to join forces with IBM to develop an entirely new PC standard with which they could control the rights to the operating system software and the RISC microprocessor. Apple and IBM agreed to work together on software and hardware projects designed to change the personal computer market.

Apple's CEO, John Scully, and Jim Cannavino, IBM's top PC-executive, agreed to develop jointly a new object-oriented operating system for use in a new generation of work stations and servers that would use IBM's RS/6000 as the processor. This operating system would be designed to work well with IBM'S OS/2 and the Mac Operating System. They also sought a platform-independent, multi-media environment. They planned to establish a joint venture that would deliver the new operating system to Apple, IBM and other companies that wished to license it.

Borland, a software company, could provide the object oriented tools on which IBM-Apple's new object oriented operating system would be based.

Borland could be on the verge of becoming a new Microsoft, owning the new small orifice through which the whole industry must pass in the 1990s. Apple and IBM would share microprocessor technology, object-based operating system, networking technology and multiplatform computing environments (technology that allows computers manufactured by many vendors to run the same software).

2.2 Distinctive[3] and core[4] competence

What can we learn from this microcomputer saga? Five important concepts show up repeatedly in this juggle for standards: distinctive competencies, core competencies, core technology, core products and integration strategy.

Distinctive competencies are the skills that an organization acquires in solving its problems. Microsoft's competence in developing operating systems (DOS) and widely accepted software like Windows 3.0, provided the company with two core products that were not only profitable but also dictated the pace at which old technology was replaced. In the microcomputer industry these skills separate Microsoft from other software companies; however, they are not exclusive to Microsoft, Borland also excels in these skills. So, distinctive competencies are the skills mastered by a company (people skills, policies and assets) that set it apart from the pack – but they may not be unique.

Clearly the distinctive competencies of a corporation may not be useful, nor needed, for competing in all of the industries in which it is present. For instance, in 1991, DEC possessed distinctive competencies that were insufficient for competing in the systems integration consulting industry. Consequently the company had to reorganize and realign its skills in preparation for doing business as a consulting practice.

Prahalad and Hamel introduce three additional concepts: core products, core businesses, and core competences. *Core products* are components of an end product (final) that are central to its functionality – for instance, motors for cars. *Core businesses* are the business units which are organized to produce core products. *Core competencies* are people skills, policies and assets, managed in these core businesses. These competencies in performing key activities must be closely protected and cultivated by core organizational leader-managers. Losing too many of these leaders, i.e. people who carry these skills, jeopardizes the corporation's core competencies. DEC, for instance, lost David Cutler to Microsoft. Cutler, one of the world's top programming minds, was the brains behind DEC's VAX programming, which permits the networking of computers made by different manufacturers. Similarly, Lew Eggebrecht, IBM's brilliant systems engineer, left the company after he built IBM's first micro-computer in the early 1980s. Eggebrecht and others – 'the dirty dozen' – had built the new machine in less than a year; obsessed with the product, he was the architecture and hardware driver in the team. Although both computer giants have enough

[3] Selnick, Philip, *Leadership in Administration: a Sociological Interpretation*, Harper and Row, 1957.

[4] Prahalad, C.K. and Hamel, Gary, 'The core competence of the corporation', *Harvard Business Review*, May–June 1990.

talent to survive these losses, the problem is that scarce, outstanding people tend to be recruited by competitors eager to build a competitive edge in carefully targeted core technologies.

2.3 Core technology

Consider again IBM's and Apple's decision to join forces in the exploitation of IBM's RS/6000 RISC processor. In 1991, Intel, which had previously been 40 per cent owned by IBM, dictated the perceived technological obsolescence of the PCs by introducing, as it saw fit, new generations of the 80n86 processor. In an attempt to regain control of the speed of perceived technological obsolescence of its end products, PCs, IBM sought to license several chip manufacturers with its RS/6000 RISC processors.

Core technologies are simply the technological base needed to cultivate core competencies. IBM possessed the RISC core technology and was organizing competencies to exploit it. Thus, core technologies facilitate the creation and/or mass manufacturing of core products and services. Dominance in core products such as logic processors provided one key for managing the perceived value of the end products, PCs. Clearly the people that cultivate core technologies form an important part of the core competencies of a corporation. Their work needs to be protected.

So, it is possible to possess a core technology but not the competence to exploit it, but not vice versa; possession of a core competence also implies possession of the core technology on which it is based. This is why we disagree with Rappaport's 'The computerless computer company'.[5] Both core competencies and technologies may be possessed by several competitors with varying degrees of competence at exploiting them. Consider Sun Microsystems who, in September 1991, announced plans to create its own version of the Unix operating system for the most powerful IBM-compatible personal computers. With them, three groups struggled for the PC-standards of the 1990s: Sun, the Ace consortium led by Compaq and Microsoft, and the IBM-Apple alliance. They all announced RISC processors, better graphic capabilities, simultaneous tasking, and built-in networking capability. The key to success in this competition for standards was to design an operating system that would attract software houses. The operating system of the future – a core product – will determine the software's characteristics for the new standard personal computer.

The enterprise system helps to identify and select the key technologies to monitor in its different elements. When considering future technology it seems useful to examine present and future market needs; the needs of the competitors in all elements of the enterprise system. For this we must identify the activities that are needed in the present and thought to be important in the future. One way of doing this is to look at which technologies are mastered by the most successful competitors in each element of the industry's enterprise system; this way we can break down the system into a chain of technologies whose trends need to be examined.

[5] Rappaport, Andrews and Halevi, Shmuel, 'The computerless computer company', *Harvard Business Review*, July–August, 1991.

In the microcomputer industry, for instance, the enterprise system was dominated by a few key players. Upstream we found specialized component manufacturers in logic chips, hard disks and memory chips where the barriers to entry were the incredibly high investments required to develop and set up production plants. Next, we found groups of subassemblers who put the components together in mother boards, monitors, and so on. Their competitive advantage was also protected by the low delivered-cost generated by mega-investments. As computer assemblers' costs were mostly variable, there were hundreds of them competing in the marketplace. Software companies also sought to serve this market with differentiating strategies because there were no real barriers to entry. Any group of capable professionals with a good idea could set up shop for a couple of years; the problem was: how to survive the copycats.

Today's core technologies are clearly related to today's core activities and products; thus a competitor needs simply to ask: which core technologies do we need to master and which are we missing? Similarly, future technologies are clearly related to future core products and activities; the problem is to identify in the present the technologies needed to perform future core activities, and manufacture future core products. For this, visionary technological leadership, coupled with industry experience, constitutes the best recipe. What is the minimum size needed to develop these future core technologies?

2.4 Integration strategies

The most common prescription for strategy is to direct the business unit's competencies towards perceived opportunities in a dynamic marketplace. So, the reasoning goes, we have to identify both the opportunities in the environment, and the distinctive competencies of the business unit.

The opportunities in the competitive environment are identified by studying competitor performance in the different elements of the industry's enterprise system. Clearly, returns will be highest in some elements, and most players would like to reap profits from them, but for structural reasons they might find this impossible. Similarly, in elements with the lowest returns, only a few players will venture in as they might get better returns somewhere else.

However, for 'strategic' reasons a company may choose to participate – or not – in both highly attractive and not so profitable elements of the enterprise system. IBM, for instance, chose to protect its PC-microprocessor technology and PC-software development capabilities during the 1980s, despite the decision to subcontract both core products to outsiders. In 1991, although IBM had distinctive competencies for the development of operating systems and controlled cutting-edge technology in logic chip development, it chose to exploit these competencies via alliances and the subcontracting of both core products.

So, we can see that a strategic issue would be whether to focus solely on a firm's core and profitable businesses and subcontract needed inputs, core products and services, or whether it would be better to own these businesses.

A company may choose to participate in a business node because it represents the means to protect a core technology; an element may be attractive because the company needs to understand the cost structure of the companies in it; or because it intends to gain economies of scale; or because its presence pre-empts other competitors from entering that node; or because it is able to command the evolution of the industry.

In the 1970s, for example, General Electric decided to subcontract manufacturing of microwave ovens to Samsung, then a small Korean company.[6] At the time this seemed to be the right thing to do, for once they had mastered microwave oven technology, Samsung was able to deliver ovens at a lower cost than even the Japanese, so strengthening GE's hand. However, expanding their activities with a delivery network throughout the US was the logical next step for Samsung, and so, by the 1990s they had displaced GE from the microwave oven markets, and had themselves become the world's largest producer. Clearly, the integration strategy of a company defines:

1 The business nodes in which it will compete.
2 The technologies that it will cultivate and exploit.
3 The set of suppliers or subcontractors it will work with.
4 Its sourcing, processing, and delivery activities.
5 The set of client companies it will service.
6 Its costs structure.
7 Its value added chain.
8 The distinctive competencies it chooses to cultivate, etc.

A company's integration strategy lays out the foundation upon which all other generic strategies are based.

Opportunities in the competitive environment can be identified by studying the enterprise system, as exemplified above. This process, called industry analysis, consists of: first, understanding what successful competitors do well, their generic ways of competing and what is required to do this well: the key success factors (KSF). And second, considering what the generic strategies and key success factors will be in the future.

By comparing the KSF of the generic strategies with a company's capabilities, managers choose the generic strategy that best fits company competencies and core technologies. From this comparison managers identify investment projects which could strengthen the chosen KSF. Company capabilities are derived from a SWOT (Strengths, Weaknesses, Opportunities and Threats) analysis.

A company's distinctive competencies should be the KSFs that are needed to meet current strategy and sustained future profitability. Thus, company capabilities are the portfolio of current people skills, policies and assets, but they aren't necessarily the key success factors needed for the company's strategy. This is why we first assess the KSFs needed for each generic strategy and then, the company's capabilities; by comparison we decide upon the set of skills and policies needed to develop for successful competition with a chosen generic

[6] Magizaner, Ira and Patinkin, Mark, *The Silent War: Inside the Global Business Battles Shaping America's Future*, Random House, New York, 1989.

strategy. IBM, for instance, protected its core microprocessor technology and software development competence because it planned to use it to control the pace at which core and end products will reach obsolescence in the PC-industry of the 1990s.

2.5 The business system: a company's value activities

To understand a company's integration strategy four generic activities need to be examined: sourcing activities, processing activities, delivery activities and support activities.

A company's integration strategy determines its activities in design, manufacturing, logistics, marketing, distribution, wholesaling, retailing, service and the various support activities that add value to their product/services. These activities determine both the cost at which the products/services are delivered and the value perceived in them. Michael Porter introduced the value chain as the basic tool with which these different activities could be examined. At IMD, my colleagues Jan Kubes and Xavier Gilbert introduced in our MBA the teaching of McKinsey's concept of the business system.[7]

> **Definition 7:** *A company's business system is defined by the sequence of activities, used to deliver the product/service, between the supplier of raw materials and the final consumer of the product/service.*

The idea is to disaggregate a business into its strategically relevant activities and try to understand the costs and value delivered by them. This chain of activities determines total value and costs, including overhead and profits. From these findings we can see that the way a company chooses to participate (or not) in different elements of the enterprise system determines its activity chain, its overhead costs and profits.

The way each activity is performed defines the company's relative cost and value position in comparison with its competitors. Understanding the way in which these activities add value and create costs is essential to the construction of the business system. In the words of Michael Porter:[8]

> Value activities are the physically and technologically distinct activities a firm performs. These are the building blocks by which a firm creates a product valuable to its buyers. Margin is the difference between total value and the collective costs of performing the value activities. . . Every value activity employs purchased inputs, human resources, and some form of technology to perform its function. Each value activity also uses and creates information. Value activities may also

[7] For a discussion of this concept read Gilbert, Xavier and Strebel, Paul, 'Developing competitive advantage' in William Guth (Ed.), *The Handbook of Business Strategy, 1986–1987 Year Book*.

[8] Porter, E. Michael, *Competitive Advantage: Creating and Sustaining Superior Performance*, The Free Press, 1985.

create financial assets such as inventory and accounts receivable, or liabilities such as accounts payable.

Porter divides value activities in two broad types: *primary* and *support* activities. For us *primary* activities are: sourcing, processing and delivery activities; whereas *support* activities are: developmental, organizational and legal activities.

Clearly there are companies in which there is little processing, service or marketing. In some industries these activities are not very important. Some industries however may be service driven, marketing driven, IT driven, etc. and we must identify which functional activities dominate the particular industry. In Japan, for instance, it is common to follow value activity accounting methods to keep track of the relative importance of all primary activities.

2.6 Sourcing activities

The coordination of the value adding activities along the business system is obtained through the management of four flows: people, information, goods and money. To be successful, the core company in a strategic network must cultivate competencies necessary for managing these flows.

Benetton, the Italian clothing giant, has chosen to dominate in the management of the flow of goods: they use their economies of scale to purchase raw materials, to provide strong logistic support for their subcontractors, and to ship the finished products from a $30 million central warehouse at Treviso, Italy directly to the shops.

Benetton also manages the flow of money through the system, for example, they begin delivery of the Autumn/Winter collection products at the end of April, but the starting point for credit to shopowners is 1 September. This is when the clock starts ticking (30, 60 and 90 days credit). The first payment is due at the end of September, the second at the end of October and the third at the end of November. The peak of indebtedness to Benetton occurs when they have completed production and delivered the goods, but have not yet received payment from the shops. This happens between May and the end of September. Benetton takes 90–120 days to pay its suppliers, whereas it takes only 30 days to pay its subcontractors. 'The subcontractors can't handle the strain of extended credit, but the raw material suppliers can', said a former managing director Aldo Palmeri. Furthermore, since raw material suppliers benefit from guaranteed volumes, they are asked in return to take charge of the inventories and be flexible and responsive to Benetton's needs.

Obviously, financial flows follow the flow of goods. In this sense, it is not uncommon for a network's core to cushion the impact of financial pressures on the smaller companies in the network. One of the most important financial roles of a core company is to assure the smooth growth of its smaller partners. Benetton did this by creating leasing, factoring, insurance, banks and other independent financial services companies conceived specifically to support the growth of its partners, because they understood that the growth of the core is dependent upon the growth of the smaller associated companies.

Information provides the links that coordinate the enterprise system. Advance information technology has facilitated coordination throughout the business system of many companies. For example, the *Nordwest Zeitung*, a newspaper in North-West Germany, coordinates the allocation of national advertising to a group of 12 smaller local papers; and Benetton uses a world transaction system to manage shipments, accounts receivables and orders. However, coordination can be achieved without particularly sophisticated systems. Benetton agents, for example, have seasonal meetings both at headquarters and with their store owners in which they determine which items should be produced for the season; an information exchange on what the 'market mood' will be.

People, as usual, are at the core of all systems. In practically all the cases we have studied, personal relationships kept the system working. It is impossible to try to capture the complex information content of interpersonal relations within a written contract. At Benetton, for instance, brother Carlo chooses which plant managers are allowed to become subcontractors, and Luciano Benetton does the same for the agents. Senior agents – the between six to ten closest associates of Luciano Benetton – in turn choose from among their store owners who will qualify as a junior agent, and finally all agents select store owners.

Clearly, this type of social network has a pyramidal hierarchy inherent within its relationships, but it is not a rigid one, positions are not created by reporting lines, but rather by joint risk-taking. In fact, it is not rare to find Luciano, a junior agent and a storeowner involved in a venture. The movement of entrepreneurs through the enterprise system and across continents is based on the common desire to invest and take risks coupled with the mutual trust which is absolutely essential to keep the system working.

2.7 Processing activities

Processing activities are not only concerned with decisions that link the manufacturing posture of a corporation with present and future technology but also with the shaping of all other processes that lower the costs or increase the value of the product/services. Manufacturing processes are concentrated in the upstream elements of the business system: raw materials, component manufacturing and assembly. But processing activities are also concerned with downstream activities like finishing, packaging, delivering and service.

Traditionally, two processing strategies have been identified to capture value added: either by serving a market segment better at higher costs–prices, or by serving the market at lower costs-prices but higher volumes. In the former the company expects to increase its profits by increasing its price–volume more than its cost–volume; in the latter the company expects to increase its profits by decreasing its cost–volume more than its price-volume.

Low Delivered Cost (LDC) and High Perceived Value (HPV), concepts as developed by my colleagues Xavier Gilbert and Paul Streble, extend the above ideas to processes used along a company's business system (see Figure 2.1).[9]

[9] Gilbert, Xavier and Strebel, Paul, 'Developing competitive advantage', in William Guth (ed.), *The Handbook of Business Strategy, 1986–1987 Year Book*.

LDC and HPV convey a dynamic meaning since they remind us of the cost incurred at each element of the enterprise system and the value perceived by the different participants in the enterprise system. The participants in an element of the enterprise system worry about both: the delivered cost of their products/services throughout their business system, and the value perceived by their customers. As customers, competitors compare how much value they are getting for a given price level. However, as managers of a certain value added they look at what it costs to deliver their products at different price levels.

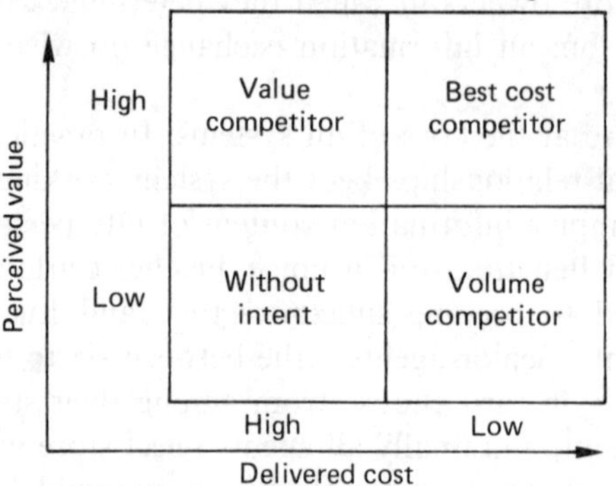

Figure 2.1 Processing strategies
Source: this figure was inspired on the ideas discussed by Xavier Gilbert and Paul Strebel in Developing Competitive Advantage. The Handbook of Business Strategy. 1986–1987 Year Book. William Guth, Editor.

Thus as shown in Figure 2.1, there are the two generic ways to compete: through perceived quality (usually high price–low volume products) or through low delivered costs (usually low price–high volume products). Most companies are able to follow only one of these strategic drives at a given point in time. However, as Gilbert and Strebel argue, sometimes we can achieve high perceived value at low delivered costs; this 'outpacing' combination is difficult to obtain, and even more so to maintain.

Two things should be noted: first, that the qualifiers 'low' and 'high' are relative to competitors, and not to the company's past performance; a company may have lowered its costs consistently throughout the years, without achieving a relatively low cost position in its industry. And second, the more a business unit succeeds with these postures, the more difficult it will be to introduce new technologies and a change in posture.

Consider Apple Computer's drastic change in October 1990 from its former HPV strategy to its new LDC strategy. The new low price hurt Apple's profitability. As a result, the company underwent a reorganization in the first half of 1991, which resulted in layoffs of about 10 per cent of the workforce. Apple consolidated its five American regional sales divisions into three units. Mass producing low cost Macintoshes requires that the company is also able to mass merchandise them; sourcing, processing and delivery activities must be coordinated. Apple found that it did not have enough manufacturing capacity, its marketing costs were too high, its distribution channels could not handle the increased volume and that they encountered a shortage of components and peripherals. Thus Apple's transformation from high price–low volume vendor to low price–high volume vendor created serious problems for the company.

While Compaq was profitable with margins around 40 per cent, and Dell with 30 per cent or less, Apple had traditionally enjoyed margins of 50 per cent. The Classic provided a margin of only 30 per cent, which was too low to pay for Apple's cost structure. For instance, in 1990 Apple spent about $750 marketing each Macintosh, just about the retail price of the Classic. The overhead costs associated with supporting the dealer network were too expensive for the new product strategy.

Clearly, when most costs are fixed, the only determinant of unitary costs is volume; in such cases going for volume at low prices (forward pricing) is the smart way to compete. But for computer assemblers most costs seemed to be variable, hence Apple's difficulty in achieving a sustainable low cost position.

Porter, Gilbert and Strebel and others propose that the product's life cycle is a guideline for important turning points in processing strategy; it is argued that at the beginning of a product's existence, when there are no standards, the customer's perceived value is the driving force in the market. But then, when a major player introduces an industry standard – like IBM did in the PC industry – innovative efforts should take second place, because the thing to do is to build volume with standard products, lower the cost and race everyone else along the learning curve.

To sustain successful processing strategies the technological environment must be monitored to make sure that the corporation does not miss a shift in core technology. For example, technological innovation redefined the integration strategy of both the Swedish furniture giant, IKEA and liquid packaging master, Tetrapak. Likewise, new electronic technology destroyed the value added by electromechanical calculator manufacturers Friden and Monroe. In the 1990s, we may see the demise of some traditional computer monitor manufacturers as they lose their mega-investments to new field emission display (FED) technology, which has the potential to produce lighter, cheaper, higher quality flat screens than LCD technology.

Simple frameworks are needed to help decide which technologies should be followed and adapted, and which not; here we are interested in a review of the technology in all elements of a company's business system. The consequences of technological change in one element of the business system must be evaluated in all other elements of the system, and then matched with complementary technology. For instance, some years ago in the Philippines, rice yields quadrupled in one season because of a new hybrid seed. On that occasion the agricultural enterprise system could not handle the expanded demand in the flow of goods, and most of the crop rotted away in the fields, because of the rupture in the physical flow.

2.8 Delivery activities

Delivery activities are concerned with decisions that deal with how to get a product and its services to customers or end consumers. Two distinct sets of decisions define these activities: strategic marketing decisions and strategic service decisions.

Broadly defined we either sell to everyone or we focus on a special niche; this segmentation has been proposed as the two generic market strategies. There are many more concepts including promotion, product, channels, advertising, pricing and others for the construction of marketing strategies. These ideas, developed many years ago, need to be integrated into any competitive analysis.

In doing this, two views of marketing need to be considered: industrial and consumer marketing. The task is to see how these ideas are applied in the different elements of a company's business system and many questions must be answered: What channels exist in each element?; What segmentation is used?; What are the pricing approaches?, etc. The enterprise system must be viewed through a marketing eye in order to establish what is happening in each element from a marketing point of view and how the company's marketing strategies are being coordinated along its business system. This book does not pretend to discuss this. Answers to these questions can be found in the work of my colleagues Derek Abell and Kamram Kashani.

Besides the services provided to end consumers, there are many industrial services, like forwarders, bankers and so on, adding value in all elements of a business system. Clearly, services are part of HPV strategies, and they need to be integrated into our analyses. But how far back in the business system do back-office activities go? And what are the generic service strategies? Are they different for HPV products than for LDC? Why? Is there room for services in all elements of the business system? What services are the different competitors delivering? In what elements of the business system do they provide services? Again, this book does not discuss the topic. But answers to these questions can be found in the work of my colleagues Christopher Lovelock and Sandra Vandermerwe.

2.9 Support activities

As mentioned above, support activities depend upon the way legal, developmental and organizational strategies are put together. One of the most important competitive support systems is provided by the legal structure of the different companies involved in the business system. Corporate law and organizational structures are closely interlinked.

Issues, like control of ownership and taxation, determine important costs that may undermine the competitiveness of a company. For example, it is possible to assemble products in tax free zones or base companies in countries providing income tax holidays. Many other legal issues affect the way companies are organized. In practice, these decisions are usually taken by teams of legal and business experts.

Companies tend to be strong in the country and element of the enterprise system in which they originated; and this is also dependent upon the legal strategies adopted. An activity-based analysis yields the best understanding of how the different competitors are organized to deliver their goods and services.

Consider the microcomputer industry in Europe. By mid-1991, most companies were drowning in inventories of hardware which in less than 6 months had reached perceived obsolescence. They were unable to sell these machines in the West, but Eastern European distributors were keen to take them at considerable discount. Yet, instead of taking a write-off by selling these machines at a loss, the accountants in one manufacturing company recommended taking a full write-off and crushing all the new machines. Transfer prices and accounting practices led these administrators to the 'rational' decision of crushing new machines, in spite of arguments for gaining market share and brand-name exposure in Eastern Europe.

Two things need to be noted: first, overhead costs may destroy value with parochial 'rational' decisions; and second, the bigger an organization, the more difficult it becomes to coordinate the strategic posture in the different elements of its business systems (for instance manufacturing with sales).

A well-managed strategic posture is capable of creating and directing quality and cost drives in different elements of the business system simultaneously, because it coordinates the activities of the different units involved. Value activities represent potential areas in which distinctive competence can be developed for the business unit; if so desired, they may be protected with the creation of value adding overhead costs, i.e. organizational structures in which overhead costs protect and cultivate the value adding activities of the business.

The study of the organizational strategy demands answers to the following questions: What are the generic ways in which competitors organize themselves and why? Do high volume players adopt different organizations than those of low volume players? Do high quality competitors have special organizations? What is different? What do these organizations do well? What can't they do? Are the organizations in the different elements of the company's business system complementary? What different ways of coordinating the business system are available? When are they used?

2.10 Key success factors

Each generic strategy mentioned above demands certain company capabilities for its successful execution. If a company wants to follow a specific set of complementary generic strategies there are certain things, key success factors (KSF) of that set, which the executives of the company must be able to manage well. Clearly, these KSF change for different combinations of generic strategies. Thus the distinctive competencies of a company are defined by the KSF of the strategy chosen by the company.

Given that we have so many upstream, processing, downstream and support activities, the company will have to watch carefully the complementarity between these activities, a problem studied in big corporations as the management of interfaces. Complementarity means the selection of a strategic posture that coordinates upstream with downstream competitive behaviour among the company's executives.

A robust and congruent strategic posture would not follow a high quality-cost product strategy coupled with a discount price–delivery strategy; processing, product, market, channel and price decisions must be complementary, a posture often difficult to achieve in big corporations. In fact, this is what general management and the shaping of business policies is all about. Coordinating activities along the business system can be achieved with the management of flows: people flows, information flows, flows of goods and money flows. It is through the management of these flows that congruence between all generic strategies is obtained and sustained.

2.11 Conclusions

In summary, the answers to the question 'How do we add value in this business unit?' are found in two steps. First, we investigate the systemic question, how are the different businesses participating in this industry linked? This leads us to understand the structure and dynamics in the industry as well as the alternative coordination mechanism found in the management of the flows of people, information, goods and money. The *enterprise system* emphasizes the understanding of the links between the raw material suppliers, the intermediate businesses and the final consumer. It is clear that the industry's definition depends on the businesses included in the enterprise system, clearly a personal decision. The enterprise system is industry related, it defines the industry and describes how the different businesses are linked.

Second, we investigate the integration strategies being followed by the most successful competitors and the activities they chose to perform themselves in their search for profits. This defines the *business system* used by the different competitors. Understanding their business system permits us to also understand the way these companies have chosen to add value – *their value adding activities*; the technology used in these activities – the *technological chain*; and the cost incurred with these activities – *their cost structure.* The business system is company specific, it describes how specific competitors have chosen to deliver their products–services to the final consumer.

To compete in today's demanding environment, companies must make sure that the business system that they choose to manage can deliver the desired goods/services with the high perceived quality and low delivered cost of world class competitors. This can be achieved if the whole system is coordinated. But coordination does not necessarily mean ownership; it really means strategic management. In fact, ownership, while theoretically providing control, is often a source of inefficiency. Mere subcontracting is not a solution either; the system still demands coordination. Therefore, the company must make sure it is choosing the right integration strategy in the enterprise system; and the way to do that is to recognize and adopt – over time – those generic strategies that yield the most profitable system in the long run.

In this sense, vertical integration decisions are at the centre of a company's strategy: they not only determine the shape of its activity chain but they also determine the long run overall efficiency of the business system that the company adopted and the coordination mechanisms required to manage the company's strategic posture.

Assignment questions

1 What is the difference between distinctive and core competence?
2 Define core and end products?
3 What is a core business? A core technology?
4 What is defined by a company's integration strategy? Is it important? Why?
5 What is a key success factor?
6 What is a business system? How does it differ from the enterprise system?
7 What flows are used to coordinate the activities along the business system?
8 What are the generic processing strategies?
9 What delivery and support activities can you think of?

Appendix A
Doing a strategic analysis

A.1 A strategic analysis approach

The process of strategic analysis is straightforward. It begins by understanding the possible integration strategies as well as the possible sourcing, processing, delivery and support strategies in an industry. That is, it identifies the generic ways of competing within the industry and the corresponding key success factors (KSFs).

The importance of these generic strategies varies among industries. Their impact on profitability also varies because the returns in different industries do not depend upon the same key success factors. A company that chooses to compete with one set of generic strategies must be well able to identify the KSFs. By matching the strengths of the company with the KSFs of each generic strategy we can determine which of the many strategies may be followed by the company. Clearly, for each different set of strategies, there may be some KSFs in which the company is weak.

Strategic investment projects are generated in the following way: they are projects conceived to increase company capabilities in key success factors that are precisely defined for use in the chosen generic strategy.

In summary, to understand the strategy of a company, consulting teams start with a set of hypotheses about the generic strategies in the industry and the key success factors for each strategy. Then they check their understanding of the industry by comparing their hypotheses with documented facts. Once they are satisfied with their understanding of the industry, they compare the company's capabilities with the KSFs of the generic strategies. By identifying the strategy that best fits the company's capabilities, consultants are able to select and recommend investment projects necessary to build strengths in those KSFs in which the company is weak.

At IMD, my colleagues Jan Kubes and Xavier Gilbert introduced project consulting within our MBA courses and followed a process similar to those used in professional services companies. Our students perform a strategic analysis of a company and its industry during the last 4 months of their programme. By 1991, we had completed analyses for some 130 companies, with findings that proved extremely interesting to both students and faculty.

A.2 Process consulting

Organizations, like sick people, require professional diagnosis in order to identify and prioritize problems that need to be cured. There are two generic ways to approach a consulting assignment. In the first method, consultants act as they normally do and become heavily involved in the task of finding a solution to the problem. In the second, they avoid direct involvement in problem-solving and assume the task of guiding the client team in the process of solution-finding instead. We call the latter *process consulting* and the former *problem-solving consulting*. There are, of course, many combinations of emphasis on process and content.

Process consulting consists of group problem-solving processes that we assume that managers and employees, through participative processes, are able to:

1 Identify organizational problems.
2 Identify creative solutions.
3 Choose a feasible strategy.
4 Implement a chosen strategy.
5 Improve the organizational climate.
6 Select achievable objectives.
7 Obtain commitment to specific action plans.
8 Evaluate strategic progress.

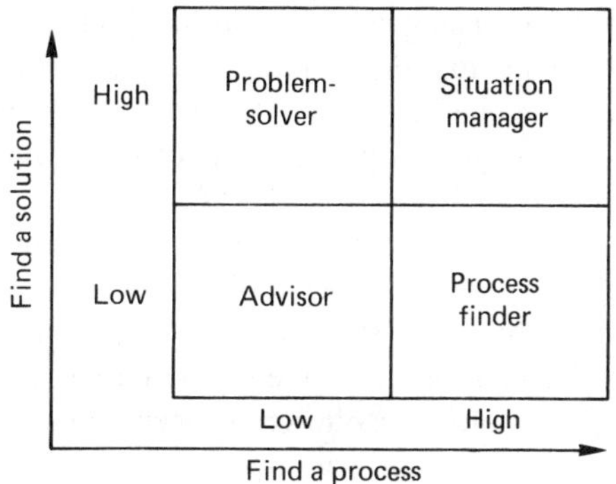

Figure A.1 Consulting approaches

Creative thinking is based on proactive attitudes; it requires curiosity, desire and the commitment to invest in exploring new ideas. Everybody possesses creativity; what is important is how we encourage ourselves and others to be creative. We believe that everybody understands the importance of what they do at work and is therefore capable of inventing original solutions. Participative processes untap a company's vast resource of employee creativity, provided that management allows these to happen.

Process consulting uses intervention techniques that release the creative energies of top and middle management and other employees. In most cases, creativity consists of the simple rearrangements of known facts and work methods into ingenious new ways that produce superior performance. Using participative processes, hidden information, facts and problems are identified by employees of the organization.

In strategic consulting we have used, with considerable success, participative processes in the form of *strategic review workshops*. They consist of three phases. First, consultants instruct the management team in the basic concepts and ideas used in the enterprise system. Several 'case' studies are reviewed and thoroughly discussed while, at the same time, team building is created in the workshops.

Second, under the guidance of the consulting team, executives actually perform an analysis of their industry and determine the generic strategies and corresponding key success factors in that industry. Lastly, executives analyse the strengths and weaknesses of their own company *vis-à-vis* the key success factors identified in the second phase. At the end of the workshop, a consensus is reached on the realistic and available courses of action for capitalizing on these strengths and overcoming weaknesses.

These strategic review workshops emphasize process over content, that is, we believe in unleashing the information, creativity and abilities of the management team as they develop a strategy. Rather than telling them what they should do, we guide them towards discovering and shaping what the company could do. Once the process is over, the company will implement what these managers have decided.

What is needed for a good process?[1]

1 A successful strategic workshop is based upon the belief that there is nothing wrong with having problems. Participants recognize and accept the existence of strategic problems in the organization. From the start people must permit themselves to have strategic problems. They must realize that having strategic problems is all right, it is natural: it is okay.
2 Participants must also allow themselves and others to solve these strategic problems and stop looking for scapegoats.
3 For the workshop to be successful, top management must be interested in and committed to the process. This means that their presence and participation in the strategic problem resolution process must reach the 'ownership' level, i.e. they must take responsibility for strategic problems and corresponding solutions.
4 Top management must be prepared to involve all those members of the organization who relate to the causes of strategic problem and solutions.
5 Early in the process, management must include those members of the organization who will implement the decisions being made. Resistance to change is reduced if the strategy is created by those who implement it.

Top management should be aware that participative consulting processes arouse people's expectations and these should not be frustrated; discontinuation or lack of commitment to the identified solution leads to demotivated managers and employees, and a lack of commitment to whatever strategy the company decides to follow.

[1] Ulshak, L. Francis, *Finishing Unfinished Business: Creative Problem Solving: The 1979 Annual Handbook for Group Facilitators*, University Associates.

A.3 Clients, participants and the facilitator[2]

There are three basic groups that should be involved in the participative consulting process of a strategic workshop: the client, the participants, and the facilitator.

The client, is represented by top management, who 'own' the problems and determine which should be solved. The client must be receptive; he must permit himself to listen to ideas and have others work on the problem. The client evaluates the ideas and alternatives and examines them as they are presented.

The participants are typically a group of subordinates, peers or outsiders working for the client on a particular problem. They allow the facilitator to direct the problem-solving process; let responsibility for the problem stay with the client; provide useful facts for problem-solving; offer possible solutions for consideration; recommend actions; and maintain a high level of energy and creativity.

The facilitator manages the process and comes from outside the organization. He is concerned with maximizing the organization's ability to conduct this type of self-diagnosis and solution identification.

The facilitator decides when to do what. He decides on the sequence of steps in the process, and makes sure that the problem-solving process flows smoothly. The facilitator creates cooperative climates by:

1 Preventing discounting: negative comments about a person, his ideas or his department.
2 Avoiding offensive/defensive behaviour among the participants.
3 Protecting people from critical interventions.
4 Evaluating interactions.
5 Encouraging positive interventions.
6 Keeping energy levels high.

A.4 The synthetic process

How do the management team start their analysis? For which consumers should they build the enterprise system? Which raw materials should they end up with? Clients and participants face the issue of industry definition. The first insights into these questions lie in the company under analysis. Here we find out what the different competitors in the system are doing, how they compete and what the typical strategies are.

From the start, it is essential to admit that they will be dealing with an iterative process. They will start with a product/market definition and follow the flows needed to market the product throughout a business web, and eventually, end up at some raw materials. Clearly, only the most important intermediate businesses will be considered as belonging to the business web in the system.

[2] Ibid.

Although experience is the best guide for selecting the businesses to include in the analysis, the following may be useful. We ask:

1 Which set of upstream supplier technologies are key for low cost strategies?
2 Which set of upstream supplier technologies are key for high quality strategies?
3 Which set of upstream supplier technologies are key for future low cost or high quality strategies?

Clearly, for every business some qualitative judgements will be passed as to its importance and its technologies. Once the raw materials are reached, the next step is to make the journey in reverse; that is, beginning with the raw materials we proceed to identify the most important downstream businesses that lead to the selected consumer set. At each business node we ask:

1 Which set of downstream customers of the node's product/services are key for low cost strategies?
2 Which set of downstream customers of the node's product/services are key for differentiation strategies?
3 Which set of downstream customers of the node's product/services are key for future low cost or differentiation strategies?

Repeating the process a few times generates a service, product, market and technology set that presents a robust definition of the businesses in the enterprise system. This definition must have a clear product, service and market scope, including the geography and technology. The clients and participants are asked to define the limits of the industry in terms of products made, sold and consumed; technologies and processes used; markets and needs served; geographic areas covered; and the competitors in the industry's enterprise system.

Depending upon the time and money available, they can expand or shrink the scope of the industry's definition or competitor analysis. Eventually they will reach a situation where their understanding of the system is satisfactory.

Specifically, we recommend the following processs. First, following the logical framework of our enterprise system, hypotheses arising from the following questions are examined by the team performing the study:

1 What is the shape of the enterprise system?
2 What are the generic ways to compete?
3 What are the KSFs for each generic strategy?
4 How are the flows through the system managed?

Second, the team reviews their hypotheses on the above with information found in general magazines. This part of the process leads to a refinement of their suppositions. Third, the team reviews their new hypotheses by referring to information found in trade magazines. This iteration refines their theories even further. Fourth, this iterating process continues until the team feels that they have achieved a satisfactory understanding of the enterprise system and the strategic issues in the industry.

Then, the team turns its attention to the company and proceeds to study its capabilities: First, they look at the way the company has defined its business system; then, they examine the complementarity between the activities being followed in sourcing, processing, delivery and support. In this step the team usually discovers things that can improve the congruence between the activities in the business system; next, they compare the company's capabilities in these activities with the KSFs needed to follow the generic strategies identified in the industry analysis phase; from this comparison they select the strategy best fitted to the company; and, finally, they recommend investment projects that will close the gap between the present way of doing business and the KSFs of the recommended strategy.

A.5 Support documentation

To analyse a company's strategy we follow the iterative process described above. Our analysis is generally supported by an industry file similar to those ordered from strategic intelligence centres.

These data files include information found in varying media, formats, quantity and quality. Special efforts are required to complete and update the information; at IMD we use our own documentation centre for additional information. It is realistic to expect that a better file can be organized with more time and expertise than those normally available to you, so we recommend the use of professional services.

To facilitate the use of a file we organize it in three sections:[3]

1 *General industry information.* Articles from business newspapers and magazines including *The Economist*, *Fortune*, *Business Week*, etc.; industry surveys and statistics. These give an overview of the industry and are useful because they provide an holistic view of what is happening in the industry.
2 *Information on competitors in the enterprise system.* A collection of articles culled from industry studies on various issues; annual reports; and direct interviews with experts. The emphasis is on what seems to be working well, and what is no longer working. Thus, we look for success and failure stories, for reports explaining the strategies followed by today's competitors and technological trends as seen by specialists. We collect details on how the enterprise system is organized, what successful companies are doing, in what part of the system they are operating and the activities that generate value or cost differentiation.
3 *Information on activity and technological dynamics.* Articles taken from industry trade magazines. They are used to discover and understand intimate details of the activities performed by the competitors in the industry; they specify how technology is changing in certain elements of the enterprise system. For example, changes in sourcing and processing activities, technology used, information systems, distribution channels, etc. It is important to group here articles describing industry shifts and changes in business practices.

[3] For a more detailed description review Appendix B 'How to conduct an industry analysis' in Porter, E. Michael, *Competitive Strategy*, New York, Free Press, 1980.

While studying these articles, answers should be sought to the following list of important points:

1 *The economics in the enterprise system.*
   (a) How much value is being added in the system? Where? Who is making money? How much? Why?
   (b) Where are the economies of scale? What is the critical size? What are the maximum number of players? What are the barriers to entry and exit? Are investment levels high or low?
   (c) What are the generic strategies: integration, sourcing, processing, delivery and support strategies? And the key success factors for these strategies?
2 *Processing activities through the enterprise system.*
   (a) Availability of supplies, who is doing what?
   (b) How easy is it to copy a component?
   (c) How fast are standards created?
   (d) What technologies predominate in sourcing, processing, delivery and support?
   (e) Which activities are cost or value drivers?
   (f) How are the flows being managed through the system?
3 *What changes are occurring in the various elements of the enterprise system, such as:*
   (a) Technology driven changes.
   (b) Product obsolescence.
   (c) New competitors.
   (d) International competitors.
   (e) Subcontracting practices, integration strategies.
   (f) Alliances and partnerships.

Part Two
International Business Strategy

The reader should be familiar with the following concepts discussed in Part One: business nodes; strategic posture; enterprise system; value added chain; generic strategies; key success factors; distinctive competencies; core competencies; core technologies; core businesses; core products; company capabilities; integration strategies; company's business system; sourcing, processing, delivery and support activities; and the process for strategic analysis.

In this part we introduce alternative ways of doing business on a global scale. The tone of the chapters is narrative; they deal mainly with interesting ways of getting organized for global competition. We want to recognize the contributions of Michael Porter, Gary Hamel, C.K. Prahalad, Criss Bartlett, Henry Mintzberg, Aldo Palmeri, Sumantra Ghosal, J. Carlos Jarillo, Jim Baughman, Giorgio Inzerilli, and many other colleagues whose ideas form the backbone of this section.

In this overview we specifically summarize some of the findings of Bartlett and Ghosal.[1] In their study of corporations doing business around the world they found that the most important factor influencing the strategic posture of a corporation was the generic way in which they *organized* for worldwide market dominance. Their generic organizational strategies were characterized by typical structures, management systems and corporate cultures.

They classified nine corporations into three groups of similar organizational forms. First, the classical form, which they named *multinational organizations* who decentralized their assets and capabilities to facilitate their subsidiaries' adaptation to specific market conditions. As a result, resources were dispersed and most responsibilities delegated to country managers. Philips, Unilever, and ITT were their examples of multinationals which functioned as loose *federations* of country businesses.

Second, the Japanese model, which they named the *global corporation*, was comprised of companies like Matsushita, NEC, and Kao, who are characterized by their investments in centralized global-scale factories geared to manufacture standard products under a centralized worldwide market strategy.

Third, the *international corporation*, a group of corporations like General Electric, Procter & Gamble and Ericsson, whose organizational strategy managed to transfer and adapt the core company's know-how to foreign markets. The core maintained influence over the subsidiaries, but to a lesser extent than the global corporation, whereas the subsidiaries were able to adapt products and policies coming from the core, but less than in the case of a multinational corporation.

Bartlett and Ghosal proposed that it was the *transnational corporation* that was able simultaneously to develop global efficiency, adapt to market needs and learn from all markets. The transnational corporation is capable of learning in all the markets in which it is present and of exploiting this knowledge in other markets, by adapting it to the local country conditions, while achieving cost efficiencies on a global scale.

[1] Bartlett, Christopher and Ghosal, Sumantra, *Managing Across Borders: the Transnational Solution*, Harvard Business School Press, 1989.

In summary, multinational corporations evolved from trying to adapt themselves to local market conditions; the global corporation evolved from the need to achieve world-wide cost efficiency; and the international corporation was best equipped for transferring knowledge from the centre to its markets.

In this part we take an additional step to those taken by the above mentioned students of management, as we discuss some of the hidden assumptions in 'strategic speak', as well as propose new organizational forms for corporations engaged in selling solutions to customer problems.

3 What do we mean by cooperative advantage?[1]

Military jargon has been bandied about for years in business circles as a source of metaphors in strategic discussions. 'Redefining the battlefield' or 'outsmarting the competition' are still commonly used when describing strategies. One can understand the use of militaristic language by managers in the 1950s and 1960s – it was about the only education they had received – but in the 1990s, militaristic explanations of the success of Japanese and German companies seem less appropriate. It was argued that corporations could have 'outsmarted' Honda in the motorcyle industry, Toyota in the car industry, Sony and Matsushita in the home electronics industry, and so on. Even now, in the 1990s, similar advice is being given to western companies on how to redefine the 'battlefield' to 'outsmart' Fujitsu, Hitachi and the like.

In these popular analogies one either attacks competitors frontally by outflanking them, or in some other way – possibly by parachuting in sales people – in order to understand the battlefield (schlachtfeld) before entering the market. Central to these beliefs is the tenet that companies compete with their suppliers, customers and anyone else in sight, for opportunities to make profits for as long as investments generate required rates of return.

An alternative belief to this militaristic wisdom proposes extremely complex sets of business relations. This view suggests that the Japanese have outsmarted no one, but rather that they were under-managed by some western companies. The problem with these western companies is not the Japanese, but instead, their 'smart' management teams and their 'raubritter mentalität'.[2]

Some highly successful companies, such as the *Nordwest Zeitung* in Germany, IMS and SEMCO in Brazil, Benetton in Italy, and many others, don't share this competitive 'raubritter' view of business. Rather than fighting everybody, they create internally cooperative climates and choose their external competitors carefully. For such companies, cooperation in achieving negotiated agreements is a distinctive competence.

3.1 IMS

Industrial Mecanica de Salvador S.A. (IMS), is a family company situated in Salvador, Brazil – Lambada country. IMS sells about US$12 million annually in circular valves, mainly to the country's oil industry. In 1988, IMS owner

[1] This chapter was influenced by the working IMD-Perspective for managers 'What do you mean by a negotiated strategy?' prepared by J. Carlos Jarillo and Werner Ketelhöhn E., October 1990.

[2] Robber Baron mentality.

and CEO, Victor Manuel Faulkerts, decided to make some changes in his company's traditional command structure and to introduce a participative management approach.

To this end, Eduardo Oliveira Santos, who was to become the architect of the new scheme, advised his old friend and new boss, Faulkerts, to introduce a quarterly profit distribution plan whereby 7.5 per cent of profit would be paid to workers in proportion to salary levels, and another 7.5 per cent distributed evenly to all employees. Thus even the lowest paid employee received a significant share of the company's profits.

The results of Faulkert's action were electrifying. Within weeks of the first profit distribution, a cost reduction programme and an in-house training scheme that would improve their skill base and upgrade the quality of the product were introduced by the work force. There was a dramatic change in worker management relations. Antagonistic personnel attitudes and poor working conditions gave way to a climate of cooperation and improvements in the workers' cultural, emotional and spiritual life. IMS managers and employees worked together to create a happy and prosperous family environment.

By 1991, a typical quarterly employee meeting started with a review of the financial results and continued with clarification of the meaning and implication of the costs and sales. This was followed by reports from employee representatives and finalized with a discussion about what the company was doing well, and what was not being done correctly. Everyone shared in the discussion on how things could be improved.

For instance, in the April 1991 meeting, two machinists complained that their supervisors took too long to respond to requests for help: 'When downtime like this occurs, we are idle and we lose money', exclaimed the employees, looking indignantly at the supervisors. A 30-minute debate ensued after which the employees' assembly proposed to eliminate the role of supervisor, replacing it with the job of 'consultant'.

Although hesitant at first, the employees now feel free to call upon the best 'consultants' whenever they have a problem. The consultants, in turn, have an incentive to provide quality service to their 'clients' because if their services are not in demand, they have no right to be in the factory. By June 1991, the creativity of these employees had changed most procedures in the plant, improving both delivered costs and product quality. Moreover, most management positions had been substituted by consulting roles so that the whole company is run with only five managers; CEO, sales, finance, design and manufacturing. Today, most executives are highly appreciative of the value adding activities of sales and machining.

The general feeling at IMS is that the quality of life, including life in the work place, is reflected in the quality of the product. A second belief is that both investors and employees have a right to part of the profits; hence the profit sharing scheme. But a right to part of the profits must also include shared responsibility in case of loss (loss sharing). At IMS workers help absorb the company's losses by deferring overtime payments. In this way, everyone helps protect IMS from downturns in the Brazilian economy. Clearly none of the above can happen without frank and open information sharing – *transparency* – which helps everyone's understanding of the company's performance, its activities, costs and profits.

This is why, in 1991, IMS was the only profitable company in Brazil's metalworking industry. It also explains why Victor Manuel Faulkerts, who once worked 12 hour days, 7 days a week; now leaves his office every day at 4 p.m., and on Fridays he heads for one of Brazil's fabulous beaches!

3.2 SEMCO

IMS is not the only company with a strategy negotiated internally through participative management. Ricardo Semler, 32-year-old owner and CEO of Brazil's $50 million per year SEMCO corporation, believes that an interdependent set of relations should be established to enhance internal cooperation. His proposal begins with the participation of employees in decision-making. This releases their creativity, and in order to maintain mutual trust inside the company, he keeps employees informed of the effects of their actions. This is complemented with a reward system whereby SEMCO's workers receive 23 per cent of profits as an incentive to increase their performance.

In SEMCO's internal structure, groups of associates (workers and employees) are led by coordinators (supervisors) who report to partners (plant managers). Partners, in turn, report to counsellors (business unit managers) who report to the CEO. Clearly, changing titles will not produce a more cooperative internal climate. A lot more is needed, as has already been explained above, to put the right incentives in place.

To ensure that the value-adding activities are maintained, the following principles are observed: first, the 23 per cent after-tax profit sharing programme sustains workers' motivation levels. Second, business units are kept small (150 people) so that close personal ties and familiarity exist among employees. Third, because supervisors report directly to the partners, with no one in between supervisors and partners, there are no intermediate managers intervening in the value-adding activities. In this way, the value-adding activities are protected, and the familiar western syndrome, managers of managers, and supervisors of supervisors is eliminated. At SEMCO, all employees from counsellors down, contribute to the value-adding activities.

These basic principles of cooperative management have helped dissolve the traditional command structure, substituting it for a set of negotiated relations between workers, employees and consultants, as in the case of IMS; and associates, coordinators, partners, and counsellors in the case of SEMCO.

3.3 Outsmarting

What can we learn from these stories? These companies are much stronger with their internal 'partners' than they would be on their own. Their moneymaking is based on participative management: a cooperative advantage. Both economics and experience are involved in choosing when participation is advisable or when top-down decisions would be a better choice.

The moment a successful company – for instance – comes up with a new strategy, the rest of the business world starts weighing up the pros and cons of copying it. If Toyota changes its sourcing, processing or delivery strategy, there is a fair chance that its competitors will soon be doing the same. The irony is that the ideas used to 'outsmart' the competition can be copied because once they are rolled out, they become available to everyone. Outsmarters' ideas are simple quantum jumps in products, processes, costs or quality, which is why executives complain of 'me-too' strategies and 'bandwagon' competitors.

Participation–cooperation – instead – can only be sustained if two basic conditions are met: first, if the size of the pie is increased by creating more wealth, either through increased revenues and/or, by being more cost efficient than the company would be with a command structure. Second, if the enlarged pie is split to everybody's satisfaction. In short, everyone must be happy and the deal must work for a long time. IMS and SEMCO, for instance, increase the pie by releasing employee creativity and efficiency through profit sharing, transparency and empowerment through participation.

Consider Honda, which came into the US market chasing competitors in the big bike segment but succeeded in the lowest end of the market by selling 50 c.c. models.[3] Kihachiro Kawashima – designated in 1959 as president of American Honda Motor Company – recounts his impressions of how Honda's dominance of the American motorcycle market was achieved. In summary, he confesses, 'we had no strategy'. Honda's large bikes were simply not good enough to compete with the likes of Harley Davidson. However, as demand for small bikes soared and Honda was able to solve quality and cost problems, the Japanese company drifted towards a high volume, low delivered cost strategy. Through the years, they displaced all established competitors until, by 1980, all American competitors were facing extinction. Honda could not be described as planning a 'smart' global strategy. They entered a highly competitive market cautiously and adjusted their strategy as market demand developed, solving large and small internal and external conflicts as they went along.

YKK, the famous Japanese zipper manufacturer, followed a path similar to that of Honda in its takeover of world markets. Carefully selected young Japanese managers were sent overseas to start new companies and manage them to market dominance. These Japanese expatriate managers were simply the best men that the founders of their companies could find to handle conflict resolution.

In conclusion, since we don't just ignore what Honda, YKK, Sony, Toyota and the like are doing, and these Japanese companies seem to be ahead, then business success must be about more than 'outsmarting'.

3.4 Out-managing: internal cooperation

Major research findings confirm that most corporate managers do know what needs to be done – no one is outsmarting them – but, instead, their major

[3] This example was taken from Honda (B) a Harvard Business School case no. 9-384-030, written by Richard T. Pascale, Copyright, 1983.

problem is getting around, and rid of, the organizational structure, procedures, systems and culture that constrain their actions. Successful companies out-manage the companies they choose to compete with in their industry.

To become a top competitor a corporation needs world class workers, engineers and managers, not soldiers and generals. For instance, from the moment he took charge, Lee Byung Chull – Samsung's chairman in the 1970s – invested in better minds; a distinctive competence for cutting edge technology. He sent waves of young Koreans to American universities, but not to West Point military academy.[4]

Consider the approach commonly used in German and Japanese companies to upgrade their people's skills. Workers and middle management go through intense in-company apprenticeship programmes. Moreover, many of them recruit their top cadres among holders of PhDs in economics or mechanical, electrical and industrial engineering. Some American companies have also understood the advantages of learned leaders – some 5 per cent of the CEOs in *Fortune*'s 500, according to a June 1991 *Fortune* magazine article – hold PhD degrees.

The apprenticeship scheme, for example, is at the centre of Germany's cooperative work culture. In Germany, it is expected that firms have apprenticeship programmes so that young people can join the company for 2 to 3 years of in-house instruction, shop-floor training and some schooling before moving on as qualified technicians. German industrialists invest in their people's development with programmes meant to pass skills and processes to younger generations of employees; by drawing on the experience and creativity of the 'senior' work force and middle management. In this way the employees determine how the work must be done. At IMS, for instance, the same goals have been achieved through participative management and profit sharing.

Sanyo Electric, the Japanese consumer electronics maker, decided to send Yutaka Hayashi to round off his scientific education by spending a few years at Stanford University, California.[5] To develop Sanyo's strategy for solar batteries, known as project Sunshine, Hayashi reviewed 20 years of documents on solar energy. He did not read Patton's or Rommel's campaigns. Dr Karl Angst, for many years head of Nestlé's corporate research centre was a scientist; and William Shaver and Robert Maurer, of Corning Glass Corporation, in the USA, held PhDs from MIT. None of these successful builders of core corporate technologies drew on military strategies; they were/are eminent scientists and engineers – not Samurai warriors.

Effective management consists of a series of never-ending improvements that helps unleash employee creativity and productivity and so improves both products and processes. The objective of out-managing is to establish processes for continuous improvement and change. But 'out-managing' is frequently perceived as a set of boring interactions performed to build trust among obscure 'operative' types (those who actually make or sell things) so it does not receive the strategist's attention and as a result is not cultivated in some western companies.

Instead, outsmarting the competition implies a one-off 'move' which made at

[4] Magaziner, Ira and Patinkin, Mark, *The Silent War*, Random House, 1989.
[5] Ibid.

a particular point in time seems logical and correct. As in football, these discrete actions attract people's attention and executives can quantify, see, control and imitate the 'moves' of the best 'players'. This is no doubt very convenient for people who strongly believe in 'outsmarting' competitors: it provides them with a sense of false security, because by imitating they may believe that 'we are at least as good as our best competitors'.

Unfortunately, the management of incremental improvements (internal negotiations), is indeed the source of a sustainable advantage that remains largely hidden inside the corporation. Furthermore, management conflict resolution is something the 'outsmarters' cannot see or control, let alone imitate. Because they don't identify these distinctive competencies, some western executives subscribe to convenient, popular business mythology. In the early 60s we heard, 'the Japanese can't really produce quality products', then in the 70s and 80s it became, 'everybody knows that the Japanese are weak at design', and now in the 90s we hear, 'not to worry, the Japanese can't really write software'.

3.5 Nordwest Zeitung[6]

The *Nordwest Zeitung*, in Germany, provides an example of an externally negotiated strategy. In 1987, the newspaper, situated in the Oldenburg region, captured a record 84.4 per cent of the population as readers of one of the daily newspapers belonging to the *Nordwest Zeitung*'s partnership. From the start – after the Second World War – *NWZ* had adopted a zoning strategy by publishing seven editions of one paper, one for each main locality served by the newspaper. Mr Gerhard Koeser – owner and CEO – believed that in order to be successful a newspaper had to have local coverage, so the *NWZ* followed the readers' needs and provided what they wanted most, local news.

The zoning strategy was devised by adapting a practical newspaper format: four different sections in which one was exclusively devoted to local news. The other three sections were the same in all seven editions: international, regional and entertainment; the fourth section contained news for the local community. Each edition was easily recognizable as the most important local story was always on the front page.

In 1950 the *NWZ* established a cooperation with the Ostfriesen Zeitung in both editing and advertising. By October 1969, several small local papers had joined *NWZ* in a partnership. The editorial cooperation consisted of selling the non-local sections of the paper to the partners, while the small papers developed only their local sections. When local editorial activities of the partners overlapped, the *NWZ* closed two of its small editorial bureaux. Several combinations of *NWZ* sections and self-produced sections were marketed by members of the partnership in response to market demand. Some editions of the *NWZ* competed locally with newspapers in the partnership, but it was minimal and not a real threat to either side because editors competed only on the quality of their local news.

[6] Taken from the *Nordwest Zeitung*, written by Research Associate Amy Webster under the supervision of Professor Werner Ketelhöhn E., Copyright by IMD, March of 1988.

A clear example of increasing the economic pie and splitting it is provided by the partnership cooperation in local advertising which prevented aggressive competition in this field. *NWZ* monitored the allocation of national, recruitment and real estate advertisements for the 12 members of the partnership, as the newspaper received ads directly from agencies and customers who refused to deal with small newspapers. *NWZ* served as a newspaper-space wholesaler, having advertisers use a price list to choose the combination of publications in which they wanted to advertise. In this way, smaller newspapers secured advertising revenues that they would not have received otherwise, while *NWZ* generated extra income through a 12 per cent commission for this service. Besides savings in overhead and direct costs, the small newspapers registered a growth in advertising revenues as high as 50 per cent after they entered the partnership; in 1988 this growth averaged 5 per cent a year.

3.6 Benetton[7]

Consider now, Benetton's dramatic growth from nothing in 1955 to 1.9 billion dollars in sales in 1990, proving wrong those who had predicted that the company's unusual system could not be exported. Benetton developed its 'industrial fashion' by first focusing on sweaters for the youth segment, and then gradually expanding its clothing to attract children and adults in the middle income bracket all over the world. For Benetton, being 'industrial' means the pursuit of volume to achieve economies of scale. These economies allow the company to offer its consumers products at acceptable prices.

Normally a global strategy forces product standardization that goes against the product's adaptation to different tastes around the world. Benetton, however, derives its strength from the simultaneous pursuit of two contradictory objectives – economies of scale and manufacturing flexibility – through a negotiated strategy.[8]

Aldo Palmeri – Benetton's former CEO – describes the company as 'vertically de-integrated'. That means that upstream, the company subcontracts most (close to 95 per cent) of its activities in manufacturing to independent or partially owned 'Indotto'. In this ways Benetton can still respond flexibly to changes in market mood. But, by centralizing the purchases of raw materials, Benetton – the world's largest purchaser of wool – also obtains considerable cost advantages.

Upstream, manufacturing is taken care of by more than 700 small subcontractors who receive their raw materials or semi-finished goods from Benetton and send the finished products back to the centralized distribution facility. The only activities Benetton keeps 'in house' are those where expensive high technology, that benefits from economies of scale, can be used. These include

[7] Taken from IMD case series on Edizione Holding Sp.A. written in 1991 by Bob Howard under the Supervision of Professor Werner Ketelhöhn E. Ketelhöhn Werner and Howard Robert, 'Building the Benetton system', *IMD Case GM*, 437, 1990.

[8] A negotiated strategy is based on choosing competitors and partners carefully: partners that will – in the long run – increase the pie and agree to split it fairly; and competitors that are better dealt with at arm's length.

complex chemical processes for creating colours, Computer Aided Design and Computer Aided Manufacturing which deliver efficiency and quality in cutting. A US$30 million automatic warehouse provides economies of scale in logistics. In summary, Benetton keeps within the company only those core activities that benefit from economies of scale.

Benetton makes sure that its subcontractors operate at full capacity, supporting them with standard prices and costs. The company allows some of its own plant managers to run subcontracting outfits on a part-time basis but demands total dedication from all of its subcontractors. In order to create specialized subcontractors with no salesmen, marketing and finance costs, etc. (and correspondingly low overheads) Benetton needs the full capacity of its production network to be utilized.

Benetton's upstream cooperation with its subcontractors produces clear advantages over what internal production could offer: flexibility and low costs. The flexibility to produce more than expected of a certain item since subcontractors can easily work overtime; and low costs in labour-intensive, low-skilled operations, where close supervision is essential to achieve high levels of labour productivity. Benetton guarantees a 10 per cent profit margin on the average costs (set by Benetton) that are incurred by subcontractors. Thus, these hundreds of profit-motivated small entrepreneurs find ways to cut costs. The effects on productivity are clear. Subcontracting is a way to lower Benetton's own overhead costs, and operating at full capacity sustains subcontractors' efficiency drives and specialization.

Downstream, Benetton's negotiated strategy extends to wholesale and retail as well. The company sells only through Benetton named shops. Except for about ten flag-stores these shops are owned by entrepreneurs. This 'network' of shops benefits from close owner supervision and profit motivation. They are owned by about 1000 small entrepreneurs who are highly motivated to get the market mood right because they buy all their inventory from Benetton and are not allowed to return stock.

A key feature of the Benetton system is the entrepreneur-agent. A group of about 80 people, the agents, set up the retail network in each country and act as the link between Benetton's corporate headquarters and the shops. They perform their job better than company employees because they are free and encouraged to own shops. Experience with their shops provides them with first-hand knowledge of Benetton's client (shop-owners) and final consumers. They are extremely motivated: their investment in shops is important and they become very rich.

This network enables Benetton to pursue its strategy of low cost, high quality and quick response to market moods. At each element of its business system, the company has made a conscious choice as to whether make or buy. Thus, Benetton derives competitive advantage from its negotiated strategy. The Benetton set-up comprises a network of highly motivated entrepreneurs who risk their capital either as subcontractors – who provide flexibility and low costs – or as agents and shop-owners, whose main concern is to correctly identify the market's mood and feed it back to design.

3.7 The battlefield: external cooperation

In the above examples we have seen external cooperation in the *NWZ*'s partnership and at Benetton. The *NWZ* increases the pie with new advertising revenues, whereas Benetton does it mainly by reducing its own overheads and those of its subcontractors and store-owners. In 1991, thirty executives manned the Benetton headquarters, the same number as in 1982, when the company was selling about US$350 million a year.

Once again, these companies are much stronger with their external 'partners' than without them. Their money making is based on negotiating agreements with prospective competitors. Considerable business acumen is required when deciding whether cooperation is advisable, or when competition with suppliers and distributors is preferable.

However, in their search for a sustainable competitive strategic posture – position or formula – some writers have gone to the extreme of recommending Prussian military author Von Klausevitz, or 'Five Rings', a book written by Japan's Musashi's, and lately Sun Tsu's *The Art of War* – a book written by a Chinese general around 500 B.C. – as advanced readings on how to outsmart competitors in business. This may lead us to believe that the best managers, and management education for that matter, are to be found in Soviet military academies. Why then bother with seminars and recruiting at IMD, Harvard, Stanford and other business schools?

This obsession with military metaphors in the business world has culminated in the CIA being asked to file a report on Japanese business practices. In June 1991, newspapers reported that Japan is basically an amoral society which seeks peace only because it needs peace for trade purposes.

Imagine, a society in which workers and managers share the same goals, where they talk to each other and don't spend much energy on inside fights; corporations where employees concentrate on delivering the activities entrusted to them; an economy where companies cooperate with some of the participants in their industry instead of declaring war on everybody; companies who build alliances with financial groups, the media, subcontractors, and sometimes even with competitors, seeking to market extremely high quality products at very reasonable prices. These are things that the CIA reputedly claims make Japan an amoral society.

Things are not so simple, and certainly not so militaristic. The minimum size to gain economies of scale and the maximum size before starting to lose them again, and not amorality, are really the reasons why a company finds that for some activities in the business, it is too large to be as efficient as small companies and so it may want to subcontract; whereas for other activities, it is too small to obtain the economies of scale available to a larger company.

In the former case, of being too large to equal a small company's efficiency, we considered Benetton for the assembly of semi-finished garments, and *NWZ* for the editing of local news. These are activities with a high component of direct labour and small potential for achieving economies of scale. The critical activity is the management of labour, and maximum efficiencies will be achieved by the companies that have more incentives to perform: small specialized subcontractors.

In the second case we have the small German newspapers and their sales of advertising. *NWZ* can attract national advertising because it offers the buyer a circulation of 300,000 newspapers, something the small paper cannot do.

3.8 Why the predominance of battlefields

Why don't we find a lot of negotiated arrangements with external partners? And why don't we see more companies following the employee participative management practices of IMS? Internal battlefields exist because negotiation processes (management) are time consuming activities which demand consistent use of participative skills. It is a lot easier to command when you expect to be obeyed and to create control mechanisms (carrots and sticks) than to manage processes that lead to internal cooperative climates.

People are attracted to command structures, and the immense internal transaction costs designed to 'control' employees, because of the illusion created that everyone does his part. In the end, the number of people managing each other increases geometrically (Parkinson's laws), whereas the number of people actually doing some value adding activity, like producing and selling, actually diminishes. This, an inescapable law that is at work in large corporations, ends up creating the Christmas tree organization: a pyramid of managers supported by a few workers and salespersons (see Figure 3.1).

Figure 3.1 The Christmas tree organization

In a 'Christmas tree' organization managers of managers earn a lot more money than the team leaders of key value-adding activities and we should question whether this is right. Within such organizations, corporations need to nurture champions to bully a project through the bureaucracy (this became common wisdom in the 1980s) instead of questioning the very existence of the pyramid of managers of managers that make the execution of value adding activities so difficult. We should also query whether champions are required to deliver value. At SEMCO, for instance, Ricardo Semler got managers out of the way of the value adders: between the producing and selling activities there are no managers subtracting value from the efforts of the value adders. Thus at SEMCO there is no need for champions.

Externally, battlefields exist because even when internal costs are higher than external prices, many companies prefer not to cooperate with external partners. They may do this out of greed or because of 'transaction costs'. In the former case the greed to capture the potential value added in the external operation blinds managers into preferring higher internal costs. Moreover, even if it is cheaper to subcontract, the final result may be more expensive, because there are costs in performing the subcontracting transaction. When these costs are included, it may really be cheaper to make than to buy. Thus internal costs must be compared to the sum of external prices plus transaction costs.

Transaction costs are the costs of negotiating, monitoring and enforcing contracts with external parties and internally with employees. They are also the costs of internal and external coordination of the different activities in a company's business system. For instance, if a supplier has to deliver different products according to a complex and uncertain schedule, it may be better to do it internally, so maintaining control over deliveries and product quality. Subcontracting is possible when the firm is able to coordinate, at acceptable costs, large amounts of information with third parties.

So, even though external prices are lower than internal costs, the costs of coordination have forced companies into vertical integration. As these transaction costs disappear, thanks to new IT solutions, cooperating companies may obtain costs and quality advantages over less efficient or effective integrated companies.

However, there are transaction costs other than those caused by coordination of internal and external activities. These can arise from the fear of irresponsible or opportunistic behaviour of a supplier, employee or channel such as; suppliers charging more, the workforce slacking without supervision or partners joining another partnership. With a negotiated strategy companies run the risk of having their distinctive competence 'captured' by a partner or 'destroyed' by employees because they trusted them. Trust originates in the belief that – in the long run – they will make more money with the partnership than without it.

Thus an externally negotiated strategy is preferable if the costs of buying things are low enough and transaction costs can be kept to a minimum, so as to make the total cost less than the alternative cost of making things. If these two conditions prevail, a company relying on cooperation will obtain lower costs than an integrated company for so long as they maintain trust – internally, among employees, and externally among the members of the network.

3.9 The advantages of negotiated strategies

Internally, a negotiated strategy allows a company's management and work force to concentrate on the value adding activities in their organization, while avoiding unnecessary overhead costs and diluted energy in political fights. As at IMS, employees in companies following internally negotiated strategies concentrate on adding value.

An externally negotiated strategy allows a company to concentrate on its distinctive competence while benefiting from efficiencies in other firms which, in turn, concentrate on their distinctive competences. The specialization choice is based on a complicated blend of motivation, participation, information and technology. Benetton is able to invest in big warehouses and telecommunication technology while its subcontractors do so in labour intensive activities; the *NWZ* is able to concentrate on national news editing, printing and advertising while the local partners concentrate on what they do best, local news editing and newspaper distribution; and IMS machinists are able to concentrate on improving their skill base and manufacturing processes while management gets the space to pursue a bigger client base.

Building a negotiated strategy is based on Kupia Kumi[9] – the attitude of letting others prosper while we prosper – in fact, successful growth in cooperative networks can only be achieved if all members of the partnership can grow and prosper simultaneously. The reason for this is that the core company has chosen not to compete with them, but rather to concentrate its efforts on specific and complementary economic activities: managing the flows of people, information, goods and money.

Assignment questions

1 Why are militaristic metaphors criticized?
2 What does outsmarting the competition imply?
3 What is special about IMS and SEMCO?
4 What do we mean by outmanaging?
5 What is special about *Nordwest Zeitung* and Benetton?
6 What is wrong with a Christmas tree organization?
7 What is an externally negotiated strategy?
8 What is an internally negotiated strategy?
9 What does 'Kupia Kumi' really mean?

[9] 'Kupia Kumi' a Nicaraguan Misquito Indian expression for 'eat and let all eat'.

4

Effective organization

4.1 More network organizations

Looking at the Benetton case study we could be led to believe that entrepreneurial network organizations are a very Latin way of doing business and can only work where there is a sense of 'family'. But when we also consider the network of newspaper partners built by the *Nordwest Zeitung* in Germany, we can see that quite patently, entrepreneurial networks are not confined to Latin countries at all. At the *Nordwest Zeitung* partnership, a negotiated strategy enhances the economic pie and distributes it among the partners in a mutually agreed proportion. And as we shall see, the *Nordwest Zeitung* is not the only non-Latin network of entrepreneurs.

4.2 Lithonia[1]

Lithonia Lighting, a subsidiary of National Service Industries, is one of the world's largest manufacturers of lighting products and systems, with a turnover of US$700 million per year. The US lighting industry possesses a distinctive enterprise system whereby the downstream element of the enterprise system includes specifiers, contractors, distributors and agents. Specifiers design the technical specifications of required electrical equipment; contractors order their components from distributors who carry various makes which they source from independent sales agents. It is usual for sales agents to market a single make, but Lithonia allows its agents to carry products that complement their own range.

Lithonia's senior vice-president, Charles Darnell, decided to exploit this apparently minor difference and reorganized the company to feature Lithonia's agents at the forefront of the service network. These agents would be in direct contact with the entire downstream network. The objective of the new organization would be to support the agents by helping them to improve the service to their customers – the specifiers and contractors – and thereby to increase efficiency and profitability. Put simply, Lithonia's success depended on the success of its independent agents and their ability to create strong relationships with their clients and get Lithonia's products specified and used.

To facilitate these aims, the entire organizational system was overhauled. Computer links were installed between agents, factories and warehouses. Specifiers were able to use a Lithonia CAD system to design their projects and Lithonia used computers to respond quickly to market demand by incorporating customer feedback obtained by the agents. By linking contractors and distributors to Lithonia's product divisions and warehouses, tracking orders through

[1] This example was taken from 'Lighting the way', an article in the Management Focus section of *The Economist*, 6 October 1990.

the enterprise system was possible, and general efficiency increased to such an extent that lead time was reduced from an average of 9 days to less than one.

Lithonia's successful management of information flows was popular with the agents, as they became more profitable and efficient. The technology meant that they needed less people to handle more business and as a result their loyalty to Lithonia was strengthened.

In 1990, Lithonia was planning to link its upstream suppliers into the information network. By having the whole system interconnected it was believed that product design would be improved and inventory control would become obsolete as 'just-in-time' would prevail throughout the system.

4.3 State farm[2]

State Farm, the second biggest insurer in the United States, based in Bloomington, Illinois, was founded in 1922. Its business culture and aims have not changed over the years and the company has built its success on the activities of a network of agents. Owned by its policy-holders, in 1991, State Farm had grown to be the seventeenth largest company in the US, with equity of US$18 billion and sales of premiums US$26 billion. Moreover, State Farm has grown through retained earnings without the need to raise capital.

Run by the Meherele and Rust families since its foundation, State Farm operates mainly in life, motor and domestic insurance markets. Over the years its management has developed a bias for capitalization in order to maintain the safest ways of protecting policy-holders' interests. They have a conservative approach to investment, believe that the policy-holders' interests are paramount and have a loyal and stable work force; perhaps as a result of these attitudes, the company has grown at an 18 per cent compound rate over the past 20 years.

At the heart of State Farm's success lies a remarkable agent network. In 1990, 25 million households were purchasing 57 million policies from 17,500 agents. As at Benetton, these agents are not State Farm employees; they are independent entrepreneurs who have permission to sell the company's products and nothing else. They are not allowed to sell another company's policies to rejected clients. Why don't they risk making such deals?

Agents understand that State Farm occupies a special affection in the minds of the public. Its policies tend to be cheaper and its claim settlement system is perceived as being better than its multiproduct competitors'. This makes the agents' job easier and offers them long-term business – if they don't behave opportunistically. In addition, State Farm provides a great deal of agent support in the form of 28 independent regional offices, reporting direct to the CEO, that handle the paperwork generated by billings and claims. It also pays well. With substantial percentage commissions on policies sold and maintained over the years, average agent earnings in 1990 were $140,000. The company reserves the right to add agents in any location, with each regional office responsible for hiring agents and promoting the strategic direction chosen at the core.

[2] This example was taken from Carol J. Loomis, 'State farm is of the charts', *Fortune*, 8 Apr. 1991.

New agents are selected with great care and their reputations and entrepreneurial attitudes are closely examined. Many are graduates or ex-teachers rather than experienced insurance salesmen who tend to find it too difficult to change their ways to the policy holder motivated approach favoured by State Farm.

4.4 Participative management on a grand scale

We need to ask whether management by participation and consensus can also work in mammoth corporations; or are participative management techniques of such a nature that they may only be used in smaller companies like SEMCO and IMS? We believe the answer to be no. Participative management, like creativity, is a state of mind; it flourishes if the leaders of the organization are genuinely interested in capitalizing on the knowledge and experience of subordinates, and if they are prepared to follow up on recommendations from people in direct contact with the problems. The correct attitude is to manage, not to outsmart the organization.

Consider General Electric's latest drive towards the coordination of business policies in their operating units through employee participation.[3]

A US$58 billion company with about 300,000 employees, GE was in 1991, one of the world's largest diversified industrial concerns. Chairman John F. Welch Jr., 55, appeared to be changing the traditional command organizational structure for a IMS-SEMCO inspired culture: respecting and counselling of people, cultivating their talents and implementing their recommendations.

In the early 1980s, Jack Welsh reduced GE's jungle of 350 product lines and businesses into an organizational form of just 13 big business industries. In the process (reported in the excellent Harvard Business School cases and videos), he hacked at GE's nine layer high Christmas tree organization (see Figure 4.1), and by 1988, pruned it to a more simple five levels.

Figure 4.1 Liberating a corporation from value subtracting overhead

[3] This example was reported in Thomas A. Stewart, 'GE keeps those ideas coming', *Fortune*, 12 Aug. 1991.

However, the command culture was still around; employee creativity and cooperation and management transparency can always be improved. So Jack Welsh and James Baughman, GE's director of executive development, set about changing Welsh's monthly meeting with GE executives, to a constructive discussion of the company's business.

In an article in *Fortune* magazine it was reported that the central belief behind the GE approach was that by getting everybody in the organization involved, the best ideas would surface in the places where they should be applied. So, to untap the vast resource of innovative ideas in the minds of GE's employees, two management intervention techniques were designed: 'work-out' and 'process mapping'.

Like everyone else's management development workshops, work-outs are held outside a unit's premises, usually an hotel, where a group of up to 100 employees, picked from all levels and sectors of a business unit, get together to discuss company problems and search for solutions. At least three things happen in such forums: first, managers and employees get a better understanding of how their unit works; second, they have a chance to simplify the way they are doing things; and third, they can engage in specific group problem-solving.

According to *Fortune*, work-outs typically start with a speech given by the 'boss' of the unit – essentially giving permission to work on a series of problems, i.e. simplify processes, minimize meetings and so on. After setting the agenda and giving his permission to work on his problems, the 'boss' leaves the meeting. Led by a facilitator, the group proceeds to solve these problems in small groups and plenary sessions for a couple of days. On the third day of the work-out the 'boss' and some senior executives arrive to listen to the results; the rules of the process appear to allow only three responses: agree on the spot, disagree, or ask for more information. In the latter case a deadline is set for a team's report and the 'boss's' decision.

To strengthen its skills in executing value adding activities, GE appears to use process mapping, an industrial engineering technique, which consists of a flow chart showing every step, whether small or large, that goes into making something. Activities are depicted in various value adding shades to distinguish what is really needed from 'nice but unnecessary' activities, and value subtracting overhead costs. A well thought out process map involves all levels of the unit, from management to plant workers, who are the people that really make things. It demands commitment, and takes time to be completed. But once finished, the productivity gains can be startling.

The details of these programmes are not available to the public as they are company confidential, but *Fortune* magazine reports that they are expected to pay off handsomely from 1991.

But a change in culture can only be expected to happen in about a decade, because for 300 thousand GE employees to adopt a new IMS-SEMCO-like culture, three things need to happen: first, the *unfreezing* of old working habits and culture – a reason for Welsh's *Neutron Jack* behaviour; second, to *teach* the new successful behaviour – partially achieved with work-outs, best practices, and process mapping and last; to *freeze* and reinforce the desired behaviour. All this takes several years in a mammoth corporation. But *it can* and *is* being done at GE and IBM.

4.5 A different organization[4]

The business environment of the 1990s will be characterized, more and more, by simultaneous drives in contradictory directions. Corporations will be implementing quality programmes under intense cost-reduction plans; short-time product delivery under just-in-time constraints; quick response to market needs with shortened product life cycles, while facing increased market entrance by large integrated corporations and closely knitted groups of small entrepreneurs. These pressures must be matched with innovative corporate organizational strategies.

It has been stated that a corporation's organization can be changed to optimize different objectives, for instance, quality, efficiency, quick response to market needs, creativity, etc. Obviously this is the case, but why change? One answer is to help optimize the corporation's long run sustainable profits. The problem is that changes in the objective to be optimized cannot be accompanied by correspondingly drastic changes in organization, because changing the organization of companies like IBM, GE or Nestlé takes a number of years. This means that quality drives, cost drives, market orientation drives, creativity drives, and so on, will have to be executed by the existing organization (a constraint), adopting small incremental changes, using task forces, or some experiment.

Consider the major obstacle to Nestlé's merger with Rowntree. Financial matters were not the problem, but Rowntree's management demanded an independent organization, that could retain some of its proven market punch, as a chocolate division of Nestlé. The CEO at Nestlé, Helmuth Maucher, and his team agreed to experiment with the proposed organization, in the hope that some lessons could be learned and transferred to other product divisions; some of which had gradually lost their flexibility and punch when compared with smaller food specialists. A similar experiment was set up with their pasta division one year later. By 1991, Nestlé's chocolate division – including R&D and other value adding overheads – was based in York, the UK home of Rowntree. This puts the entire Nestlé corporation one step closer to worldwide learning from the UK chocolate subsidiary.

Therefore, to maximize the long run profitability of a corporation we have to find an organization that best facilitates the pursuit of different, and sometimes contradictory, drives. It is not a question of putting in place a rigid organization that optimizes a particular objective, but rather, the challenge is to find an organization that will simultaneously 'best' perform several of these objectives and, moreover, effectively lend itself to switch emphasis from one drive to another (a flexible structure). Consider Philips, a company apparently organized to maximize creativity and innovation in the consumer electronics industry. They created video disks and the like, but were unable to mass produce, let alone market, these products in the way that Sony and Matsushita

[4] Based on Ketelhöhn, Werner and Burdet Taylor, Juliet, 'Aldo Palmeri: taking charge (A) and (B)', IMD cases GM 463 and GM 464 1991; Ketelhöhn, Werner and Burdet Taylor, Juliet, 'Aldo Palmeri: managing growth', IMD case GM 467 1991.

did. A corporation's organization should be able to be creative and innovative in some elements of its business system and a low cost manufacturer or mass marketer in other elements.

Since it is difficult to imagine a corporation that will be creative during five weeks, and then reorganize itself and become a low cost producer of the new products in the following few weeks, it seems clear that different parts of the organization must be able to carry out these different and sometimes conflicting drives simultaneously. We need to identify the type of organization that allows both R&D and manufacturing to perform their jobs optimally. In short, how can a big corporation be entrepreneurial?

Our answer to the above is the activity-based organization, where overhead activities are conceived to provide support to the managers of the value-adding activities; the core of the organization being formed by the activities that support the value-adding activities. In this organization, sourcing activities consist of the management of four flows through the business system: people, information, goods, and money; processing activities consist of R&D, manufacturing and technological activities throughout the business system; delivery activities consists of marketing and service activities throughout the business system; and finally, support activities consist of organizational, management development and legal activities.

An activity-based structure provides organizational flexibility. Obviously, if managing these four flows is the corporate task – a distinctive competence – then a radically different form of formal structure is needed. Thus, from fuctional, or even divisional, structures, the corporation evolves towards a form in which three functions acquire new importance: logistics, finance and information systems. The management of human resources requires the attention of all top executives. An example of an activity based organizational structure is the network organizations created at Benetton. The managerial implications of this network organization are manifold:

1 This arrangement defines two independently coordinated organizations: the *social organization* formed by the network of entrepreneurs, and the *professional organization*, staffed by managers whose role is to support the entrepreneurial activities of the members of the network. We call this twin arrangement the *Hammock organization* because the graph of the professionally managed flows supporting the risk-taking of the entrepreneurs resembles a hammock (Figure 4.2).
2 A network organization clearly distinguishes between entrepreneurial and professional activities. In fact, managing information, financial and physical flows becomes the professional's distinctive competence, whereas coordinating social interactions becomes the distinctive competence of the senior entrepreneurs.
3 The management of these flows generates what we call activity-based overhead, that is, overhead created to support value adding or money making businesses and activities. Clearly, Benetton storeowners gladly pay for the charges generated by their POS system, because it increases their full price sales; similarly, the *Nordwest Zeitung*'s partners gladly pay a 12 per cent commission on national advertising to the core newspaper.
4 The organizational chart, and overhead cost structure of the core company,

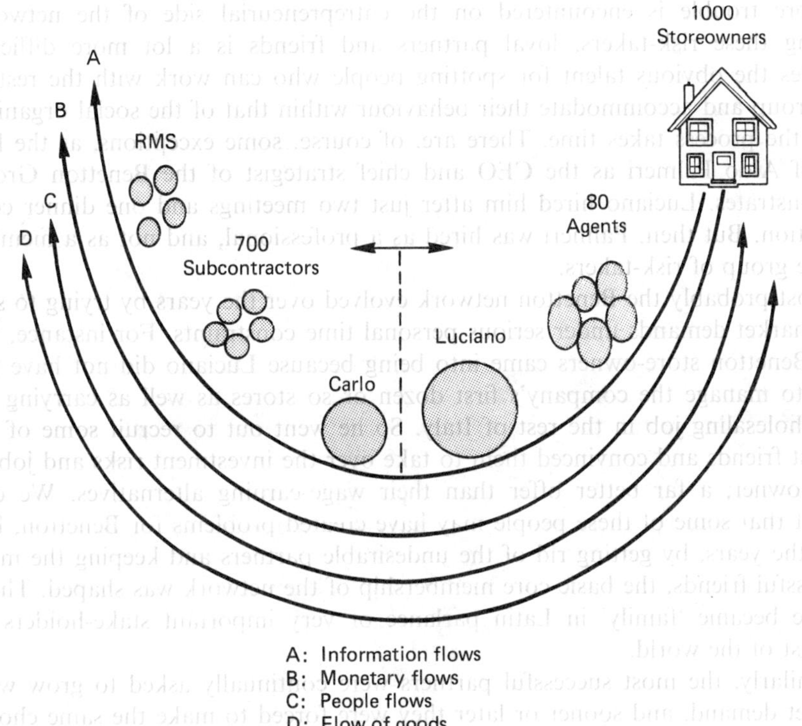

Figure 4.2 Benetton's group hammock organization

does not include marketing, sales, production and personnel. There are four vital executives: the CEO, the information manager, the logistics manager and the manager of financial flows; all other positions take a secondary, or advisory role. Benetton, for instance, would surely be a behemoth with close to 15,000 unionized workers and more than 36,000 store employees were it not for its network of subcontractors and agents. Thus, at Benetton, there is no need for several layers of managers and the huge personnel department that goes with the traditional structure needed in an integrated company.

4.6 Creating a network organization

To create a network organization two parallel structures must be reproduced: the professional structure and the entrepreneurial network. The professional side of a network organization can be reproduced without much trouble; information, logistic and finance managers can be found and trained in the 'ways' of the network and so support the money-making activities of all entrepreneurs in the social side of the network. Aldo Palmeri did this for Benetton between 1983 and 1984 with great success. His biggest problem was convincing these managers to move from Milano, on the West side of north Italy to Treviso, on the East!

More trouble is encountered on the entrepreneurial side of the network; finding these risk-takers, loyal partners and friends is a lot more difficult. Besides the obvious talent for spotting people who can work with the rest of the group and accommodate their behaviour within that of the social organization, the process takes time. There are, of course, some exceptions, as the hiring of Aldo Palmeri as the CEO and chief strategist of the Benetton Group demonstrates. Luciano hired him after just two meetings and one dinner conversation. But then, Palmeri was hired as a professional, and not as a member of the group of risk-takers.

Most probably the Benetton network evolved over the years by trying to satisfy market demands under serious personal time constraints. For instance, the first Benetton store-owners came into being because Luciano did not have the time to manage the company's first dozen or so stores as well as carrying on his wholesaling job in the rest of Italy. So he went out to recruit some of his closest friends and convinced them to take over the investment risks and job of store-owner; a far better offer than their wage-earning alternatives. We can expect that some of these people may have created problems for Benetton, but over the years, by getting rid of the undesirable partners and keeping the most successful friends, the basic core membership of the network was shaped. These people became 'family' in Latin parlance or very important stake-holders to the rest of the world.

Similarly, the most successful partners were continually asked to grow with market demand, and sooner or later they were forced to make the same choice that Luciano had made in order to improve the effective use of their time: they convinced some of their friends and employees to take risks as store-owners. So, the first agents were born, they concentrated, probably substituting for Luciano, in wholesaling products to groups of stores, including their own. This led to the first store-owners in partnership with agents or Luciano.

Eventually the agents had to divide their territories among the most successful store-owners-partners and a third tier of wholesalers came to be known as junior-agents. It took Luciano Benetton about 20 years to have the core group of agents in place by 1975. By 1991, the system had a pyramidal structure with Luciano at the vertex, followed by about ten 'senior' agents interacting with him, about ten 'junior' agents following each senior agent and about ten store-owners following each junior agent. On average, the direct span of social control of these people was ten. As the system developed, the people most competent at these social interactions were closer to Luciano.

The whole system was based on personal knowledge of each individual. Downstream, Luciano was followed by about 1,100 independent risk taking entrepreneurs who invested their money in Benetton garments and followed the strategy set at its centre. But intimate knowledge also meant trust, interpersonal understanding, intimate comprehension of people's motivations and feelings. The latter can only be developed through time. Thus time and intimate interpersonal understanding are necessary for the replication of the social organization.

Clearly, the span of social control of Luciano included many more than ten senior agents – he had to deal with professional managers, acquisition strategies, legal strategies, joint ventures, licensing and family relations. For us the key word in all these relations is not control, it is '*followed by . . .*'. Control implies a command relationship that does not really exist in a social network. For a social network to exist four things need to be true:

1 A risk-taking *leader* must be willing to take on bigger and bigger challenges – dreams – with a group of trusted, risk-taking junior partners. Luciano sets the strategy.
2 This group of trusted, risk-taking junior partners must in turn be willing to *follow* the leader in the search of his collective dream: it must become a shared dream. The members of the network follow the strategy set by the core company.
3 The bonding material must be made from a *mutual trust* between the members of the partnership that neither the Benettons nor the agents will behave opportunistically.
4 The motivation of the core company is to help the growth and prosperity of the members of the network; without it, the core company cannot grow or prosper.

4.7 Concentrating on a strategy

Conceiving an outpacing strategy is not a terribly difficult task. The time-consuming and permanent top management job is to manage the consistent execution of a chosen strategic posture. The harmonization of a complex set of strategies is usually done through the adaptation of simple and clearly understood formal and informal rules that guide the decision-making in the company.

Since the idea is to coordinate the thousands of decisions taken by executives working in downstream, support and upstream elements of the company, these 'decision rules' should be complementary, that is, they should assure the generation of synergistic decision-making in all elements of the business system: decisions taken upstream must complement decisions taken downstream, even when they are taken by people who don't know the existence of each other, let alone that they are taking decisions that add up to a strategic direction. These formal and informal decision rules are called 'business policies' of the company, and the task is to create these so that thousands of people take smaller complementary decisions.

Strategic management is about managing business policies. Most of the time these policies emerge upstream, downstream or in support functions by adapting and keeping the things that work well in those elements of the business. Clearly, there is a risk that the uncoordinated adaptation of these emergent policies may produce a strategic posture that is incongruent, produces no synergy, or still worse, destroys value.

Hence, there are two main company needs demanding strategic management: first, the need to create explicit policies in all elements of the business system; complementary policies that create and do not destroy synergy; and second, the need to select, adopt and adapt emergent policies in all elements of the business system, without destroying synergy. Strategic management is about creating and adapting complementary business policies.

Contrast this view with the often presented problem of managing interfaces. Functional interfaces are needed when isolated management functions exist, or are created. You don't have a problem if you don't get organized to have it. The need to manage interfaces arises from poor strategic management, that is, from a lack of processes that create complementary business policies in all elements of the business system. Quite the contrary, the corporation gets organized in carefully separated and independent compartments (called functions, business units and divisions) that are not only managed at arms length but also housed in far away physical locations (cities, countries and continents).

Clearly, an organized team is capable of creating and adapting policies for producing low-cost, high quality products in the upstream elements of the business system, whereas in the downstream elements a niche or mass market strategy is being followed by a completely different group of people in a coordinated way. A well-managed strategic posture is capable of simultaneously creating and directing quality and cost drives in different elements of the company's business system while still maintaining a congruent posture.

4.8 Conclusions

The network organization seems to be an effective answer to the question of how to inject entrepreneurialism into mammoth corporations. We have seen how Lithonia and General Electric are in the process of creating external networks and internally negotiated strategies respectively. We believe that after careful study of a company's industrial environment, some type of network partnership can be developed in its industry. The advice we offer is: go out and look for potential partnerships that have not yet been created.

Assignment questions

1 What is a network organization?
2 What is needed for participative management?
3 Describe the Hammock organization.
4 How is the social organization created?
5 How can a corporation be simultaneously entrepreneurial and cost effective?

5

The missing link in the solutions business: managing flows through business systems

Over the last twenty or so years, the West has watched in amazement as Japanese low-cost suppliers have systematically displaced well-established western corporations, first in motorcycles, then in automobiles, and more recently in the sophisticated computer industry. It has been argued that the Japanese threat can be avoided by concentrating on products in which they were weak such as, bigger motorcycles or more luxurious cars, because: 'the Japanese are weak at design'. Today, in the early 1990s, equivalent myths are beginning to permeate the computer industry: 'they can't write good software' and 'the Japanese will never make it in the expensive car segment'.

History has shown that the ostrich approach is no answer to the challenges of the Japanese. To face the threat of new low-cost, high-quality entrants into an industry, established market leaders must devise ways to match the newcomers' products both in price and in quality, denying them the privilege of exploiting the price umbrella created by leading-edge technological products. Let us consider three established western market leaders.

5.1. Uponor Oy

Uponor, a conglomerate of about 60 operating companies had sales of around US$800 million in 1990. The corporation tripled its sales between 1987 and 1990, while maintaining double figure returns on net assets. This strong growth was achieved by acquisitions and the research and development of plastic materials in piping transportation systems, as well as in the delivery systems themselves.

Uponor specialized in the development and manufacture of plastic pipes systems for a wide range of industrial sectors, including construction, municipal engineering, agriculture and forestry. The company expected to continue to increase the use of plastic and its composites as a material for pipe manufacture.

Uponor was organized in four major business areas:

1 The Hot Water Systems division manufactured cross-linked polyethylene pipes for heating and tap-water systems. A range of products was marketed through independent companies or subsidiaries as semi-finished or as complete systems. The best sales were obtained by Velta and Polytherm, both successful brand names in the complete systems German market. Extensive investments were made with clients and specialists for the development of new types of pipe fittings, industrial applications and complete

systems. Several new products for use with underfloor heating, radiator heating and tap-water systems were introduced.

2 The main products for the Piping Systems Divisions were sewer and pressure pipes for municipalities; soil and waste-water pipes for housing; and plastic pipes systems for construction, agriculture and forestry. These divisions operated in Finland, Scandinavia, Central Europe and the USA. Increased competition, especially from Scandinavian and East European manufacturers, within the polyethylene pipe sector as a whole, led to severe pressure on pipe prices. Price competition among wholesalers of plastic pipe systems also accelerated in the late 1980s.

3 Uponor introduced new products among which was its breakthrough Ultra-Rib system, which comprised a new infiltration system, a new chamber system and a new electrofusion fittings system for water supply. Investments were made for the development of extrusion, injection moulding and Ultra extrusion lines, in an effort to build the technology for large-scale production of pipes and components.

4 The Gas Systems divisions manufactured special plastic pipes and systems for the transportation of a variety of liquid gases over long and short distances.

Strong manufacturers emerged in the world market for plastic pipes, coupled with an evolution towards a new class of competitor: those who were allied to raw material suppliers and who continuously strengthened and consolidated their position in competition against other materials.

As a result, by 1990, there was an extrusion overcapacity of 400 per cent of the market's needs for hot water pipes in the West European market. Overcapacity of installed extrusion in Western Europe led to intense price competition in plastic pipes during the 1980s. In response to these competitive pressures a number of systems suppliers appears and ended up dominating the industry. By 1991, the sequence of businesses serving the end consumer of the hot water division started with the supplier of raw materials (pellets), followed by extrusion companies, component suppliers (manifolds, electronic controls, panels, fittings, etc.), systems suppliers, wholesalers, installers, contractors, and finally the end consumer.

Installers could purchase cross-linked polyethylene pipes and all other components directly from a manufacturer or from wholesalers. Uponor's delivery strategy was typical of the largest competitors in the industry: they sold both pipes and complete systems to wholesalers and systems suppliers. In 1991 Uponor was the market leader in systems sales and owner of the strongest brands in the West European market.

5.2 ABB Robotics[1]

In 1990, ABB operated in 20 countries and had 25,000 industrial robots installed around the world. It was the world's largest industrial robotic manu-

[1] This example was taken from the industry note prepared by research associate Robert Howard under the direction of Jean-Pierre Jeannet, visiting professor at IMEDE, Copyright in 1989 by IMEDE, Lausanne, Switzerland.

facturer in a global industry tentatively assessed at around $US2.5 billion; with an annual growth rate of nearly 15 per cent between 1987 and 1990. Its sales in the same year were about US$350 million and they sold 2,000 robots worldwide. Despite an industry slump triggered by the global retraction of the motor industry, ABB's profits strengthened significantly by following a product strategy that combined the sale of 'naked' robots and integrated systems.

Sales increased in the Far East and Europe, and included orders from Nissan, Citroën and Volvo. The acquisition of Cincinnati Milacron's robotics division helped to strengthen their presence in North America. ABB's new super IRB 6000, a robot designed for the motor industry and material handling business, was launched in the early 1990s.

Although some industry experts have predicted slower growth within the industrial hardware segment during the 1990s they have been rather more optimistic about systems. Ten years ago ABB's billings were split 30/70 systems and hardware. In 1990, the split was 55/45 in favour of systems.

Industrial robots[2] are a part of the large manufacturing automation industry segment, that includes computer-aided design (CAD) and microprocessor-controlled industrial machinery. The full range of robots includes varieties that can perform space exploration, mining and underwater work and even housekeeping. Their uses are endless. They can perform dangerous, monotonous, dirty work. They can be re-programmed to adapt to new product designs rather than retool or replace existing machinery. Usually, such robots are sold 'naked', i.e. without engineering but with articulated limbs, sensors, vision systems and a built-in computer with software for specific tasks.

Plants that use mass production techniques and incorporate industrial robots in the manufacturing process consistently outperform non-robotized plants. However, as manufacturing technology approaches perfection, the value added by machine tool proficiency falls. Consequently it becomes important for a robot producer to develop other abilities such as electronics and software.

Japan leads the world in robotic hardware, largely because of its superiority in customizing them for specific applications, an ability the western companies lacked. Japanese design skills also allowed them to offer greater choice and flexibility at cheaper prices. However, they were less able to supply software that can compete with many US firms and this undermined their overall competitiveness in systems integration (SI).

A robot was generally purchased from a manufacturer or a systems integrator. Installation of a robotic system called for a long-term investment in capital and would take about 2 to 4 years to break even; 5 years to make a return on R&D. Systems were often built from a number of robots sourced from different manufacturers and could vary widely in their complexity. Engineers are required to design systems that would enable these robots to work together and meet the exact needs of the client. Achieving this type of integration entailed either cooperation between the various manufacturers or the use of an independent systems house.

[2] The International Federation of Robots in Stockholm, has defined an industrial robot as 'An automatically controlled, reprogrammable, multi-purpose, manipulative machine with several degrees of freedom which may be either fixed in place or mobile in use in industrial automation applications'. Let's just call them industrial robots.

The second option was a path often taken by the Japanese who lacked their own systems houses and as a consequence their customers had become used to either dealing with integration themselves or calling upon the services of independent system integrators, or system houses, who occupy the same sort of position in this industry as third-party programmers play in the computer world. These people were responsible for specifying the robots and related equipment necessary to do the job at hand, often from different suppliers.

ABB's Robotics division operated a typical distribution system, with 'Robot Centres' or sales centres supplying both hardware and the engineering capability to set up an entire system, including service and training. These services were included to discourage customers from going to an independent systems integrator who, because they could recommend products from any manufacturer, could end up competing with the robot manufacturers themselves by selecting only a limited amount of their accessories.

ABB Robotics, whose growth rate was well above the industry's average, also believed that good training was key to the success of a robotic supplier. If introduced right from the start, it prevents the misuse of robot technology and minimizes errors in operations, errors that are all too often blamed on the robot itself. ABB Robotics had been so successful in training users that it decided to sell training separately. In 1990, 10-12 per cent of ABB Robotics' billings came from training, and the company estimated that it trained 2.5 persons per robot sold.

5.3 IBM

The major offerings of the computer manufacturers over the past 30 years: the main-frames of the 1960s, the minis of the 1970s and the PCs of the 1980s – still continued to play an important role at the beginning of the 1990s. However, by 1991, the industry was rapidly adapting itself in the face of new competitive forces, which combined software and hardware produced by a variety of vendors. Backing their products with intense, customized service, this new generation of suppliers was able to offer cost efficient solutions.

In this mature computer industry, competition and technology combined to drive down the costs of computing power and the price of end products. The hardware business looked more and more like a commodity market, with several American, European and Japanese competitors supplying state-of-the-art computers and components. The US Industrial Outlook (1990) identified three clear trends as the major forces that would drive the change forecast for the industry in the 1990s:

1 Maturation of the hardware business with a shift from high-margin main-frames to low-margin workstations and personal computers, positioned software and services as differentiation factors for future growth.
2 Increased competition among vendors using off-the-shelf parts and contracted labour to avoid the immense investment associated with vertical integration for the manufacture of equipment.

3 Elimination of proprietary software architecture resulting in a move to open standards that would allow the mixing of equipment from many vendors.

Consider IBM's competitive posture in the early 1990s. During the 1980s, Japanese computer manufacturers led by Toshiba Corporation, Fujitsu Ltd/ICL, Hitachi Ltd and Mitsubishi Electric Corporation became a major challenge to IBM's worldwide dominance, grabbing a 20 per cent market share in Europe in 1990. With the sole exception of Japan, IBM was market share leader in every major market in which it was active.

With sales of US$67 billion and 387,000 employees, IBM faced falling market shares, particularly in Europe where it fell from 21 per cent in 1980 to 16 per cent in 1990. This trend, and a drop in profits, prompted a restructuring of its organization through staff reduction and the forging of business partnerships. The aim was to improve profits and to strengthen ties with customers. From 1989 onwards, IBM gave top priority to changing from its original product-oriented (boxes or hardware) sales strategy to a new customer-solution oriented approach.

The systems integration market (solutions) had high growth and high value added. However, its complexity and high margins made it a high risk business as well. IBM's new end-product strategy meant delivering turnkey solutions to customers' system integration problems, which for most customers meant integrating systems and applications to provide a unified operating environment.

A number of independent system integrators, like Andersen Consulting, CGS, Sema, SD-Scion, Siemens, Logica, EDS, Digital, and others, were quick to grasp the opportunities offered by the fast growing and lucrative ($4 billion), West European market. A similar situation prevailed worldwide. In 1990, one systems supplier defined a solution as 'necessarily including the selection and provision of the best hardware and software for the job; and the initial contract must be worth more than US$ 500,000 and take more than 9 months to implement'.

According to an IBM marketing manager, a solution was composed of: hardware (IBM or others), basic software (IBM or others), standard applications (IBM or others), special applications (IBM or others) and services which included conceptualisation, analysis, programming, maintenance, education and value added networking.

The sales objective was to solve the customer's problem with a turnkey solution including hardware specification, software adaptation or development, and services. Working with a sales person, a specialized group defined the project, assessed the skills required and decided what had to be subcontracted.

About half of the solutions sold in 1990 to the West European market were provided by professional services organizations, like Andersen Consulting, about one-third were provided by vendors of computer equipment, like IBM, and the rest by vendors of other hardware. The equipment vendors exploited their products, technological skills and access to the market through their existing customer base and sales force. Professional service organizations exploited their consultancy, project management and application skills as well as their multi-vendor experience.

5.4 What do they have in common?

In spite of the vast differences in size between Uponor Oy, ABB Robotics and IBM, similarities can be found in the dynamic of the competition in their industries. In summary, the three industries were reflected in an enterprise system[3] that included hardware component suppliers (HCS), hardware suppliers (HS), solution component suppliers (SCS), software houses (SH), and solution suppliers (SS); where the value added tended to concentrate around the solution suppliers. Forward integration changed the nature of competition, both in the delivery strategies of solution-services and in the processing strategies of hardware producers.

Specifically:

1 *Hardware products are turning into commodities.* All three: plastic pipes, robots and computers, once protected by patents or proprietary technology, were becoming commodities in all market segments. This meant that competitors had to excel in low-cost manufacturing and high delivered quality, since patents no longer protected processing inefficiencies through high margins.

Historically, IBM provided software services to its customers in order to sell its hardware products; there was not only a scarcity of systems talent but also many products had proprietary patents that maintained the use of complex know-how inside the corporation. In the 1990s it will make no difference who supplies the 'boxes', so long as they perform the job in accordance with specifications. By the same token, the manufacturing technology of cross-linked polyethylene pipes and other components, patented by Hewing and Wirsbo at the beginning of the 1980s, became a commodity at the end of the decade. In 1991, most pipe producers could offer similar quality products, and only in special projects, such as wide diameters or composites, did plastic pipe technology make a difference to supplier selection.

Since the late 1980s the manufacturing technology of many hardware products has become increasingly accessible. This caused the appearance of Japanese low-cost hardware manufacturers, like Fujitsu in the computer industry, who eroded the market shares of the traditional market share leaders.

2 *The new end products are solutions to customer problems.* Recognizing how complex it was to come up with customized solutions to complicated management or industrial problems, independent service organizations started providing solutions to these customer problems by sourcing components from several hardware vendors.

Why do these solution markets come to exist in the first place? In the plastic pipe industry, the installer obtained value from the wages saved by an easy to install product solution; while the contractor also found value in the security of having eliminated risks and the lower costs associated with shorter installation times. In the robotic and computer industries, customized SI solutions required

[3] Defined as the sequence of existing businesses (starting with raw material suppliers and ending with retailers) which are involved in delivering goods/services to final consumer groupings.

project management know-how to blend complex technologies. Most customers considered themselves ill-prepared and ill-equipped to do the job. Thus, they preferred to concentrate on what they could do well; for instance, Volvo manufactured cars while ABB Robotics installed robots, and as a result, Volvo avoided the risks inherent in the development of a complex system.

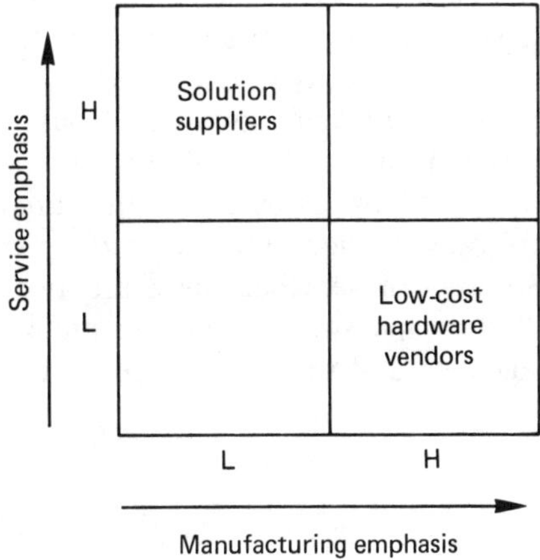

Figure 5.1 Business emphasis in the solution business

Two dimensions, illustrated in Figure 5.1, facilitate the understanding of the differences between the solution and hardware businesses. On the vertical axis we note that solution suppliers have a higher service content in their end products than hardware suppliers, that is to say, they operate *people* businesses. On the horizontal axis we note that hardware suppliers have a higher content of manufacturing abilities than solution suppliers, that is to say, they operate *process* businesses.

In addition, Figure 5.2 helps us understand the different types of solutions in

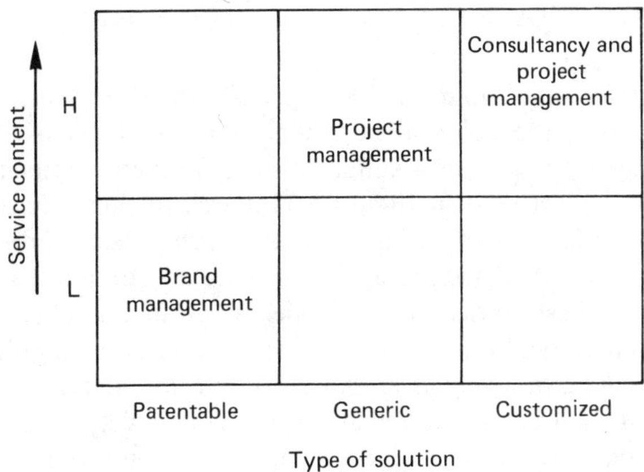

Figure 5.2 Generic solutions

the plastic pipes, robotic and computer industries. The vertical axis shows the degree to which the customer requires services to obtain his customized solution. The horizontal axis measures the degree of uniqueness of the solutions, from standard patentable plastic pipe systems at one extreme, to unique, tailor-made highly complex SI solutions at the other.

When standard and patentable solutions can be produced, as is the case in the plastic pipe industry, a key success factor (KSF) in the business is a company's ability to manage the brand names originating in the patents. However, when each solution is tailor-made to satisfy customer needs, then all development costs, including marketing and research, should be recovered immediately, making project management the KSF for competition. In the former, patents become industry standards as over time they are available to everybody and, in the latter, hardware-solution suppliers end up competing with consultancy partnerships. So we can see that there are two important differences between patentable plastic pipe systems and customized robotic-computer SI solutions: brand management and project management.

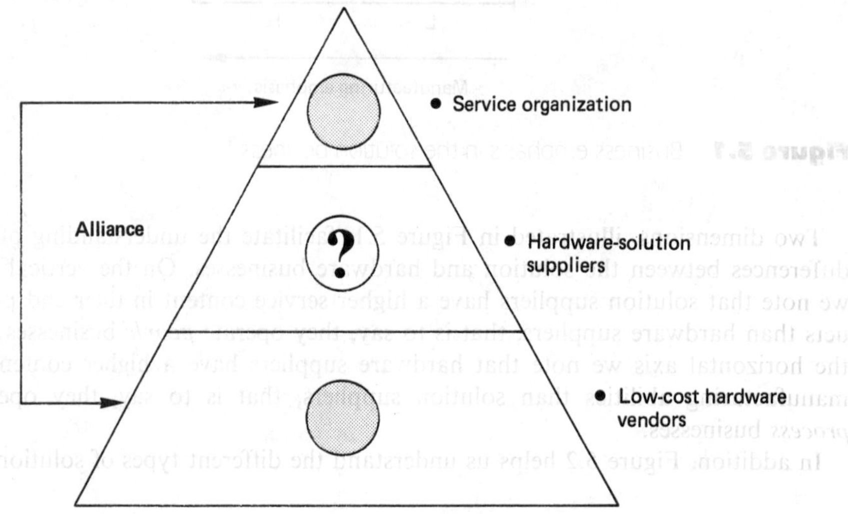

Figure 5.3 Potential alliances

3 *Solution-service suppliers are increasingly dictating an industry's strategy.* In the three industries, the solution suppliers solve a problem and proceed to select the hardware vendors best suited to become the equipment suppliers for their solutions, as illustrated in Figure 5.3. It was in this way that Velta marketed its floor heating system using pipes and components produced by competing suppliers; and Andersen Consulting, selected computer and component vendors that were best suited for their clients' solutions. Thus the bargaining power in these industries shifted into the hands of solution suppliers.

4 *Traditional hardware suppliers have decided to integrate forwards in an attempt to become hardware-solution suppliers.* This is why competitors in solution markets have two historical origins: hardware vendors like IBM, Uponor and ABB Robotics who have integrated forwards in an effort to capture the value added located downstream of their main businesses; and systems suppli-

ers – service organizations or entrepreneurs – who identified a market need and created a solution (new service).

5 *The traditional organizational structures of hardware vendors are insufficient to deal with the new competitors and end products.* This clearly poses two interrelated questions: how should the traditional hardware supplier reorganize its corporation and how should the change to this new organizational structure be managed?

5.5 Two generic ways of competing

Hardware vendors were historically successful because they were organized to excel in making money by managing their fixed and current assets. That is, they managed their return on equity (ROE) superbly by protecting their profit margin, turnover and financial leverage.

Thus the key success factors were usually linked to the ability to manufacture high-margin proprietary products that permitted profitable operations with relatively low financial leverages. Accordingly, executive incentive systems were generally related to revenue, cost-quality measures and profitability. When these high-margin advantages are sustained for a long period of time, the corporation ends up developing considerable overheads in the form of staff positions at headquarters, for the simple reason that it can afford it.

However, when these high margins shrink away because it is no longer possible to differentiate your product from the competitors', one way to compete is to become the lowest cost manufacturer in the business. This strategy was followed by the Japanese computer and robotic manufacturers but not by most of their Western counterparts. The latter preferred to add some service layers to their core hardware products in an effort to capture some of the value added by systems suppliers located downstream of their businesses (refer to Figure 5.4). For both these strategies the overheads accumulated during happier days subtracts value.

Figure 5.4 Generic businesses

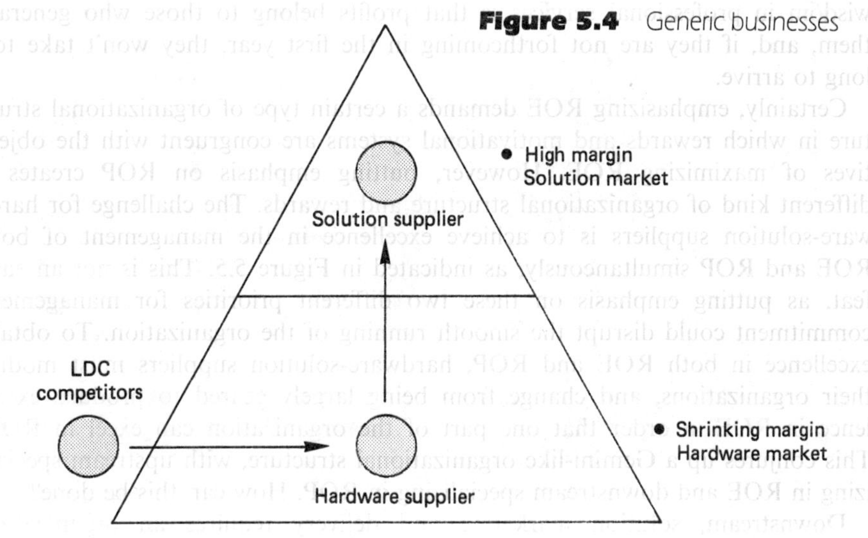

In the hope that 'the Japanese can't write software', some computer companies are shying away from low-cost Japanese new entrants in the familiar hardware market, by choosing instead to compete with professional service organizations dominating an unfamiliar service market downstream of their businesses. This decision provides the Japanese low-cost manufacturers with a price umbrella under which they can both prosper and gain market share.

Professional service organizations prosper by making as much money as they can on their partners' time. The key to their success is the management of this time. That is, they manage their return on partners (ROP) by protecting their efficiency (profit margin) and their partners' effectiveness (sales per partner).

$$\text{ROP} = (\text{Profit/Gross Fees}) \times (\text{Gross Fees/No. of Partners})$$

One key success factor in a service organization is the ability to manage high value-adding projects within cost and time constraints. Thus, professional services can be viewed as partnerships that specialize in project management. In this way, the partnership's efficiency is reached through close management of the time of the professionals working on all projects.

Another equally important key success factor in a professional service organization is the partnership's effectiveness. This is obtained through repeat business and internal promotion of those professionals able to maintain repeated client orders.

The partnership's prestige and the partners' time can be leveraged if junior professionals carry out the project activities under the supervision of senior partners. The concept of leverage in a service organization is to leverage the partners' time; a completely different notion from financial leverage.

Thus all three, efficiency, effectiveness and leverage depend on the partners' abilities and sustained efforts through the years. Workaholic habits occur because the profits that are gained as a result go to the partners. Thus when selfish behaviour by a partner, or partners, impedes the promotion of star junior consultants, the latter simply pack up and start new practices, capitalizing on their well earned relations and 'savoir faire'. Therefore, the overriding wisdom in professional services is that profits belong to those who generate them, and, if they are not forthcoming in the first year, they won't take too long to arrive.

Certainly, emphasizing ROE demands a certain type of organizational structure in which rewards and motivational systems are congruent with the objectives of maximizing ROE. However, putting emphasis on ROP creates a different kind of organizational structure and rewards. The challenge for hardware-solution suppliers is to achieve excellence in the management of both ROE and ROP simultaneously, as indicated in Figure 5.5. This is not an easy feat, as putting emphasis on these two different priorities for management commitment could disrupt the smooth running of the organization. To obtain excellence in both ROE and ROP, hardware-solution suppliers must modify their organizations, and change from being largely geared to produce excellence in ROE in order that one part of the organization can excel in ROP. This conjures up a Gemini-like organizational structure, with upstream specializing in ROE and downstream specializing in ROP. How can this be done?

Downstream, solution marketing and delivery requires an organization

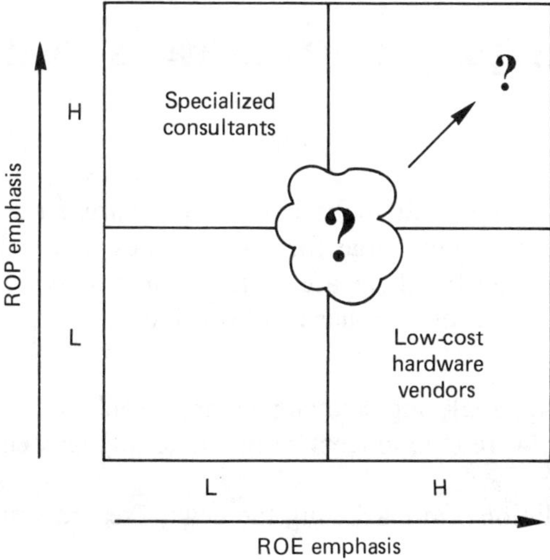

Figure 5.5 Caught in the middle?

designed to identify and then respond quickly to evolving market needs. Rapid response to customer needs is cultivated through appropriate reward systems. A system needs to be implemented that can standardize and introduce these solutions into all the markets in which the corporation has a presence. Major consulting partnerships are good examples of the type of organization required, and the kind of incentives that are key to the success of such ventures.

5.6 Corporate strengths and the marketing of solutions

Clearly, the major advantage in marketing solutions instead of hardware is the opportunity to exploit the high value added that becomes available with the delivery of professional services: about 25 per cent in the robotic industry, about 30 per cent in plastic pipe systems, and between 30 per cent and 60 per cent for SI solutions in the computer industry.

A second advantage is that corporations like Uponor, ABB Robotics and IBM are well positioned in world markets with broad customer bases, well-recognized brand names, knowledgeable and well connected sales forces, and, except for Uponor, wide installed bases of equipment. Thus, these organizational strengths present a basis upon which the marketing of solutions can be built.

Finally, three additional, organizational strengths can be created and exploited by corporations involved in the marketing of tailor-made solutions: first, data banks of successful generic solutions that can be accessed by any manager trying to solve a customer's problem; second, data banks of capable and reliable service partners in specific areas of expertise; and finally, data banks of corporate project and marketing managers (a skill base) who have successfully delivered complex SI solutions.

5.7 Three major pitfalls in the solution business

In their haste to occupy what looks like a high margin business, some hardware-solution vendors undercharge for the activities in which they add value. In the plastic pipe industry there are at least three activities prior to project execution where the solution supplier creates value:

1 Understanding and analysing civil engineering problems.
2 Defining the hardware components to manufacture, as well as the associated investment risks.
3 Patenting the solution and marketing the newly created system.

In the pipe systems business the value added by solving the technical and hardware problems is recognized by the market, and profited on by solution suppliers through patents on systems. In this way Uponor and its systems competitors capitalize on their experience, expertise, knowledge and efforts, through patents and brand management of these patented product-solutions.

In the robotic industry there are at least four activities where the solution supplier creates value before project execution:

1 Understanding and analysing the industrial engineering problems and risks.
2 Defining the technical hardware and software needs, as well as associated risks.
3 Putting together the project team.
4 Trying to patent a generic solution for a class of industrial engineering solutions.

In the robotic industry, generic solutions to industrial engineering problems could be leveraged by systems suppliers through either the use of solution-data banks or attempts to patent some of them. Otherwise, if the time spent in these activities is not billed to the customer, the corporation loses the up-front investment in proposal preparation, i.e. the industrial engineering work, the technical work and project team preparation.

In the computer industry there are at least three activities before project execution (illustrated in Figure 5.6), where the solution supplier creates value:

1 Understanding and analysing business problems and risks.
2 Defining the technical hardware and software needs, as well as associated risks.
3 Putting together the project team.

Most customers' problems demand tailor-made solutions that require the type of skills in which consultants excel: leveraging out the time of the part-

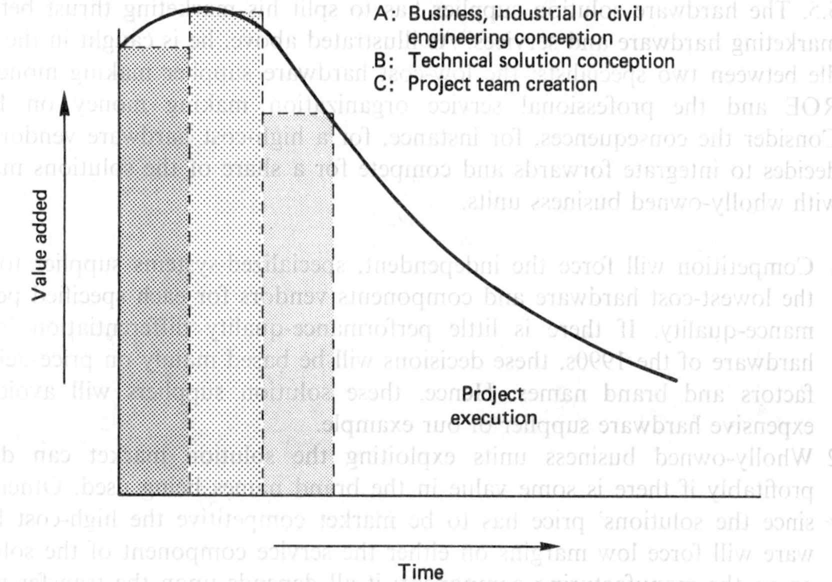

Figure 5.6 Value added in the solutions business

ners. Professional service organizations recoup this up-front investment in two ways: first, by using a multiplier on the time spent by everyone working on a project's execution (counting the number of hours spent on a project and multiplying them by, say, three times the hourly fees). This multiplier, say three, is calculated so that all overheads and yearly working-hours, including selling time, down time, development time, execution time, and so on are paid for at execution time.

A second, and complementary system, often used to recover marketing expenses, is to break down big projects into smaller sub-projects, i.e. first, a sub-project to determine the scope of the study; next, a sub-project to solve the business/engineering problem; then, a sub-project to conceive the technical specifications; next, a sub-project to deliver the final solution. In this way consultants not only recover the value added by proposal preparation and solution conception but also diminish to a minimum the risks assumed with each sub-project.

However, some computer-solution suppliers do not recover the value added during their marketing efforts, solution conception and development activities, as shown in Figure 5.6. If the contract is not won, they lose these investments, which can provide up to 50 per cent of the value added to the customer. Put simply, once a customer knows what his business problem is; understands what IT solution would help solve it; and knows which combination of subcontractors can deliver the solution; most of the value has been added, and all he has to do is have various service organizations bid for the management of the project, which has been excellently specified – free of charge.

The second pitfall is getting stuck in the middle, as shown in Figures 5.3 and

5.5. The hardware solution supplier has to split his marketing thrust between marketing hardware and services. As illustrated above, he is caught in the middle between two specialists: the low-cost hardware supplier making money on ROE and the professional service organization making money on ROP. Consider the consequences, for instance, for a high-cost hardware vendor that decides to integrate forwards and compete for a share of the solutions market with wholly-owned business units.

1 Competition will force the independent, specialized-systems supplier to find the lowest-cost hardware and components vendors for each specified performance-quality. If there is little performance-quality differentiation in the hardware of the 1990s, these decisions will be based mainly on price-delivery factors and brand names. Hence, these solution suppliers will avoid the expensive hardware supplier of our example.
2 Wholly-owned business units exploiting the solution market can do so profitably if there is some value in the brand names being used. Otherwise, since the solutions' price has to be market competitive the high-cost hardware will force low margins on either the service component of the solution or on the manufacturing component; it all depends upon the transfer prices used. Clearly there is no free lunch: a high-cost hardware supplier participating in the solution business cannot siphon margins from ROP to ROE and pretend to be doing a good job; it really is stuck in the middle, hurting ROP margins with illusionary ROE margins.
3 This policy harms the corporation in the long run. As shown above, high quality professionals – those developing the ROP part of the business – hold all the negotiating power, and will eventually set up independent shops if part of the ROP profits do not come their way. The illusory transfer of margins may work temporarily, but only until the exodus of the firm's best solution creators starts, fuelled by either recruiting raids from systems suppliers or by spin-offs from new, competing houses. Therefore, the corporation must seek a low-cost hardware position in order to make money on ROE without having to milk the margins made by its service organizations.

There is little hope to be found in seeking refuge from the low-cost Japanese hardware vendors in the solution business. To remain competitive, a hardware-component vendor must seek a low-cost position or a proprietary, technological innovation that the market is willing to pay for, as is illustrated in Figure 5.6. In summary, when proprietary technology is no longer available, and hardware component vendors sell similar commodities, it is imperative that they develop a low-cost 'box' that competes in price–quality with the new entrants and deprives them of a price umbrella.

Clearly, the third pitfall in the solution business is to compete with an organization designed to maximize revenue (ROE-based, high profit margins) in a service. That is, using an organization designed to research hardware technologies, develop hardware products and promote these products, to compete in a market place dominated by successful service specialists.

5.8 Five distinctive competencies to cultivate

To become dominant competitors in the solution business, corporations like Uponor, ABB Robotics and IBM must refine their business systems so that upstream they are organized to manufacture and sell low-cost, high-quality hardware components (computers, naked robots, and plastic pipes, etc.) to all participants in the solutions business; while downstream they are organized to sell and deliver solutions to customer problems. Both products – hardware and solutions – have to add real value to succeed: in hardware, the value added will be reflected in the price, while in solutions it will be reflected in their high quality performance. This double-edged product/market strategy can be accomplished in the long run if the following five distinctive competencies are nurtured and cultivated.

First, the corporation has to encourage and protect the value-adding activities in their business system. In an activity-based organization the top of the pyramid is occupied by the business units performing the activities at the core of the success of the corporation, whereas staffing is placed in a support role (as it should be). This has the following implications:

1 Managers will be out in the field adding real value to customer solutions or low-cost, high-quality hardware, research, development and manufacturing. Managerial positions are assigned only to value-adding activities.
2 Positions incurring overheads disappear from these organizations unless, of course, they add value to some activity. In the robotic and computer industries, for example, overheads created by research, development and internal services must be guided – and if possible hired out – by the activities using these services. This way, the managers in charge of these support activities will respond directly, with nobody in between, to the users of their services. This clearly implies a lean organization, capable of responding to market needs, and not one with everyone busy writing memos to each other and interfering with the value-adding activities performed by the service units and hardware manufacturing and selling units. In an activity-based organization, executives manage activities and not other managers; likewise, researchers don't manage other researchers, they actually *do* research.

The second distinctive competence is the ability to protect the four core generic activities that eventually transform pyramidal organizations into entrepreneurial organizations: these are sourcing, processing, delivery and support activities. One successful way of doing this is found in network organizations, like Benetton, who create processing and delivery networks of entrepreneurs and centralize those activities where it pays to be big: sourcing and support activities. Figure 5.7 illustrates how a corporation can organize its business system in order to encourage specialization in its core activities: via a network of interlinked but independent business units. The key to such organizations lies in the support provided to the money making activities of the different units.

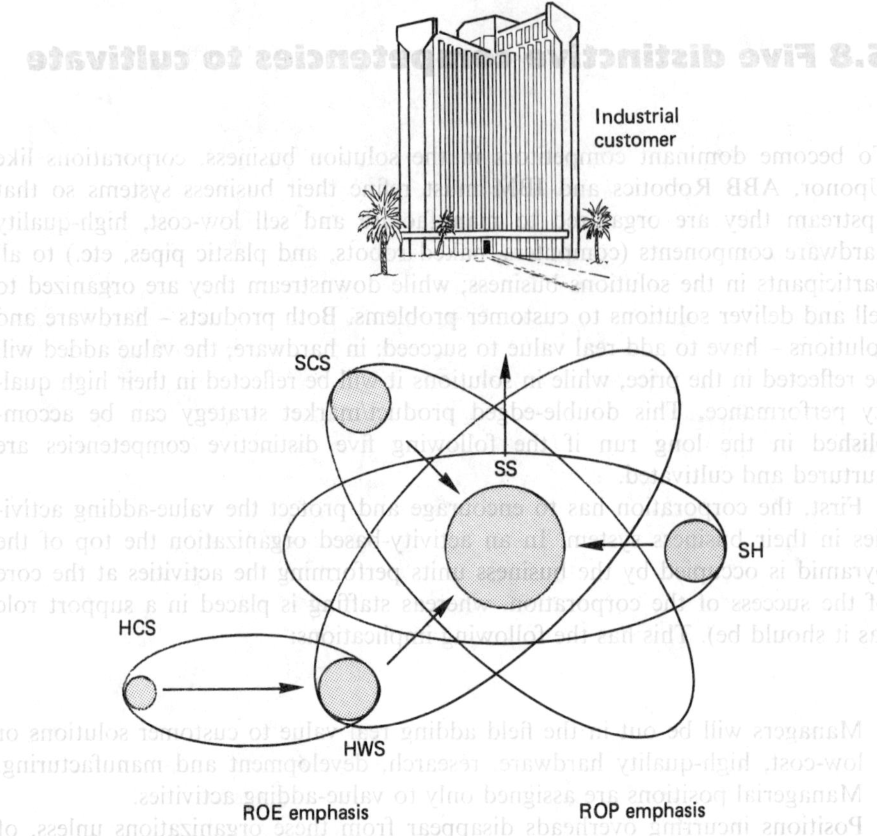

Figure 5.7 A network organization

The third distinctive competence is the corporation's ability to identify and nurture the core technological competencies that enable the creation of leading-edge hardware products, both in a planned and unexpected manner. Two major questions guide the protection of these competencies: what is the future leading-edge quality hardware technology and what is the lowest-cost processing technology? Other key questions that must be answered are concerned with where to invest; who should be protected; who should be freed from value-adding activities to become a part of the corporate research and development overheads; and how long should they be freed from these activities? Answers to these questions are both industry and company specific.

A fourth distinctive competence to cultivate is the corporation's ability to deliver both solutions and hardware products to its customers. In each market, clear decisions have to be made concerning the partners to which the corporation will sell hardware products, the independent subcontractors with which the corporation should work, the partners that should be partially or totally owned, and the alliances that should be maintained. The corporation's integration strategy in the delivery elements of the business system plays a key role, both in the profitability of the business units and in the ability to keep the best solution-creating talent within the corporation.

The delivery strategy of a global corporation is a complex matter that can be streamlined in an activity-based network organization. Partially-owned and independent service practices could be made responsible for the delivery of the corporation's solutions. In these practices, executive reward systems must be allowed to follow consulting standards: consultancy remunerations should be shared between the partners of the different practices and the corporation. But why would a partnership allow a corporation to claim part of its profits? An economic answer, that is, the value added by the corporation, must be found for this question. For instance, the corporation must provide value-adding services to the solution suppliers in return for its share of the profits and its minority stake.

Like everyone else, corporate executives who add value with their services expect a share of the profits. This is why consulting remuneration packages must be adopted by any corporation expecting to retain its best SI talent. It is an illusion to say, 'our people are not interested in money, they have such a strong, achievement-oriented culture that they won't set up an independent shop'. When in doubt, review the remuneration packages of the top 50 people in the corporation to check whether or not 'our people are not interested in money'.

The fifth distinctive competence to protect is the ability to add value to the network of partners through the management of four flows through the business system. One way a partnership would be willing to share part of its profits with a corporation is if its partners receive value-adding support from the corporation. In exchange, corporations like Uponor, ABB Robotics and IBM can select the strategy to be followed by the members of the network. Entrepreneurs will follow if they receive value-adding support in terms of information, goods, people and money. These four critical links provide the umbilical cords that sustain the prosperity of the different participants in the enterprise system.

It has been argued that hardware-solution suppliers add a substantial amount of value with the management of information on generic solutions (solution data banks), skill bases and project team selection (partner data banks). To achieve this, solution-banks, partner-banks and skill-banks must be protected, updated and used on a worldwide scale. Moreover, the people in possession of the experience must be available and willing to help when needed. These are clear examples of activity-based overheads that can be directly financed by the units using these services. Two things are encouraged: first, the data bank managers are motivated to provide the best service money can buy – because their income will depend on it; and second, the business units will demand certain inputs that improve the usefulness of the information. Clearly, end-users will be happy to finance value-adding overheads.

By breaking down a solution into value activities it can be shown that these activities add value by managing information and people flows during proposal preparation and project execution. For example, during the preparation of a proposal for a tailor-made solution, integrated systems suppliers draw on their expertise, knowledge and relations to identify alternative ways to approach the problem, and most importantly, the resources capable of doing so. This is accomplished through: in-house expertise, data banks, electronic communications media, good relations with partners, and so on. That is, by having the ability to manage information flows or put simply, knowing what has to be done and who is capable of doing it.

Similarly, during the preparation of the proposal and the assembly of project teams, the integrated systems supplier also makes a decision, based on past experience, data banks and networking, about who is going to participate in the execution of the project. So we can see that solution suppliers manage the flow of capable people (consultants) through the project.

Clearly, once a project team is accepted by a customer, most of the value created by these activities has been added, and project execution becomes a matter of controlling delivery times and containing risks. This creates a pricing issue. The value added by deciding what activities need to be performed and who can deliver them needs to be charged for. Although these activities are developed with the collaboration of the end-user, the fact is that the customer cannot take these decisions alone. It is precisely because they want to eliminate the risks inherent in the solution that a tremendous value is added by these decisions, and hence the right to a fee for the service. Moreover, these two activities – if performed well – eliminate most of the risks assumed in the project.

Monetary flows are essential for financing proposals and project execution, especially when smaller partners are involved. Financial muscle is central for company qualification in mega-projects. In addition, multi-vendor expertise is crucial when it comes to providing the best hardware for satisfying customer needs, a technology-based value activity.

Professional service organizations, with a multiplier of three, can be conceived as charging one for the professionals' fees, one for overheads, financial and hardware flows (project management) and one for the management of information and people flows (knowledge and experience funnelled to the project). Thus one view of the value being added in a solution is to assign 33 per cent of the value added to the work itself, 33 per cent to project management and 33 per cent to experience, i.e. the people and information flows.

In summary, a dominant hardware-solution supplier should support the sourcing strategies of all partners in the business system with outstanding management of four basic flows: information and people flows at project conception and execution; and money and hardware flows during project execution. This creates the Hammock organization illustrated in Figure 5.8. The Hammock organization, unlike pyramid organizations, is designed to support the activities of the different business units, whether subsidiaries or independent, participating in the business system. This not only facilitates the management of the risks inherent to the solution business but also protects the distinctive competencies of the corporation.

5.9 Conclusions

The marketing of solutions to customer problems does not provide a fundamental answer to competing against low-cost hardware manufacturers. Adding new service layers to the core hardware product brings high margins. However, the high risk nature of the business and the new market in which the corpora-

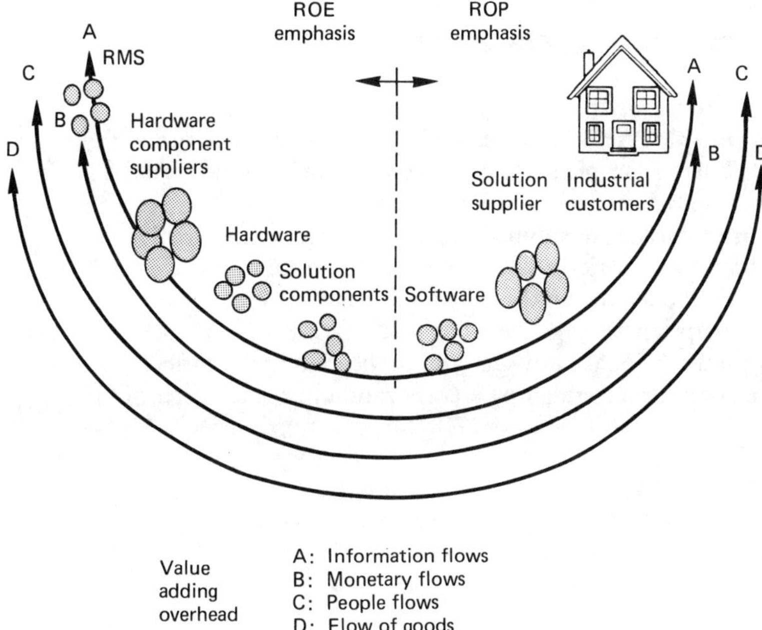

Figure 5.8 The hammock organization

tion gets involved, changes the basis for profitability. We can't pretend that the exploitation of this additional value added costs nothing. In fact, if exploited to perfection, none of the additional profits generated should go to the hardware vendors; they should all belong to the partners of the service organizations. Thus, if a corporation wants a share of these additional profits, without degenerating into a simple distribution channel of value-adding service subcontractors, a new form of industrial organization needs to be created: the Hammock organization.

More importantly, the corporation cannot avoid facing the low-cost hardware competitor in the hardware market by taking refuge in the illusory high-margin service market. They must eliminate the protective price umbrella under which the low-cost hardware competitor prospers, and proceed to add at least as much value with their own low-cost, high-quality hardware; that is, of course, if they want to survive in the long run.

Thus, to remain competitive in the marketing of solutions in the 1990s, a corporation needs to implement a dual market strategy: first, exploit the top of the pyramid by offering solutions that really add value; and second, face the lowest-cost hardware competitor with low-cost, high-quality, commodity hardware, and compete with them in exploiting the price umbrella created by proprietary top-of-the-range models.

Assignment questions

1 What do IBM, ABB Robotics and Uponor have in common?
2 What different people skills are needed in the solution business?
3 When is brand management important?
4 Why is the hardware-solution supplier caught in the middle?
5 What are the generic ways to compete in the solutions business?
6 What are the major pitfalls in this business?
7 What competencies must be cultivated?
8 How do the KSF of hardware and service industries differ?
9 What value can be added by a corporation in the solution business?

6

Global corporate strategies

6.1 The global corporation of the twenty-first century

Consider Sony's purchase of CBS Records for about US$2 billion in 1988. This was followed by their 1989, US$3.4 billion purchase of Columbia Pictures, and by Matsushita's purchase of Universal Studios in late 1990 for US$6.1 billion. What were these Japanese consumer electronics giants pursuing?

Two things need to be noted. First, these Japanese companies may have concluded that to become truly global competitors, the electronic Godzillas of the future, they have to control the software that is used in their electronic entertainment products. And second, since today's music and movie businesses are mostly based upon American culture, these software divisions should operate out of the USA.

As in most professional service organizations, the assets in the music and film businesses walk home every night. Thus, most of the profits generated in entertainment go to those who conceive and/or perform the shows: artist and producers. This is why there are some doubts over the potential synergy created by wholly-owned music and films, played on Sony's and Matsushita's high quality hardware. Why should these companies go through the trouble of lateral integration and why try to capture the value added in the complementary enterprise systems of music and films?

A trend in consumer electronics seems to be towards the digitalization of most analogue equipment. Desk-top publishing and CDs have already been digitalized, and soon most home hardware products will follow: cameras, video, HDTV, fax machines, mail services, digital fibre optics, and so on. The core technologies in these equipments are rapidly converging on digitalization, and 'the mother of all struggles' for dominance of a common core standard is beginning to take place. Canon, for instance, sells electronic cameras that display images on TVs and computer monitors; they also make printers and photocopiers. Sony makes CD players, TVs, computer monitors, CD-ROMs, disk drives and digital-optical storage products. It looks as though the VHS-Betamax struggle was just a foretaste of larger-scale struggles to come.

My friend and colleague Dominique Turpin argues that one can gain insights into the strategic thinking of Japanese corporations by understanding the game of 'Go'. In this game, he explains, the contenders try to dominate, first the corners of a board, and from there they proceed to dominate desired intersections. Following this analogy, one could argue that both Japanese consumer electronics giants are playing a game of 'Go' for the worldwide markets.

Sony seems to be building KSFs in the multimedia industry of the next century. For instance, to dominate the core products in multimedia – possibly the fastest growth industry of the 1990s – both Japanese competitors may want to occupy the following four corners of the worldwide game of 'Go':

1 The businesses related to the production and consumption of music. Thus Sony added CBS Records' music software to its already strong product offering in electronic music recorders and players.
2 The businesses related to the production and consumption of video entertainment. Through Sony's experience with Betamax, the home video standard that opposed Matsushita's VHS, they discovered that one major key to success in the selling of hardware was software availability. So Sony have added Columbia Pictures' software to its already strong offerings in the recording and display of home video entertainment.
3 Sony already has very strong hardware offerings in the form of micro-computer peripheral equipment and components; and through its alliance with Apple, the most successful niche innovator in the PC industry and for whom they already assemble Apple's Macintosh notebooks, Sony is able to learn about micro-computer and Operating System software product development;
4 Sony may have to look for a way to enter the computer software industry. As at February 1992, Sony neither owned a software development company nor manufactured a Sony-branded microcomputer; we will not be surprised if Sony or Matsushita try to buy Nintendo or some other computer software company in the early 1990s.

Although in 1991, Sony's strategic investment decisions were still guided by the motto *BMW*, meaning '*Beat Matsushita Whatever*',[1] an alternative vision for the year 2000 could be to become the home entertainment Goliath of the twenty-first century. To achieve this the following four corners would need to be developed:

1 Dominance in multimedia hardware.
2 Dominance in multimedia software.
3 Participation in telecommunications.
4 Participation in mass communication media.

Other willing or unwilling players in this game of 'Go' operate in many other industries: IBM, DEC, NEC, Fujitsu, Siemens and other computer assemblers; Philips, Siemens, RCA, GE and other electrical companies; Kodak, Xerox, Canon and other image companies; Microsoft, Borland, Lotus and other software companies; ATT, Telecoms and many PTTs; as well as thousands of component manufacturers and service companies.

We realize, of course, that the analogy of the game of 'Go' is just a device useful for communicating some exciting possibilities. We could as well have used poker, chess, skat, or some other game where the number of strategic corners is, for instance, two, hardware and people; or three, home electronic hardware, software and computers, and so on. In communicating an idea or vision, what really matters is how it can be expressed in order to guide the shaping of

[1] Turpin, V. Dominique, 'Gambare: "Never Say Die!" Why Japanese companies won't give up', *IMD Perspective for Managers*, No. 3, 1991.

business policies throughout the corporation. The important thing is to express the strategic intent of the corporation with one simple, understandable and inspiring analogy. This way, policies are shaped through the years into a congruent and harmonic whole.

6.2 Four, major, strategic decision-making areas

Four, major, strategic decision areas need continuous reviewing within corporations seeking global dominance: product/market scope, integration strategies, international strategy and organizational strategy. In a big corporation, like Sony, GE, or IBM, these strategic decisions are taken at various levels. At the corporate level one decides in which countries to compete; at the country or continent level one decides in which industries to compete; at the industry level one decides on integration strategy and product lines with which to compete; and so on.

Product/market scope

The first decision a corporation must make is whether to market hardware, or solutions, or both of these end-products. These decisions determine the product/market strategy of the corporation but they also carry important implications for the organizational strategy. Goliath corporations can afford to follow a broad-sweep product/market strategy because they can capitalize on their installed client base, financial muscle and ability to coordinate numerous partnerships with many small specialized firms. IBM, for example, can afford to serve central governments, defence departments, utilities, financial institutions, transportation, the communications industry and so on. Uponor, a big player in its markets, has to decide most carefully which solutions to market: systems for floor heating, cooling, tap-water, municipal water transportation, gas transportation, etc.

Small companies, however, are forced to seek market niches where they can offer specialized services with relatively less competition. They tend to work as specialized subcontractors for larger competitors. This is especially true in the consulting business where companies go from one-man practices, centred around a very special area of expertise, to worldwide, leviathan consulting firms with thousands of professionals. Since no consulting practice can possibly specialise in everything, most tend to hire experts to help in the solution of customer problems.

Integration strategy

Secondly, the corporation has to make another set of strategic choices: those concerning the elements of the business system in which it decides to have a competitive presence. In other words, it must develop an integration strategy for each industry in which it competes.

IBM, for example, has to decide whether or not to participate in the manufacture of chips, hard disks, micro-processors, software, telecommunications equipment and parts, robotics, etc. whereas Uponor has to decide whether or not to manufacture plastic pipes, connectors, panels, manifolds and controls. The integration strategy has many important competitive implications because, among other things, it determines the technologies to cultivate, the nature of corporate overheads, the industrial-customer set and the processes to develop. Again, these decisions have direct implications for the organizational strategy.

International strategy

Third, the corporation's international strategy is concerned with the decisions that evaluate which businesses to exploit – and how – in the countries where it competes. Based on macroeconomic and political assessments, the market attractiveness of different countries is reviewed and corporate management decides which parts of the business system to locate in each country. This means that global competitors add value by managing the flows of information, goods, money and people not only throughout the business system but also through the world's markets, as illustrated in Figure 6.1. Both hardware and solution suppliers have to manage the investments needed for the development and marketing of their products in these countries.

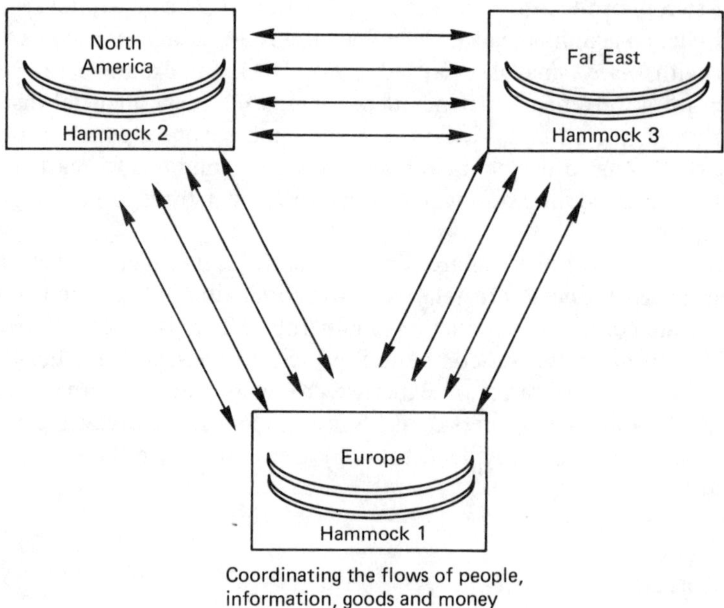

Figure 6.1 Value added by flows in transnational corporations

There are two fundamental viewpoints that corporations often leave to the random understanding of country managers: first, the macroeconomic forces of the countries in which the corporation has a presence; and second, the political and social perspectives of these same countries. However, there are entire disciplines that have developed useful frameworks to guide the understanding of both politics and economics within a country. It is a matter of applying these frameworks to host countries in order to understand the political and economic situation; why it is like that and what is going to happen in the future.

Despite the clear importance of such strategic questions as:

1 Where will we source our raw materials?
2 How, by whom and where are they going to be shipped?
3 Where are they going to be processed?
4 In which markets are these products going to be sold?
5 How will they be serviced?
6 How are they going to be financed?

Many multinational corporations do not make a coordinated effort to manage the flows through the world's economic systems and remain content to leave these decisions to random negotiations by country managers.

Organizational strategy

Fourth, the corporation needs to organize its value-creating activities in order to succeed with its chosen strategy. Although constrained by the first three decisions, global competitors still have sufficient freedom to shape alternative organizational strategies that can achieve the above objectives. For instance, a corporation may adopt an international form, multinational form, global form, transnational form or network form. It really depends on the prevailing company culture and the management's capabilities.

Hardware manufacturing and selling, for instance, require an organization designed to perform these activities at a low cost but with high standards of quality. This calls for a structure that facilitates these activities, and performance reward systems that encourage the desired objectives. In these companies research, development and processing policies cultivate the competencies that are at the core of successful low-cost, high-quality hardware suppliers. Clear examples of alternative types of organization and incentive systems for these classes of businesses can be found in Dell, Apple, Compaq, Benetton and Lithonia. However, when competition is low, technology proprietary, and margins fat, a different organizational structure develops: the Christmas tree organization, which may indeed be needed to prosper under such conditions.

The outpacing global competitor, or what Bartlett and Ghosal call a transnational corporation, coordinates the world's market needs with the world's best manufacturing capabilities and availability of raw materials. They buy the required raw materials, ship them around the world, have the goods manufactured, have these operations financed, ship the finished goods to their distributors and/or retail outlets, and service their products in all markets (as illustrated in Figure 6.1). Thus, to dominate the global industrial system, a corporation must be able not only to manage the flows in the industry's enterprise system, i.e. the hammock organization used in each vertex of the Triad, but also to control the global management of the four flows: people, information, goods, and money.

6.3 Diversification strategies

By corporate diversification we mean the acquisition of businesses which are then run by the corporation; we are not discussing investments managed by outside organizations. Traditionally, diversification refers to product/market diversification, that is, becoming involved in the management of businesses other than the corporation's core businesses. These investments are related if they share similar sourcing, processing, delivery or support activities. For two businesses to be related it is enough to share one of these generic activities; otherwise we say that the diversification is unrelated. Synergy may then be produced by sharing either sourcing activities, processing technologies – including R&D – delivery activities, or support activities. Through investments in related businesses a corporation should attempt to build a portfolio of skills that complement the strengths already existing in core companies.

Consider, on the other hand, a corporation that continues to diversify indefinitely. Eventually, it will approach the average risk and rate of return of all businesses present in the economy. The more unrelated businesses that are bought, the closer to these averages the corporation will become. Thus unrelated diversification may not lead to increased corporate rates of return; at most it can lead to decreased risk. One way in which unrelated diversification leads to increased rates of return is when the corporation abandons low-yielding businesses and keeps profitable ones; but sooner or later the economy runs out of profitable businesses and the diversification effort stops. Consider how Jack Welsh concentrated General Electric's portfolio of businesses between 1981 and 1988.

Empirical studies[2] have shown, however, that corporations following related diversification have indeed achieved higher returns on capital than those following unrelated diversification. It follows that unrelated diversification is in fact, a poorer performer than related diversification. Nevertheless, the effectiveness of related business diversification depends upon the management at the core company: it is not a formula for automatic success.

We believe, moreover, that in the long run, corporations following unrelated diversification obtain returns on investment lower than the economy's average. There are two reasons for this belief: first, the more they spread their investment money, the more they approach the economy's average; and second, even assuming that they do know how to pick high-yielding businesses, the more they diversify, the less they know about how to run these businesses, which is a force towards lower than industry average returns; in other words, the more unrelated the diversification, the fewer distinctive competencies one can use.

[2] Rumelt, Richard P., 'Strategy, structure and economic performance, and "Diversity and Profitability"', UCLA Working Paper, 1977.

In Costa Rica, for instance, Ignacio Gonzalez Hollmann, a Nicaraguan entrepreneur, says 'I understand only two businesses, oil and beer; so I invest in projects related to these core technologies, and I refuse to fool around with all other ventures, no matter how attractive they look. I just don't get involved when I don't understand a technology'. Accordingly, the management of a corporation that diversifies just to reduce business risk, is not only avoiding the management of the risk entrusted to them, but they are also diluting management talent in areas where they have no expertise. Investors choose to carry the risk intrinsic to a company precisely because they trust its management's ability to avoid those risks and exploit the opportunities presented in those businesses.

Investors can and do diversify their risk taking, and these desires should be respected by management. If we choose, for example, to invest 20 per cent in real estate, 20 per cent in gold bullion, 20 per cent in CDs, 20 per cent in blue chip stock and 20 per cent in the futures markets, we're choosing the level of risk that we're willing to carry in each one of these fields. We would certainly object if the blue chip corporation started playing the futures markets and investing in real estate to diversify its risk because they would increase the level of risk that we are willing to take in those fields. Clearly, exceptional portfolio managers can make a success out of any investment strategy, but that is not what we mean by management of a diversified corporation.

Michael Porter suggests[3] that corporations don't compete: business units do. It is through them that the corporation competes in specific industries and markets. The strategy of a business unit however, must be holistically conceived with industry and company analyses to take advantage of the corporation's skills in its core businesses. So, just as the strategy of a business unit is more than the addition of sourcing, processing, delivery and support strategies; the strategy of a diversified corporation is also more than the addition of its business unit's strategies. Once again, the optimum of the whole is more than the sum of the optimum of the parts.

That is why strategic analysis begins with questions aimed at establishing fundamentals such as: where we are coming from; the areas in which we are good; where we are going; and how we are going to get there. First we define the vision of the corporation, and then we work out how to achieve it. To answer these questions proactive reasoning goes something like this:

1 Following a logical framework for country analysis, the variables affecting industries, markets, technologies, costs and sales of the corporation are studied.
2 The above analysis leads to the selection of a general direction (goal) and specific objectives of the corporation in the different countries and industries in which it is present, and those in which it wants to develop a presence.
3 To accomplish these specific corporate objectives a number of components must be identified, such as strategic investments in: skills to consolidate; technologies to research; products to develop; markets and industries to enter; companies to acquire, etc.

[3] Porter, E. Michael, 'From competitive advantage to corporate strategy', *Harvard Business Review*, May–June 1987.

4 Industry analysis techniques are used to determine the pay-offs and attractiveness of these objectives.

In selecting the markets, industries, businesses and technologies to exploit and/or enter, corporations have to watch that these investments complement each other. They must fit a corporate concept of how investments relate to each other in all strategic senses: sourcing, processing, delivery, support and technological.

An effective corporate strategy is based upon some decision about the skills and businesses to develop, internally, in joint ventures, with alliances, and by acquisition.[4] Secondly, an explicit organizational form with which to manage these businesses and cultivate and exploit these skills, must be put in place. Finally, a set of business policies must be centrally coordinated throughout the corporation's business units, and simultaneously, another set of policies must be adapted for specific market needs. In short, some method of answering the eternal corporate-policy dilemma of central coordination versus market adaptation must be found. From this quest we find corporate strategic-management deals and the identification of related investments upon which to build similar sourcing, processing, delivery or support strategies.

6.4 Distinctive corporate competencies and the diversified corporation

We have referred to a corporation's portfolio of skills in an industry as 'the distinctive competencies' of the corporation. Below we extend this concept to the diversified corporation. A distinctive competence consists of the coordination of complex sets of people skills, policies and assets, using some mix of technologies, to deliver value.[5] Prahalad and Hamel[6] talk about 'core competence'. For instance, they discuss how Canon's core competencies in optics, imaging and microprocessor controls enable it to compete in markets as apparently unrelated as copiers, laser printers and image scanners.

Core competencies can be exploited when sourcing, processing, delivery or support activities are used in similar ways across countries and industries; thus, these four generic sources of competence can be used to find and explain the core competencies of successful corporations, e.g. Honda (motors), Canon (lenses) and Benetton (networking). The difficult thing is to decide which corporate skill to build into a core competence; since so many of them can be cultivated, it is a matter of strategic choice. Transferring and sharing these

[4] The prices paid for target companies should be below the expected present value gains from the purchase – which, as we know, is an extremely difficult number to obtain, and even more difficult to believe.

[5] The term distinctive is not understood to mean 'unique to . . .', but rather to mean 'characteristic of . . .'. This implies that several competitors may possess some of the same 'distinctive' competencies, as indeed do Motorola and Intel in microprocessors.

[6] Prahalad, C.K. and Hamel, Gary, 'The core competence of the corporation', *Harvard Business Review*, May–June 1990.

competencies among related industries is also a matter of effective strategic management.

Malcolm and Porter[7] identified seven different reasons why corporations should acquire businesses that would create better returns than those obtained from simple portfolio diversification. In essence, however, scholars argue, the success of a related diversification strategy hinges on the achievement of three strategic management objectives:

1 Corporate management cultivates consistently an acceptable vision of which skills and competencies should be nourished and protected in the corporation.
2 The skills possessed by one business unit can be applied to the problems and opportunities facing other units – the cultivation of core competencies.
3 The organizational form and incentive systems of the corporation allow and encourage the sharing of these skills among business units – the learning corporation.

The transfer and use of skills, scholars argue, often becomes entangled in a jungle of corporate reporting, planning, reward and control systems which attempt to make sure that centrally-decided policies are followed and that the adaptation of corporate policies to local market conditions is congruent throughout the corporation's businesses. Strategic management practices should try to minimize the difficulties found in adopting corporate policies in all businesses. It is in this sense that Japanese corporations – like Toyota and Matsushita – seem to have outmanaged most of their Western competitors.

In the long run, the argument goes, success derives from the consolidation of corporate people skills, policies and assets into competencies that give business units the ability to use each other's resources by learning from each other and responding quickly to dynamic market needs.

6.5 Identifying core competencies

Prahalad and Hamel[8] suggest at least three tests to identify core competencies in a corporation:

> First, core competence provides potential access to a wide variety of markets. Second, a core competence should make a significant contribution to the perceived customer benefits of the end-product. Finally, a core competence should be difficult for competitors to imitate. And it will be difficult if it is a complex harmonisation of individual technologies and production skills.

[7] Salter, S. Malcolm and Porter, Michael E., 'Note on diversification as a strategy', 9-382-129. Publishing division Harvard Business School, 1982-Rev 6/86, Boston MA 02163.

[8] Ibid.

We believe that core competencies can be found in the key success factors common to several industries; they define areas in which competencies should be developed by the corporation and they represent present and potential skills to be exploited in different industries. For instance, IBM's chip technology can be exploited in several computer segments. To succeed, however, at least two questions need to be addressed:

1 How do we identify today's competencies in the corporation?
2 How do we identify future core competencies?

The first question can easily be answered for a corporation competing in a single industry. We have already proposed that the distinctive competencies to cultivate are those people skills, policies and assets defined by the key success factors of the generic strategy followed by the corporation in that industry. Special care – we reason – should be taken to cultivate the most important KSFs. Thus core competencies can be identified with the key success factors of the generic strategies in an industry. Next, we propose that a core key success factor, in a particular industry, is the set of KSFs common to all generic strategies in that industry (see Figure 6.2), i.e. no matter what strategy one follows, the KSFs that are always needed, make up a core KSF for the competitors in that industry. This view suggests that the KSFs are both a necessary and sufficient factor for sustainable competition with a generic strategy, but that the core KSFs are necessary for all generic strategies, but not sufficient.

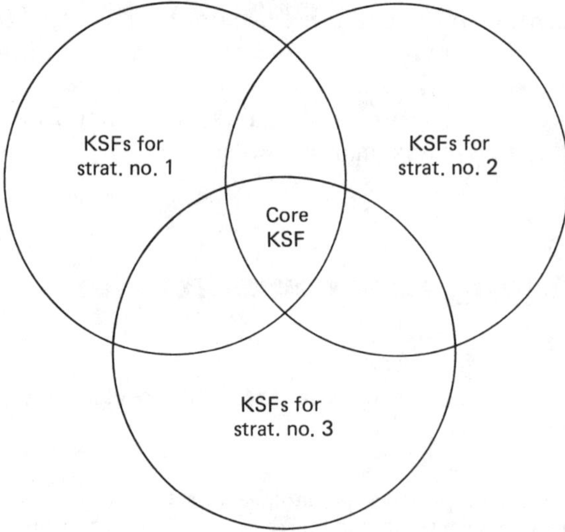

Figure 6.2 *Identifying core success factors for a corporation in one industry*

The outpacing competitor in an industry organizes its business to protect these competencies. In the clothing industry, for instance, there are three core competencies that need to be protected: first, the ability to concentrate on a chosen market segment; second, the ability to read the 'market mood' correctly; and third, the ability to respond quickly to these market needs. These competencies are needed by all competitors in the clothing industry, no matter what their generic strategies. Benetton, however, outmanages its competitors with their network of entrepreneurs supported by a professionally managed hammock organization.

For a corporation competing in several related industries, the concept of core competencies is an extension of the notion of key success factors in an industry. Thus we identify the key success factors of the different related industries in which the corporation competes. Then, the reasoning goes, the corporation should develop special skills in the key success factors common to all industries in which the corporation competes; these core KSFs are its core competencies.

This suggests that a corporation competing in several industries should first cultivate those KSFs that appear in all the industries in which it is present (see Figure 6.3). If a corporation dominates its core competencies, it masters key resources in the industries in which it competes and therefore develops a competitive edge over other corporations participating in the several industries in which it is present.

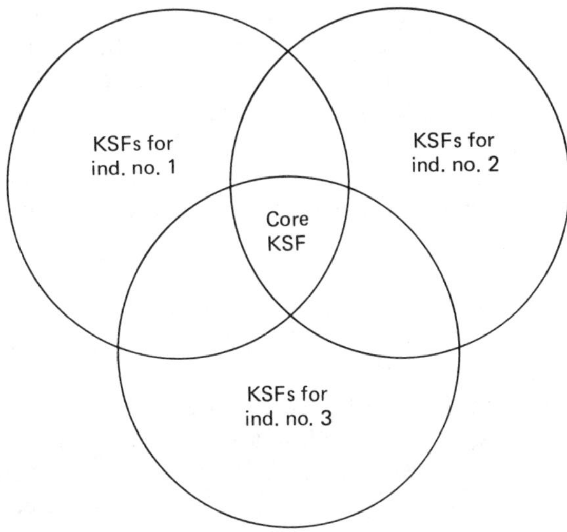

Figure 6.3 Identifying core competencies for the diversified corporation

For a corporation present in several unrelated industrial fields, like General Electric, the concept is the same. First, synergy can be created if all its businesses are clearly organized under several groups of related industries. And second, for each group of related industries, core competencies can be identified by finding the core key success factors for each group. Future core competencies are identified in a similar way:

1 For each industry we identify the future KSFs.
2 We select as future core competencies those future KSFs that prove to be important for most industries in which the corporation competes. Core competencies are those KSFs believed to be important for most future products.

6.6 Building core competencies

Michael Porter[9] has offered a prescription for a corporation seeking to build its core competencies:

1 Identify the interrelationships amongst already existing business units.
2 Select the core businesses that will be the foundation of corporate strategy – those that include the present and future core competencies.
3 Create horizontal organisational mechanisms to facilitate interrelationships among the core businesses and lay the groundwork for future related diversification.
4 Pursue diversification activities that allow shared activities.
5 Pursue diversification through the transfer of skills if opportunities for sharing activities are limited or exhausted.
6 Pursue a strategy of restructuring if this fits the skills of management or no good opportunities exist for forging corporate interrelationships.

But we can't just perform a corporate strategic audit and decide what core competencies to buy; core competencies are not for sale, they are developed over the years. What we can do is to revise corporate goals, specific objectives, generic strategies and key success factors and then review the skills of the corporation, its organizational form and management practices (as discussed above) and select investment projects that may lead to master core technologies and future core competencies.

But, since it is people who possess all the skills that make up the core competencies of a corporation, they need to be grouped as a part of the organizational strategy, in core businesses, so that synergy can take place. The thought is simple: rather than dispersing a corporation's scarce talent amongst a number of unrelated business units, the people possessing these skills should work together in core businesses. Consider Prahalad and Hamel's report on NEC,[10] who in the early 1970s declared their intent to exploit the convergence of computing and communications, what it called 'C&C'. They report that NEC chose an organizational form and during the mid-1970s communicated its intention to the whole organization as well as to the outside world.

Core competencies are shaped through the years by trying out new things and keeping only what seems to work. But they are built with consistent corporate behaviour and guided by clear corporate goals and specific objectives. NEC, we are told, determined that semiconductors would be the company's most important 'core product'. So it entered into over 100 alliances (as at 1987) aimed at rapidly building competencies. Clearly, to develop and nourish these corporate skills the holders of semiconductor technology skills had to work together in core businesses. At NEC, there was a need for centralized coordination of certain business policies throughout the corporation.

[9] Porter, E. Michael, 'From competitive advantage to corporate strategy', *Harvard Business Review*, May-June 1987.

[10] Prahalad, C.K. and Hamel, Gary, 'The core competence of the corporation', *Harvard Business Review*, May–June 1990.

From this example we see that to nourish core competencies, top management must create a vision, get people involved and obtain their commitment to work across countries, markets, industries and elements of business systems. They may be stuck, as Prahalad and Hamel point out, in functional and/or strategic business unit organizational forms. If so, they run the danger of accepting the notion of managing interfaces, which implies legitimizing isolated functions and a lack of coordination between units competing in different industries. Thus to build core competencies the corporation must learn to think and act differently.

Unfortunately corporations don't learn, it's the people within them that do; and learning only occurs if people are willing to do so. Thus managerial attitudes are at the centre of success in cultivating core competencies. In this respect top management has to learn to protect the people who carry and promote these skills: the learning organization.

To coordinate the building of corporate core competencies without interference from organizational politics, scholars agree that there seem to be four key success factors: first, care must be taken in the definition of the corporation's core businesses, business units and divisions; second, the management of core competencies calls for centralization of skills in core businesses; third, these core businesses should be run by the corporation's most effective managers; and fourth, a complementary set of business policies, which transmit the corporation's goals and objectives, must be explicitly coordinated and not left to chance.

Since competencies are in the hands of people, the understanding of core competencies is explicitly recognized by the corporation in the way its organizational form protects and nourishes the people who possess this accumulated knowledge. This includes those business policies that facilitate the coordination of diverse sourcing, processing, delivery and support activities and integrate this vast reservoir of skills into a coherent whole. Prahalad and Hamel go on to explain that by focusing on core businesses and concentrating them on core products, some Japanese corporations including Sony, Canon, NEC and others have built advantages in the components markets and then used their superior core products to invest in new and better end-products. For instance, microprocessors and MSDOS enjoyed dominant positions as core products of microcomputers, and were the dominant force in the evolution of the industry in the 1980s.

6.7 The global business group of the year 2000

Aldo Palmeri said:

> To become an important and powerful economic group in the world of the twenty-first century, some Italian, American and German business families[11] are not only pursuing dominance in their core industry, but also an influential presence in two additional industries: finance and mass communications media.

[11] Business family and business group are terms used interchangeably. They represent a worldwide phenomenon recognized in the Japanese keiretsu, in Latin America's 'grupos economicos', and under different names in other regions of the world.

That is, in addition to the core industrial base in which the family built its fortune, they should seek a presence in two other areas: mass media-communications and finance-banking. For example, the Rockefeller family went into banking; the Benetton family invested in financial services; Agnelli went into finance as well; Matsushita who are 14 per cent owned by the Sumitomo bank, invested in entertainment software; and all keiretsu include a giant bank.

The idea is clear: a business empire needs access to money to finance its growth, working capital, acquisitions, etc.; consequently it needs influence within a financial conglomerate that includes banks, insurance, leasing, factoring and all manner of financial services. This is not to say that they should pursue the control of a financial conglomerate, or diversify into banking; they just need a presence in order to influence the financing of their expanding operations. This is quite a different posture from arm's length financing and is nearer to the Japanese keiretsu. It pursues influence and protection – not returns.

Eventually, all well managed corporations will have access to the same technology, similar cost structures and production processes and the same price categories for products with similar quality. Consider what factors determine the buying decision between a Toyota and a Honda in any price category. Or the buffer that BMW must use to ensure that their cost and quality can match Toyota's Lexus. How much time does a car company need to accept and digest its weaknesses, implement effective cost drives, and catch up in delivered cost and quality with the likes of Acura and Infinity? A strong brand name provides the time needed to catch up with competitors who, over the years, introduce superior sourcing, manufacturing, technological process improvements, cost advantages, improved delivery processes and better quality features. Brand management is, thus, the essence of high perceived value (HPV).

Therefore, a presence in the mass communication media is important to influence the development of brand names and to watch and understand the development of competing trade marks. Information, about what the market wants and the different ways to influence the market's mood, tastes and quality perception, have become an essential part of successful global strategies. Therefore, it is argued, an important presence in the mass media and advertising is good for the sustainable protection of a corporation's brand names.

But why acquire partial ownership of these businesses? Is it not better to contract out these services at arm's length? Some business families would answer that this is not the case. Although they leave the management of these businesses to the experts, they insist on maintaining a presence – a minority interest – through which they can learn what is important in mass media and finance growth. But the core corporation in a business group seeks profits in its own activities; these lateral presences are put in place to guarantee learning and protect their money making activities.

6.8 Conclusions

Corporate strategy deals with four fundamental questions:

1 *The international strategy*: in which countries/markets should the corporation do business?
2 *The diversification strategy*: in which industries should the corporation compete?
3 *The integration strategy*: in which businesses of a particular industry should the corporation's units participate?
4 *The organization-implementation strategy*: how should the corporation organize the management of its presence in these industries?

Corporate competitiveness is gained by cultivating core businesses. Strategic management must identify which core competencies and supporting technologies are to be cultivated. Corporate management should then spend time nourishing, building, and protecting the people that carry the corporation's distinctive competencies. Furthermore, these people should be placed in core businesses so that synergy can take place, protected from organizational politics.

Assignment questions

1 What are Sony and Matsushita trying to do?
2 What are the four major strategic decision-making areas for a corporation?
3 Why do corporations diversify?
4 Relate diversification strategy with core technology.
5 How do we identify core competencies in a corporation?
6 How do we cultivate these core competencies?
7 In what industries should a business group be present?

Part Three

Adjusting to Environmental Pressures

There are four important dimensions on which the international manager has to build knowledge and develop skills:

1 Understanding the country's environment.
2 Understanding the industry's environment.
3 Understanding the business unit and corporation.
4 Developing management skills.

We have found that one of the most important tasks of management development programmes within big corporations is to spread a common framework for the understanding of the corporation and its competitive environment. These efforts create essentially a common language within and across the corporation's units. In Parts One and Two of this book we discussed some useful frameworks that facilitate a common understanding of both an industry and the corporation.

Normally, management development programmes also include the building of management skills under headings such as: communication skills, listening skills, negotiation skills, influencing skills, leadership skills, etc. We believe that such training efforts, which are usually coordinated to cultivate a common strategic perspective throughout the corporation, still lack a common framework for assessing country environments that would complete the corporation's strategic perspective.

To illustrate our argument further we have drawn an executive's profile, shown in the strategic management profile illustration overleaf. On a scale from zero to 100 (think about it as percentages), we drew an executive's possible mastery of each one of the four dimensions needed for strategic international management. What we are illustrating is the potential impact of neglecting one dimension in the shaping of a shared corporate perspective. Consider a corporation that leaves the understanding of the country's environment to chance and does nothing to build a shared perspective: our graph tells us that 50 per cent of the corporation's shared perspective of strategic management is left to randomness. Clearly we assume that the four dimensions are equally important, a common assumption in all the frameworks presented in this book.

Following on from this reasoning, we could argue that corporations doing nothing about some of the other dimensions are leaving more and more of their shared, strategic management perspective to chance. For instance, they reduce it to 25 per cent if they ignore two dimensions, and leave everything to chance if they work on only one dimension and ignore the other three.

Consider the executive's strategic management profile shown in Figure C. Several things should be noted:

1 No one dominates all dimensions fully: this executive has 25 per cent dominance of the country's environment and 70 per cent of the other three dimensions. Hence the importance of management teams.

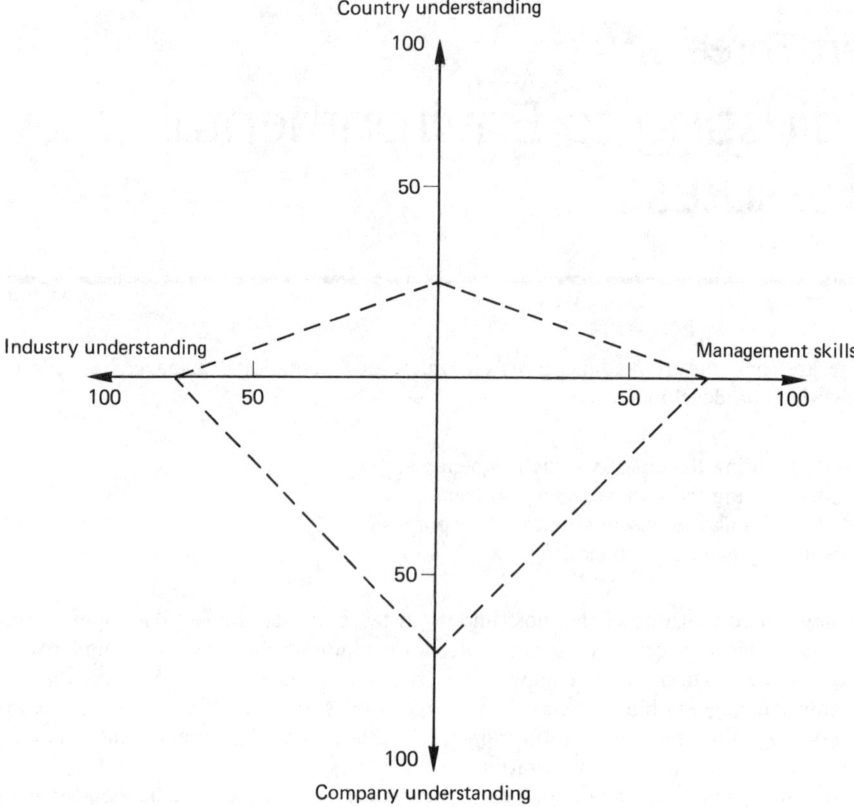

Strategic management profile

2 This means that every executive can improve his abilities in some of the four dimensions.
3 Corporations should choose common frameworks for the shaping of shared perspectives in all four dimensions.

Normally, corporations worry more about building management skills and developing the understanding of the company and corporation as a whole. Since the early 1980s, however, corporations have worked more and more towards achieving a shared perspective of the competitive environment. But even now, the whole field of environmental country analysis in management development awaits formalization because the advent of industry analysis, which was introduced by microeconomists in the 1980s, positioned the work of environmentalists relatively low. In a way, this was due to the rock-like stability of West European, Far Eastern and North American economies.

When European, Japanese, and American economies were relatively stable, scholars and practitioners of strategic management did not worry about understanding certainty, i.e. static and known rules of the game. The environment was safely assumed away and people worried about competing against Japanese, Germans and the like. But in the 1990s, this stability has gone; and markets and opportunities are disappearing and appearing. West Europe may turn into the greatest market in history; the Soviet Union has ceased to exist; Germans and Japanese may struggle for Eastern European markets; and the decade has begun with a big recession. As a result of all this activity, understanding the country environments where the corporation competes, is becoming an increasingly important area for strategic management. Therefore, to increase the robustness of their management development programmes during the 1990s, corporations should put into place the processes that create a shared perspective for all four dimensions.

Part Three of the book deals with the understanding of a country's environment and the management of some strategic dilemmas. We don't pretend to present a specialist text on either macroeconomics or political science. We are just showing how, from our own practical experience, frameworks originating in those disciplines are applied by country managers in order to understand the environment in which they operate.

We are pleased to recognize the contributions of Noel Ramirez, Marc Lindenberg, Benjamin Crosby, Fred Neubauer, Henry Mintzberg, and a number of economic and political science scholars who created the concepts and provided the frameworks used in Part Three. We are solely responsible for any misinterpretations.

7
Global corporate policies

7.1 Two strategic management approaches

The leaders of corporations doing business on a global scale face the challenge of shaping business policies that encourage decision-making – at all levels of the organization – so that congruent strategic postures are achieved. For this, top management usually develops some vision of how, when and where the corporation should go, and then communicates it to the rest of the organization. But an inevitable fact of organizational life is that lower-ranking decision-makers, the executives and employees, also develop their own vision for the corporation and then act on their understanding of where the corporation should go and when it should do so.

Thus, one of the most important strategic management areas is to communicate the vision generated at the top to the organization; this approach implies that the thinking is done at the top, and assumes that the problem is finding the right way to communicate the ideas of the thinkers to the rest of the organization; the motto seems to be *I think, I communicate, and you do.* The question that this poses is: how do we communicate and sell our vision to the organization? It is at this point that we find out that good visions are simple, inspiring, realistic, energizing and mobilize the people in the organization in the right direction.

Complementary, but often forgotten, sources for mobilizing energy in a corporation are the ideas from members of the organization who are directly responsible for the value-adding activities; the people who actually manage the activities of the corporation. Henry Mintzberg argues that many strategies emerge from the decisions taken by these people, and that the strategic management problem seems to call for identifying visions, strategies and policies that work well in the different organizational units; the motto seems to be: *you think and try it out, you keep what works, and I identify what seems to work.*

So a different strategic management question is posed: how do we identify, cultivate and adopt outstanding emerging visions, strategies and policies? Strategic decisions and business policies are guided by visions, so the achievement of a shared strategic posture in the corporation is a major challenge. One approach to this challenge is to look for processes that achieve both objectives: spreading out top management's vision and building on emerging strategies and policies, as illustrated in Figure 7.1. So one task of strategic management is to institutionalize the processes that create a shared strategic posture. This includes:

1 Finding a formal way of communicating top management's vision.
2 Finding formal ways of identifying and adopting emerging strategies and policies.
3 Finding mechanisms for arriving at a shared vision.

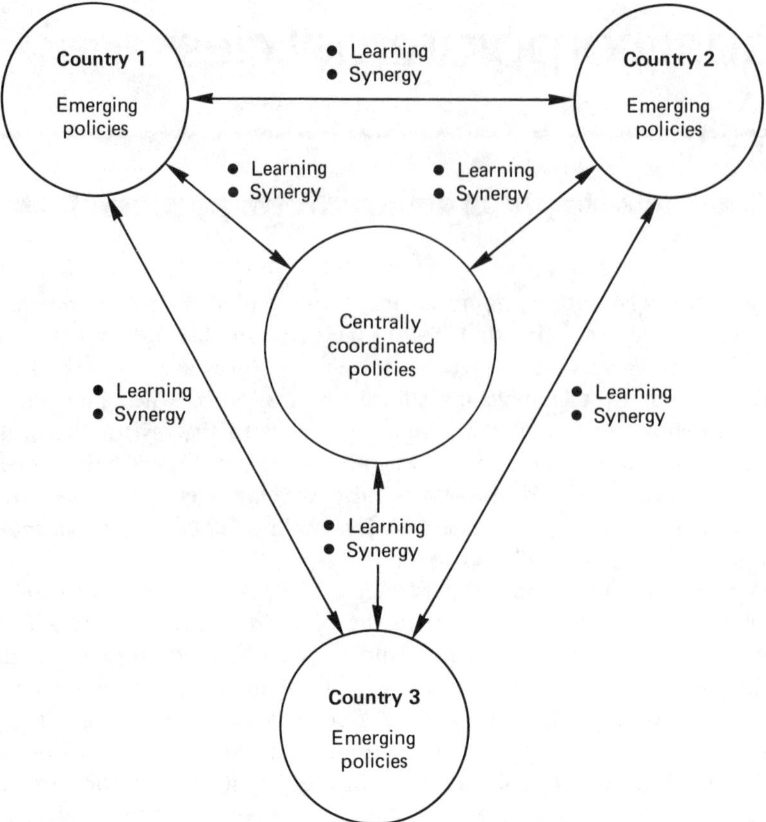

Figure 7.1 The learning corporation

4 Finding some way to examine the fit of strategic decisions.
5 Finding a way of shaping business policies that complement the shared vision and strategic decisions.

Whether we like it or not, people are guided by their interpretation of the corporation's vision, they make strategic decisions and utilize some kind of mental framework to rationalize their thinking processes. Thus frameworks are needed to create a common understanding of the corporation and its mission. They are also needed to communicate in a common language; to agree on the skills to cultivate and protect; to learn from other units in the corporation; to share successful business policies; and to give top management permission to lead. Shared frameworks constitute a corporation's 'geschaeftsanschauung'.

For instance, Henry DeNero reports[1] 'many Japanese executives use the term "middle-up management", meaning that middle managers analyse and formulate decisions and then work them "up" to the CEO as part of the consensus-building process'. He further argues that this typically Japanese strategic

[1] DeNero, Henry, 'Creating the "hyphenated" corporation', *The McKinsey Quarterly*, 1990, No. 4.

management behaviour is perfect for the low-cost processing of high-quality products; because it is based on centrally designed and manufactured Japanese products, exported to what are essentially, marketing subsidiaries. This strength or force represents the greatest resistance to becoming a 'transnational corporation'. It generates a natural resistance to learning from local markets and fails to adapt Japanese policies that are created at the centre to local conditions. Instead, it forces local employees to adapt to Japanese behavioural patterns. This is positive, in so much as it means that Japanese strategic management practices, such as their business policies and resulting company culture are spread uniformly throughout the world, but it also has an undesirable side as it impedes both learning from local experiences and the transfer of these lessons to other parts of the corporation.

But strategic management is not about choosing between local adaptation and central coordination of business policies; it is about finding the right combination of both, and the global spreading of local and centrally-generated skills. This balance should be shaped with varying degrees of centralization and adaptive learning; it is simply not correct to say that the same business policies should be coordinated at the centre for all markets. For instance, in the Triad countries, some parts of the business system can be allowed to develop their own policies, whereas in less developed countries these same policies should be centrally coordinated. In other parts of the business system the contrary could be true. At Cadbury Schweppes for instance, country managers take all marketing and positioning decisions in their markets.

7.2 Adapting a strategic posture to market needs

Country managers must create a vision that incorporates all market specific demands and pressures while maintaining the key elements of the corporate mission[2] that characterize their firm. Or in the words of Sir Adrian Cadbury:[3]

> First of all, you have to explain the company's aims and objectives: what is this company trying to do; how is it trying to work? I've put that in written words, because I feel that it is very important. But it's pretty platitudinous . . . but its still worth going through the effort of putting down what you believe in. If you don't do that, nobody has any guidance.

Executives are guided by vision; some strategic intent.
To be sure of obtaining results, effective corporations set a few well-defined objectives for their country managers. A Tetrapak executive explained: 'We've experimented a lot with packaging materials, but the bottom line for any

[2] A corporation's mission is understood as a short-term vision; it is explained better with the specific objectives in a market. The vision is the long term goal of the organization.

[3] 'Cadbury Schweppes: more than chocolate and tonic', Sir Adrian Cadbury interviewed by Timothy B. Blodgett, *Harvard Business Review*, Jan.–Feb. 1983.

country manager is very simple: satisfy our clients with the most practical and mutually profitable material'.

To create the right motivation these specific objectives must be carefully selected. Sir Adrian Cadbury commented:[4]

> Your job is to maximise profits. Okay, but over what period of time? I can maximise the profits of the company this year or next. That's a perfectly clear goal. But if you say maximise the profits of the company over the next 20 years, we're getting into a much more difficult matter. There are things that would be sensible for me to do for profit now which injure the continued profitability of the company in the longer run.

Strategic decisions are guided by specific objectives.
Effective European country managers don't spend their time in conference rooms analysing strategy; they are too busy trying to meet the specific objectives given to them. They have to adapt to technological change and look for ways to increase customer satisfaction while lowering their operating costs under the environmental conditions and manpower availability of their host country. People at headquarters should refrain from forcing their country managers to go against their own judgement. An important factor in strategic management is the commitment of the management team to a chosen strategy. A corporation can't encourage strategic adaptation to local market conditions if it controls its country managers so tightly that they cannot take strategic decisions. *Strategic decisions commit the resources of the corporation for a long time.*

Sir Adrian Cadbury[5] also believed in local initiatives: 'But I believe in the principle that you should manage in an open way: tell people what is going on and listen to what they have to offer, particularly when it concerns matters which affect them directly'. In another real-life example, Nestlé authorizes its managers to shape most business policies at country level, leaving only a few important strategic decisions and policies under central control. Headquarters staff may not intervene arbitrarily in country management, negotiation processes requiring the approval of those affected are usually instigated.

Nestlé is country/customer driven and constant contact with country-customers provides insights that direct the mission of the corporation in each country. 'When I was head of the German market I started by getting out there with the customers and trying to understand their needs' explained Helmuth Maucher, Nestlé's CEO. Managers at Nestlé believe that any person that does not meet customers regularly has little market or business feel; moreover, in their management training seminars there are always one or two successful ex-country executives making sure that the discussions transmit Nestlé policies and cultural values to trainees.

The culture at successful corporations is simple and clear. At Tetrapak and IBM, for instance, the encompassing value is customer service. During the late 1980s, Mr Maucher preached overhead reduction and productivity improvement at Nestlé until the company reduced staffing levels at headquarters by 30 per cent in 5 years. IBM reduced its staff from 405,000 to 330,000 in just five years (1987–91) without massive firings. Nestlé's country managers make it a point to drop in regularly on key country customers and interest groups, just

[4] Ibid.
[5] Ibid.

to keep in touch with market developments. Nearly every Tetrapak country manager has stories about how he took great pains to solve a packaging problem.

As Sir Adrian Cadbury[6] commented:

> In the end, the glue that holds the company together is personal contact and a belief that the company stands for something that is worthwhile. To spread the shared values, people in positions of responsibility in an international company will probably have to spend more time travelling, talking to people and building up these personal relationships.

7.3 A strategic management dilemma

Consider Nestlé, Olivetti, Exxon and IBM, who have a policy of using native country managers and native executives wherever possible. These organizations seek a better understanding of the environment of the countries in which they operate and a better understanding of their markets. Other corporations use acquisitions for market penetration and consolidation. For example, Hoechst bought Celanese, the eighth largest US chemical company; RJR-Nabisco acquired part of Britannia Industries Ltd, its Indian associate, and tailored its strategic posture to Indian priorities; and Nestlé acquired Carnation to consolidate its US operations, and Rowntree to recapture its punch in chocolates and confectionery.

The lessons drawn from the strategic management practices of excellent European corporations is that there is no such thing as a purely deliberate or randomly-generated strategic posture in corporations engaged in global competition. A business unit's strategic posture results from adapting corporate global strategic postures to the environmental pressures in a market. In short, global corporate strategic postures are sensitive to market specific environmental trends and events, human resources, leadership styles and subsidiary culture.

Therefore, the main mandate of country managers is to examine the impact on the strategic posture of their business unit from events, trends and environmental pressures occurring in their host country. What set of ideas and organizing concepts for thinking about the adaptation of a global strategic posture are available? How do country managers set their strategic agendas?

A corporate strategic posture can be conceived as being composed of a common global posture complemented by a market specific posture. This is only a complicated way of saying that corporate business practices may differ between Brazil, Japan, USA, Europe and India, and that a corporation operating in these countries should adapt its strategy and operations to local cultural conditions.

This dichotomy in the composition of the global strategic posture of a corporation provokes tension in the reasoning processes of key strategic decision-makers. A dilemma is created when they consider which components of the

[6] Ibid.

strategic posture should be globally coordinated and which adapted to specific market forces.

For instance, had the vision of Honda in the USA market remained restricted to selling large motorcycles, we would not have witnessed Honda's exploitation of the market for bikes with less than 125 cc. Honda reacted to market demand by shipping whatever was available and found by chance a market for their small motorcycles, whose volume could easily be increased.

The same tension arises when we consider which corporate-specific objectives should originate from country managers, and which should be centrally coordinated. At Tetrapak, the objectives for packaging materials and machinery are not centrally coordinated, despite a strategic decision made in 1987 to gain raw material independence. In a continuous tension, Tetrapak has so far opted for satisfaction of country needs.

On this Mr Helmuth Maucher, CEO of Nestlé, said to an attentive audience of IMEDE professors:

> I want zone managers in direct contact with the field and not at headquarters. Management must be willing to think instead of relying on formulas. I don't accept that we will always follow a certain strategy or that we will never do this or that; managers must examine each strategic decision on its own merits and remain flexible in their judgment.

Nestlé's efforts to push strategic decisions to country level without losing control of a few basic objectives further exemplifies the dilemma. In the end, it is through company policies that most of the core shared values, beliefs and attitudes that make up the common culture of a corporation, are not only transmitted, but formed and consolidated.

An elegant way to dilute the tension is to employ executives on the corporate staff/line who have managed functions in important markets. These seasoned and experienced country executives will have a thorough understanding of both headquarter's and country's points of view. It is these people who are best suited to understand the vision and specific objectives of both corporate and country executives and are most likely to transform them into acceptable policies. They are also the most able to discuss, adjust and transmit them in management development seminars. This is a common practice at Nestlé and Philips. The strength of this approach can also become one of its major weaknesses. What if these seasoned executives spread an undesirable culture, one that perpetuates the policies and processes that cause corporate decay?

7.4 Seeking central coordination

One question researched at IMD is: which components of a strategic posture should be coordinated centrally? Questions being examined hinge around the similarities of consumers in developed countries; the standardization of products for these consumers; the potential in economies of scale; the possible centralization of manufacturing, advertising and other functions; and finally, the optimal exploitation of core competencies to gain competitive advantages. The driving idea is to develop a competitive package at headquarters that is applicable in all key markets for the systematic exploitation of a privileged position across many markets.

Researchers of these questions derive their answers from studying the competitive environment. They are trying to identify the forces driving global strategic integration from the study of the competitive arenas in three major markets: Western Europe, Japan and USA. The cognitive approach being adopted is one of strategy as a plan in search of a competitive position, by which we mean, a global competitive position. The idea is that in order to benefit from the corporation's core competencies, they should be administered centrally. The assumption is that strategic coordination could be obtained through top-down imposition of a common strategic posture in the three major developed markets and that this competitive position will be found through analysis of common environmental needs and corporate competence. The philosophy of this approach seems to entail as much planning and controlling from the centre as possible, including most of the strategic decision-making. In short it creates Western European versions of what Bartlett and Ghosal call the Japanese global corporations.

7.5 Seeking local adaptation

For Nestlé, Tetrapak and other corporations, there is more to the world than Western Europe, Japan and the USA; and many more environments than the competitive one. For corporations with major operations in Russia, Ukraine, India, mainland China, Brazil, Mexico, Indonesia, Philippines, Nigeria and the like, we would recommend looking at a few of the alternative environments before deciding on a global strategic posture.

In adapting a corporation's strategic posture to the different country environments, dilemmas over technological adaptation; new product introduction; political and economic situations; and operational policies, appear for each country. In all of these situations the basic dilemma between central coordination and local adaptation holds, but the solutions adopted are not always the same; instead they are country specific.

For example, a technology is appropriate to a country, only if it is economically more productive than the challenging technology. So, how much of the technology used in each country should be decided at headquarters? Products marketed in countries with young populations are usually different from those marketed in countries with ageing populations; which products should have a global standard? The political processes of certain countries demand different strategic postures from developed western countries; what should be the global ethical posture? And obviously, financial policies and accounting practices in high inflation countries should differ from those used by the same corporations in low inflation countries.

The process of strategic adaptation is essentially a synthetic proposition: the management team only identifies key events, trends and pressures in its environment so that it can examine their impact on the strategic posture and operations of its business unit. It is a bottom-up process in which all executives in a market participate in the adaptation of the strategic posture of the corporation to specific environmental pressures in that market. The philosophy of this approach is to push strategic decision-making closer to the people with market knowledge; closer to the country/customer.

In Part Four of this book we discuss the adaptation of a strategic posture for countries subjected to violent social revolts. We call this managing in turbulent environments. In the rest of Part Four we examine ways of identifying environmental pressures in a market.

Assignment questions

1 What is a learning corporation?
2 How we adopt a strategic posture to a market?
3 What is the major strategic management dilemma?
4 What are the advantages of central coordination?
5 What are the advantages of local adaptation?

8

A framework for environmental analysis

8.1 Country environment

A country environment is composed of all of the external forces acting upon the way a unit conducts its business. To analyse it, country managers normally divide it into identifiable categories based upon easy to understand disciplines which are identified as follows:

1 *The economic environment* deals with changes in inflation, devaluation, taxation and industrial development and their impact on the strategic posture of a company.
2 *The social environment* deals with changes in population ageing, income strata, purchasing power and public investment in schools, hospitals, roads and other social services.
3 *The political environment* deals with the understanding of political parties; the political process; the resources, objectives, ideologies, and the degree of legitimacy of the different pressure groups. Political scenarios and their consequences on the strategic posture are examined.
4 *The legal and regulatory environment* deals with the evolution of the legal framework in the host country. It follows lobbying and legislation on industrial waste disposal, social costs, profit transfers, patent enforcement, licence agreements fees, and so on.
5 *The industrial environment* deals with competitive and cooperative strategies in an industry.
6 *The international environment* deals with changes introduced by foreign governments and corporations that affect a company's strategic posture both in the local and international markets.
7 *The technological environment* deals with technological changes and their impact on the processes and productivity in the different elements of the business system.

Three elements need to be examined to identify opportunities and threats in all of these environments: important events, trends and demands from interest groups.

Events are important turning points within a country. Currency devaluation and inflation are typical examples of important events. Trends are noticed in sequences of similar events; unemployment figures and GNP being good examples of important trends within a country. The expectations of the different pressure groups such as consumers, employees, unions, competitors, shareholders, etc. are revealed through their demands.

Changes in any of these three variables are important only if they somehow impact upon a corporation's strategy; otherwise they are ignored.

Environmental business conditions are realities that need to be understood and included in the shaping of a strategy. To adopt a strategic posture we must recognize, and accept, the existence of events, trends and demands from interest groups in the host country.

8.2 Environmental monitoring

In practice, we found that country managers set priorities among these environments and closely monitor only the few they consider to be important for their operations. These environments are selected because they have the biggest impact on the strategic posture of the corporation in that market and this is how country managers define their *strategic agenda.* This is simply a list of the most important strategic decisions and policies to review in the short run.

Clearly, one way to construct a strategic agenda – a very popular one, too – is to do nothing, and leave the revision of the strategic posture to the random interaction of the corporation's executives. A second approach is employ professional services and study their findings related to the events, trends and demands acting on the industry and country.

A third approach, which was used by Exxon during the Central American crisis, complements the professional's reports with formal meetings with the partners of the consulting firm, to discuss and evaluate their conclusions. This approach explores the implications of the consultant's findings on the corporation's strategic posture. We have found that such workshops are even more useful if executives from several companies meet with the consultants because much more synergy is created as different points of view are added to the discussions.

Another alternative is to concentrate these monitoring activities in formal organizations of the private sector. Several of these organizations function as problem identification and documentation centres for their industrial sector; they identify events, trends and pressures, especially by monitoring the legislative activities of the state.

These organizations command resources unavailable to a corporation. They have the authority to speak in the name of the member companies of their industrial sector and they command legitimacy in the protection of that sector's national interests. So a corporation's credibility and negotiating power increases with these two additional resources. Clearly, synergy of information, monetary resources and people skills are also increased by working through an official group.

Monitoring activities can be improved by including members of pressure groups into some of these discussions. For instance, consumers, shareholders, union members, employees, managers, suppliers, customers and other private sector organizations, can be invited to some of the discussions on the impact of events, trends and pressures on the strategic posture of a corporation. The idea is to open information flows between the various pressure groups. This allows them to explore the feasibility of specific strategies and permits the communication of corporate points of view.

There are several options for these workshops. Some companies hold seminars with several pressure groups to discuss and explain a number of company decisions. Other executives form advisory panels with members of their pressure groups that they use to review company progress on several issues identified as crucial by the panel members. Another important measure can be the creation of formal meetings with panellists and competitors with the object of discussing events, trends and pressures that are developing in the environment. Joint action may then be coordinated.

8.3 Identification of events, trends and pressures

A commonly used approach to scan and monitor environmental developments is:

1 The members of trade associations get together and agree on which events, trends and pressures to monitor with the resources of the association. This agreement can be reached through a group problem identification process.
2 The group agrees on which events, trends and pressures are the most important to the members of the trade association.
3 Finally, the members of the association assign resources for monitoring the selected events, trends and pressures.

The underlying assumption in the above, is that a group of competing, but interested, executives can do a better job of identifying key events, trends and pressures than an isolated decision-maker.

Consider, for instance, the electoral commitment of Costa Rica's President Arias to build 80,000 low-income dwelling units during his 4 years in office. This political promise was evaluated in the context of the other environmental events, trends and pressures.

1 *Economic environment.* Until 1987, Costa Rica's Central Bank had followed a monetary policy anchored in monthly mini-devaluations to maintain the competitiveness of the country's exports.
2 *Demographic environment.* Costa Rica's population was young and growing at 2.3 per cent annually. The average family had 4.8 persons in 1985 and was expected to fall to 4.2 by 1995. There was a clear trend towards smaller dwelling units.
3 *Regulatory environment.* Since 1980, several trends including scarcity of foreign exchange, fiscal deficit, inflation, and commercial deficit, forced the revision of tax laws. Furthermore, the structural economic conditions were expected to be the same for the next 10 years; this meant that tax laws could be expected to suffer further changes.
4 *Competitive environment.* Import tax barriers to foreign materials were dropping as Costa Rica was opening its markets to foreign manufactured goods.
5 *International environment.* Foreign loans and grants for the construction of the 80,000 dwelling units were channelled through the country's construction bank.

6 *Technological environment*. Low-cost prefabricated dwelling units formed the bulk of the 80,000 units planned by President Arias' administration.

8.4 Specification of events, trends and pressures

Once the events, trends and pressures are identified, the group of executives turn their attention to selecting priorities among the different phenomena. For this they usually select, for each environment, the event, trend or pressure with the greatest impact in their industry's operations.

For some of these environments there may not be a big event, trend or pressure and so it will be ignored. But for a few of them a more detailed specification of the phenomena is needed. Usually, they tend to concentrate in the same environments. For instance, all through the early 1990s, the economic and political environments of Eastern Europe created a great deal of interest.

An easy way to specify the details of important events, trends and pressures is to answer the following questions:

1 What *is* the event, trend, or pressure?
2 What *is not* the event, trend, or pressure?
3 Where is the event, trend, or pressure occurring?
4 What is the precise location of its occurrence?
5 When did it start?
6 When was is first noticed?
7 How intense are the events, trends or pressures?
8 What is their impact in our industry?

This specification process demands discipline and consistent application of an otherwise boring process. But in practice, it yields attractive payoffs to our efforts. Consider the application of the above sequence of questions to President Arias' promise to build 80,000 dwelling units for low income families. This promise was first noticed during President Arias' 1985 compaign; this event is specified in Table 8.1.

8.5 Setting priorities

By specifying the events, trends and pressures, as shown in Table 8.1, we can evaluate whether or not these phenomena have a positive or negative impact on the strategic posture of the corporation. An impact is said to be negative (positive) if:

1 It hinders (facilitates) the present strategic posture.
2 It increases (decreases) the business risks.
3 It increases (decreases) the resources needed for strategic management in the market.

Table 8.1 Specifying an event

Question	*Is it?*	*Is it not?*
What?	A campaign promise to build 80,000 dwelling units in his 4 years of tenure.	Not to build 20,000 dwelling units each year.
Where did it happen?	During Costa Rica's 1985 electoral campaign for the presidency.	In some other market
When did it start?	With the creation of Costa Rica's construction bank in Nov. 1986	Not when the promise was made.
When will construction start?	The project plans are to build as follows: 1986 16,500 units 1987 18,500 units 1988 21,000 units 1989 24,000 units	
What is the impact on the construction industry?	Costa Rica had built 17,000 low income dwelling units per year. So, the increment really was: (500) units for 1986 1500 units in 1987 4000 units in 1988 7000 units in 1989	Not to increase the volume by 20,000

For the construction industry it meant a 33% increment in construction volume in 1988 and 1989, not a doubling of demand.

4 It eliminates (increases) the need for alternative strategic postures.

Once all events, trends and pressures have been specified, a strategic agenda for the participants in the industrial sector has been created. Then, business people can act either as an association or as individuals in their efforts to influence changes in the environment through lobbying. Each industrial sector builds its own strategic agenda, as the events, trends and pressures affect them differently. A corporation's strategic agenda is a simple list of events, trends and pressures and their impact on the corporations' operations in the country. This agenda must generate action plans for different scenarios constructed by the agenda. If the pressures are too strong, the strategic posture of the corporation may be modified.

The strategic agenda defines the events, trends and pressures occurring in the environment, whose impact on the strategic posture of a corporation must be evaluated.

In a small company, the strategic agenda tends to be defined by a single decision-maker. Another alternative is to involve all executives in the company in the definition of the agenda. We recommend involving, where possible, all executives in the industrial sector because people sharing the same problem will be more likely to identify the events, trends and pressures correctly.

Assignment questions

1 How can we understand the environment?
2 How do we monitor the environment?
3 How do we understand events, trends and pressures?
4 How are events specified?
5 How do we set priorities for environmental monitoring?
6 What is the strategic agenda?

9

The macroeconomic environment

9.1 Assessing foreign investments[1]

Business people are used to evaluating investments in terms of rates of return. If an investment has an internal rate of return (IRR) higher than the minimum required by the corporation, the project is usually accepted. The IRR is an answer to the question, *how much can we expect to get out of this investment?* When international investors look at an opportunity in a foreign country, the same question pops up in their minds, *what return can we expect to get out of our investment in this country?* An obvious answer to this question depends upon estimates of the returns expected from the project; if the IRR is better than the minimum accepted by the corporation, the project has good chances of being accepted.

The way to go about this is to estimate the most likely cash flows for the project and discount them with an appropriate minimum rate of return; this way, projects with positive net present values (NPV) are accepted. Two things need to be noted in this approach: first, typical economic conditions are assumed for the estimation of the most likely cash flows, i.e. they don't include specific country risk, which is the uncertainty around these 'typical' conditions. And second, the discount rates used for foreign investments, normally include a 'risk premium', being a differential rate over the normally used rate, that punishes the projects proposed for higher risk countries.

Consider 13.37 per cent interest per year, which was the Central Bank of Costa Rica's rate for dollars on 3 May 1985; consider further an 11.5 per cent estimated yearly devaluation of the country's currency – the colon – with respect to the dollar. A country manager expects that his local investments yield at least (1.1337 × 1.115) 26.4 per cent per year in order to be indifferent to a 'risk-free' Central Bank rate in dollars or an investment's return in colones. But, shouldn't we include a risk premium for trusting Costa Rica with our investment dollars; for the uncertainty attached to getting our dollars back; and for the risks intrinsic to the project itself? Can we be sure that it really is a stable business or that it is the best alternative?

Thus the 26.4 per cent return on investment must be adjusted for two factors, first a component measuring country risk, and second, a component measuring business risk. Say that after adding both components to the basic 'risk-free' rate (26.4 per cent) we obtain 35 per cent per year; then any project with positive NPV at a 35 per cent discount rate should be accepted. But we do know that Costa Rica's 13.37 per cent risk-free rate for dollars is temporary, and that in the future this rate may increase or decrease; and we also know that the yearly devaluation rate of 11.5 per cent of the local currency

[1] Based on N. y Werner Ketelhöhn; Marín José, *Inversions Estratégicas: Un Enfoque Multidimensional*, San José, Costa Rica, Asociación Libro Libre, 1986.

with respect to the dollar is also just a temporary estimate. So, satisfaction with our estimated 35 per cent discount rate may be too simplistic. But, rates of return hold a fascinating dominance over business people's minds, so this approach is probably the most commonly used.

In 1992, for instance, investments in all Eastern European countries were punished with a risk factor of around 10 per cent by one corporation. But we know that the risk assumed by these investments differs among countries. Eastern European countries do not all have the same social, political and economic problems; the risks differ. So a different approach is needed: one that takes these differences into account. The attractiveness of the minimum return approach is that it summarizes in a single number, IRR or NPV, the perceived risk for the investment. But do we really believe that one number can represent the complex relationships of social, political and economic factors?

A second approach is to examine the uncertainty involved in each one of the variables critical to the investment and see how they behave under different economic scenarios. In this case we recommend the following approach:

1 Obtain an estimate of the 'risk free rate' in the country.
2 Identify the economic variables that are critical to the project's feasibility.
3 Estimate a most likely scenario for these variables.
4 Estimate the most likely values for the project's cash flows corresponding to this most likely scenario.
5 Estimate optimistic, pessimistic and intermediate scenarios for the country's economy, and assign likelihood probabilities to each scenario.
6 Estimate, with electronic spreadsheets, the project's cash flows for each scenario.
7 Estimate the IRR (or risk-free NPV) for the project under each economic scenario.
8 Estimate a probability distribution for the IRR (or risk-free NPV) of the project in that country.

This way the country's risk will be reflected in a probability distribution of the IRR or the risk-free NPV. What do we do with this distribution?

We have two ways with which we can estimate country risks. First, by discounting *most likely cash flows* using an adjusted discount rate: $k_c = k_f + dk_c$, (Where k_c is the country's risk adjusted discount rate, k_f is the country's risk-free discount rate, and dk_c is the country's risk premium.)

Second, by estimating the impact of selected economic scenarios on the most likely cash flows of the investment project. This way, a probability distribution for the IRR or NPV can be estimated. In the former we deal with a NPV or discount rate that reflects the risk perceived in the economy of the country; in the latter we obtain a probability distribution for the IRR or NPV (discounted at a risk-free rate).

9.2 Economic scenarios[2]

To illustrate our two approaches consider CORTURIS, a tourist hotel project in Central America. The risk-free discount rate was 9%, and the expected inflation in the country 8% per year. The project's key variables, and their most likely values under different scenarios are shown in Table 9.1. These scenarios were conceived after considering political, social and economic events and trends. These discussions led to probability assessments based on the likelihood of occurrence of each scenario.

Table 9.1 Economic scenarios for corturis

		$1000s			
Variable	*Optimist*	*Intermediate*	*Probable*	*Inter.II*	*Pessimist*
Taxes	0%	20%	40%	50%	60%
Salvage Value					
Land	1218	1218	1218	1600	2000
Improvement	120	120	120	180	240
Buildings	2346	2346	2346	3000	2500
Inflation					
Prices	12%	11%	10%	10%	10%
Costs	4%	5%	6%	7%	8%
Economy	4%	6%	8%	9%	10%
Probability	5%	20%	50%	20%	5%

Scenarios result from managerial interpretations of different political and economic decisions. Scenarios depend, of course, on people's views of events, trends and pressures, and are therefore subjected to many interpretations. Both the scenario and its likelihood of occurrence are subjects of heated discussions.

We suggest three easy-to-estimate scenarios and two that are a little more difficult. Clearly, the most important scenario would have been estimated anyway, this is the most likely scenario; it represents the country's expected economic environment. This scenario is used to estimate the most likely cash flows; those representing the project.

Two additional scenarios are also easy to estimate, they are the optimistic and pessimistic scenarios. The optimistic scenario presents the most favourable economic environment for the project; whereas the pessimistic scenario presents the most unfavourable economic environment for the project. Optimistic but realistic is the name of the game; unlikely events are not part of an optimistic scenario, they are simply unlikely; an optimistic scenario should be optimistic but feasible. Similarly, pessimistic but feasible.

Next we recommend the construction of two intermediate scenarios: one between the optimistic and the most likely scenario, and one between the most

[2] Based on N. y Werner Ketelhöhn, Marín José, *Inversions Estratégicas: Un Enfoque Multidimensional*, San José, Costa Rica. Asociación Libro Libre, 1986.

likely and the pessimistic scenario. Visualizing these two scenarios is not easy, it calls for experience of the country and an understanding of what can be considered as being between the most likely scenario and the two extreme scenarios. Understanding how the country works, its social, political and economic interactions are essential for the construction of these scenarios.

How many scenes for each scenario? Practitioners and academics create yearly scenes for the operations of the project in the form of projected operative cash flows for each year and a single environmental scene during the life of the project, as shown in Table 9.1. A more detailed analysis could be performed by creating environmental scenes for, say, every 2, 3 or 5 years, but the normal approach is to evaluate projects by creating single scene environmental scenarios, for instance, assuming one yearly inflation and devaluation rates throughout the life of the project.

Consider, now, our investors' 15 per cent minimum acceptable rate of return. It represents what they believe to be the minimum acceptable rate of return in an investment in Central America. The NPV of their equity investment is US$ (316) at this discount rate. Thus, the project should be rejected, because country risks are too high. Notice that these investors represent the country's risk with an additional 6% (15–9%) with which they punish the project's NPV.

Table 9.2 NPV and IRR for each scenario

Environmental scenario	*NPV*	*IRR* (%)	*Scenario's probability* (%)
Optimist	3,375	20.3	5
Intermediate I	2,158	17.0	20
Probable	1,038	13.3	50
Intermediate II	592	11.5	20
Pessimist	58	9.2	5

Our second approach permits a more detailed exploration of the country's risk. We simply estimate the impact of each environmental scenario on the project's NPV. For this, we discount the resulting cash flows with 9 per cent, which is the country's risk-free rate of return. Our estimates are presented in Table 9.2. For all environmental scenarios the NPV are positive when discounted at the risk-free rate (9 per cent). Thus, all IRRs are also bigger than 9 per cent, and the project should be accepted because the NPVs estimated uncertainty, which was caused by environmental scenarios, can be ignored. What do we do with these project scenarios?

9.3 Assessing country risk[3]

When the pessimistic and neighbouring intermediate scenarios yield a negative

[3] Ibid.

NPV, the question becomes one of how to use this information for risk assessment. The five NPVs can be used to estimate a probability distribution based on five point observations. A similar probability distribution for the IRRs can be constructed out of the five IRRs (some of which may be lower than the risk-free discount rate). We can then use this probability distribution to estimate whether or not the project should be accepted. This is done in the same way that one accepts or rejects an hypothesis in statistical inference. The problem is the same.

We select an *a priori* decision criteria of what constitutes an acceptable risk and what is not acceptable. For instance, consider a 10 per cent probability of obtaining a negative NPV as our acceptance limit for a particular country. Then we would reject a project if inequality 9.1 holds:

$$P(NPV<0)>10\% \tag{9.1}$$

That is, if the probability of reaching a negative NPV is greater than 10 per cent, we would not invest in the project. Otherwise, the country presents an acceptable risk level for the project.

When we work with IRR, a different *a priori* probability is required. The probability that the IRR is smaller than the country's risk-free discount rate. For instance 10 per cent as expressed in inequality 9.2

$$P(IRR<9\%)>10\% \tag{9.2}$$

The project is rejected if the probability of obtaining an IRR smaller than 9 per cent is bigger than 10 per cent. Otherwise we accept the project because it presents an affordable risk when this probability is less than 10 per cent.

In both cases the risk is measured with the probability that the random variable NPV or IRR is less than a risk-free value; zero for the NPV, at a risk-free rate, and the risk-free rate for the IRR. There are many possible acceptance limits. It is the investor's choice, but we suggest two possibilities:

1 Zero, for the NPV of the project – at a risk-free discount rate. We accept projects with less than 10 per cent probability of generating a negative NPV.
2 The risk-free discount rate for the IRR of the project. We accept projects with more than 90 per cent probability of generating an IRR bigger than the risk-free rate.

Both approaches allow for differences in risk aversion among investors. For instance, one investor could set 13 per cent as his lower limit for the IRR, that is, the country's Central Bank rate plus a 4 per cent differential rate as premium for country risk for his dollars. This investor would demand that:

$$P(IRR<13\%)>10\% \tag{9.3}$$

The interesting thing is that we can separate risk assessment from risk aversion with this approach to evaluating country risk. The project's risk is reflected in the probability distribution, whereas the risk aversion is reflected in the selected limits for acceptance. We believe this to be an interesting breakthrough, as it creates more objective discussions about risk assessment and aversion.

Our suggested 10 per cent probability also reflects risk aversion, since it imposes a limit on how much we are willing to leave to chance; it specifies how sure we want to be. In statistical inference, these limits are often set at 1 per cent or 5 per cent confidence levels. For country risk we suggest 10 per cent, as we business people gamble more than scientists. The latter seek to discover scientific truths, whereas we just seek to make money. And in money-making proaction, determination and consistent behaviour are essential.

Anyway, investors are the ultimate risk-takers and their preference curve is the one that really counts; we just give some indication of what could be used. It is useful to remember that there are no right or wrong estimates of a probability distribution nor right or wrong limits. These approaches are only methods that quantify in an orderly way, the intuitive risk assessment of the ultimate decision-maker, the investor.

In our example, the country's environmental risk has a negligible effect on the project's attractiveness. We conclude that the investment practically guarantees the 9 per cent risk-free return. Clearly, this statement holds for the environmental scenarios that were considered in the analysis; other scenarios may turn the investment sour.

What all this means is that our analytical methods, visualized scenarios, electronic spreadsheets and other techniques produce value if, and only if, the investor's experience and understanding of the environment and the business is reflected in the calculations. Otherwise, these tools and concepts may turn into dangerous value-subtracting weapons, since today's microcomputers can produce the most interesting numbers, and we may run the risk of believing them before we make sure that the soul of an experienced investor is included in the hypotheses. Our results are as good as the people making assumptions and building scenarios.

9.4 Conclusions

To believe that one number, the adjusted rate of return, represents the complex interactions of all social, political and economic factors in a country is too simplistic. Experienced business people prefer to understand these complex interactions explicitly. For this, they try to understand the country's culture, politics and economy by appealing to frameworks originating in these disciplines. They ask: why oversimplify a country's complexity when we have disciplines offering useful frameworks to understand it? This fundamentalist approach to country analysis starts with macroeconomics.

In our experience, country managers have a rudimentary understanding of how economies work – they are doers, not economists – and use their views to raise questions with experienced economic consultants. We strongly recommend using such expert advice.

To understand the macroeconomic environment, country managers must seek the help of macroeconomists who specialize in the country in which they operate. In Appendix B we present a simplistic framework for understanding an economy. In the fourth section of this book we will show how country managers cooperating with macroeconomists were able to understand the economic turning points in Nicaragua in 1979. The reasoning presented, however, does not apply to all environmental conditions; country specialists should and must be recruited to construct a fundamental understanding of an economy.

Assignment questions

1 How do we assess country risk?
2 How do we use economic scenarios?
3 Can one number represent country risk?

10

The political environment[1]

10.1 The political environment

Every time a drastic change in government occurs in a foreign country people at headquarters have a burning desire to act in response to the confusing and vague information they receive. Country managers receive desperate faxes asking: *Is it a right wing junta? Is the strong man a leftist? What plans do they have for private business?* Answers to these questions determine many hasty strategic investment decisions. Undue optimism or pessimism originates in such strangely conceived first impressions.

Instead of asking stereotypical questions, we believe that country managers should seek the help of political analysts on a regular basis. This not only provides educated analytical frameworks but also an expert analysis of the current political events, trends and pressures in the market. The political environment must be scrutinized in order to anticipate the likelihood of possible political turning-points; such events should not catch managers by surprise. When out of the ordinary events occur, three main concerns run through people's minds back at headquarters:

1 The security of fixed and liquid assets.
2 The business unit's economic feasibility.
3 The business unit's ability to move hard currency in and out of the host country freely.[2]

So, to understand what is happening on the political side and the concomitant risks generated by these events, trends and pressures, it is important to educate people at headquarters about the regime, its support groups, the political system and the country's international political and economic relations.

10.2 Leaders and support groups

Thus, the first question a country manager answers is: who is in power in that country? This is essential for understanding the way the economic pie is distributed in society. It is important to understand the ideology of the politicians, their beliefs, values and likely attitudes. Country managers learn about these things at social gatherings, Rotary and Lions' Clubs, and, in general,

[1] Based on N. y Werner Ketelhöhn and Marín José, *Inversiones Estratégicas: Un Enfoque Multidimensional*, San José, Costa Rica, Asociación Libro Libre, 1986.

[2] We are concerned with the freedom of movement of foreign exchange from the country to other markets. For instance, profits, dividends, interests, licence payments, and so on.

through friends and business associates. Clearly, these are extremely important, informal information channels.

In practice, economic decisions are taken by a limited number of people; mainly employed in the central bank, the ministry of economics and the ministry of finance. Each country has its own decision processes and country managers must be informed about the people in charge of economic decision-making. In short, who is in charge of the economy?

The idea is to understand the people in charge, their past economic decisions, their political inclinations, their ideology, their beliefs, values and likely attitudes. Our working hypothesis is that people's basic belief and value system does not change much in adulthood. Thus, if we understand 'where they come from' we will be able to forecast the direction of their future decisions.

Our second working hypothesis is that the beneficiaries of the economic decisions will be those pressure groups that support the regime – especially the economic decision-makers – in power. Thus it is important to ask: who is supporting those in power? Political support is offered in exchange for some sort of benefit. We believe that people in power distribute benefits to those that support them. Thus if we know who supports them in power, we'll have a good chance of understanding where the future economic benefits will flow.

Regimes are not eternal, they come and go; even the Soviet Union ceased to exist. Either through democratic processes or through violent means, sooner or later all regimes change. When the people in power change, the support groups also change, and the flow of benefits may change direction. Therefore, country managers should also ask: how long will this regime last?

However, even when the political parties alternate power, economic decision-makers may remain in office, for instance, the president of the central bank, because these positions demand expertise and international credibility. Eduardo Lizano, for instance, remained president of the Central Bank of Costa Rica, through two opposing political regimes. This makes the understanding of economic decisions easier, but does not help in understanding the new political will. So the basic question has to revisited: who supports those in power?

10.3 Understanding a political system

To understand the political environment, the first step is to feel how public policy is shaped in the country. To determine how open the political system is; who participates within it; which are the most important ideologies and how much support do they have.

For instance, in a dictatorship the bulk of the population does not generally participate in the political process. This unmobilized population generally turns into a source of support for dissident groups of democrats or radicals. Radicals are often able to mobilize this large section of society to attack the regime through violent methods. So, country managers must understand the political ideology of the parties participating in the political game; their ideology determines the role of the state in the economy. Also, international relations and alliances should be studied, to see where foreign support and resources may originate.

The politics in a society can be understood if we divide it into five sectors: regime, political parties, social sectors, pressure groups and the foreign sector. A political map of the relative ideological stances of these players and the direction of their support can be drawn. These political maps are constructed with the help of political scientists who study the country; it is important to use outside help to eliminate the natural bias created by our own desires and passions.

The key element in a political analysis is the understanding of how the policies will impact upon the behaviour of the country's economy. Political events, trends and pressures should be watched with an eye on their effect upon the economic environment. What matters is our ability to predict and influence the future economic behaviour and get ready for it before it occurs.

Once we understand the economic system, and the underlying political forces, we can make educated guesses as to what the future state of the economy will be. In these cases we can adjust the strategic posture of the corporation within that market. Once this understanding is reached, country managers are able to create various, educated economic scenarios for their business unit that take account of inflation rates, devaluations, available financing, growth in demand, etc.

10.4 Devaluation of Nicaragua's Córdoba in 1979[3]

Consider Nicaragua's economy in April 1979. We apply our framework to this situation because it represents the country environment from which we draw major lessons for managing in turbulent environments in Part Four of this book. We believe that this example shows how both politics and economics interact and create a company's external pressures.

Consider Table 10.1, where we show the fiscal deficits of Nicaragua from 1976 to 1979. By 1979 Somoza's (the President of Nicaragua) regime had lost

Table 10.1 Nicaragua: financial indicators[4]

	\$000,000s			
	1976	1977	1978	1979[5]
Fiscal deficit	70.8	149.2	169.1	9.3
Financing	70.8	149.2	169.1	9.3
External	52.7	139.9	9.9	8.3
Internal	18.1	9.3	159.2	1.0
Private capital movement–	–		(67.1)	(275.1)
Gross international reserves	–	158.5	164.8	80.9
Net international reserves	–	55.9	(1.1)	(225.4)

[3] Based on Doctor Noel Ramírez' dissertation.
[4] Source: Informe Anual, Banco Central de Nicaragua, años 1976, 1977 y 1978.
[5] From January to March of 1979.

its ability to finance these deficits with external resources, i.e. loans, because the country's political situation had culminated in a civil war financed by international players. In essence, Nicaragua's regime was financially blocked by President Carter's enforcement of American human rights policies.

In 1978, Nicaragua's Central Bank financed 95 per cent of the corresponding deficit, however, the foreign exchange reserves dropped by (US$225.4) because the Sandinistas' civil war created private capital flight (this was when we came to understand the meaning of 'nothing is shyer than a million dollars'). As the war progressed, the central government's deficit continued to increase, and in the first quarter of 1979, it was bigger than its equivalent in 1978.

In April 1979, economists working for organizations in the private sector estimated that Nicaragua's fiscal deficit was going to be 800 million cordobas for the year. With a rate of exchange of 7 cordobas per dollar, this meant the financing of US$114.3 million. In addition, Nicaragua's foreign exchange reserves were depleted: there were no other funds with which to finance the deficit. Nicaragua's environmental situation can be summarized as follows:

1 There was no way to influence the prices of its exports – cash crops.
2 There were no foreign exchange reserves left.
3 Since 1956, a fixed exchange rate of 7 cordobas per dollar had been used.
4 Capital flight continued to deplete any new foreign exchange.
5 Economists forecasted a deficit of US$114.3 million for 1979.
6 The country was suffering a recession created by the interruption of the production process and the GNP dropped 7 per cent in one year.
7 Unemployment was running at 20 per cent of the work force.
8 Inflation hit 9 per cent in 1978 and was getting worse.
9 A civil war was raging in the cities.

Nicaragua's economic decision-makers, the central bankers and politicians, examined the following alternatives:

1 *Refuse to finance the deficit and attempt to reduce internal credit.* This required a reduction of government spending, which was basically military in nature. Internal demand would diminish, creating even more unemployment and a deepened depression.
2 *Increase taxes to finance the deficit.* This had already been tried in 1978 and the new tax package had no effect as the economy was depressed and needed, instead, an injection of dynamism. Inflation of 9 per cent had made Nicaragua's cash crops uncompetitive in world markets. So, simply adding taxes was expected to accomplish nothing except a deeper depression.
3 Central Bank financing without the backing of foreign exchange. This was expected to increase inflation, and also paralyse the planting decisions of 1979; cash croppers could skip the year's season given their cost estimates under a runaway inflation. The economy would fall into a deeper depression.
4 Devaluing the cordoba and adding a special export tax. This was the only solution that would return the competitiveness of the cash exporters, and thus activate the economy. This way foreign exchange could be captured and used to finance the public sector; basically the money to fight the war was going to be provided by the cash croppers' export tax.

Table 10.2 Inventory of actors

Actors	*Objectives*	*Resources*
Regime		
Somoza	money, power	weapons, information, organization, money, status, etc.
Social sectors		
Peasants	survival	violence
Workers	power, survival	violence, work, legitimacy,
Middle class	power, income	violence, information, organization
Agro-exporters	money, power	experience, money, technology
Political parties		
FSLN – MDN	power	weapons, information, organization, money, status, etc.
Liberal	power	status, legitimacy, money
Conservative	power	status, legitimacy, money
Pressure groups		
Catholic church	influence	legitimacy, status
Press	money, influence	information
Army	power, money	weapons, violence
Chambers	money, power	money, technology, organization
International sector		
Latin American	legitimacy	money, weapons, status, credibility
Europe	influence	money, weapons, status
USA	status	money, weapons, troops, goods, information
USSR – Cuba	Power, influence	money, weapons, troops, goods, information

The four alternatives carried political costs. When inflation and unemployment were let loose, the winners were the Sandinistas. So, one way to understand the pressures generated by these alternatives, was to construct an Uphoff-Ilchmann political map – as explained by Marc Lindenberg and Ben Crosby.[6] For this was constructed Table 10.2, which summarizes the political actors, their objectives and their resources.

In essence, we have a table responding to three important questions: *Who are they? What do they want? Who has it?* Clearly, while trying to answer these questions there will be passionate disagreements, discussions and even fights. This is why external, neutral assistance is essential for a cool construction of a table such as Table 10.2.

Once this table has been constructed, we can proceed to identify the alliances

[6] Lindenberg, Marc and Crosby, Benjamin, *Managing Development: the Political Dimension*, The Kumarian Press, 1982.

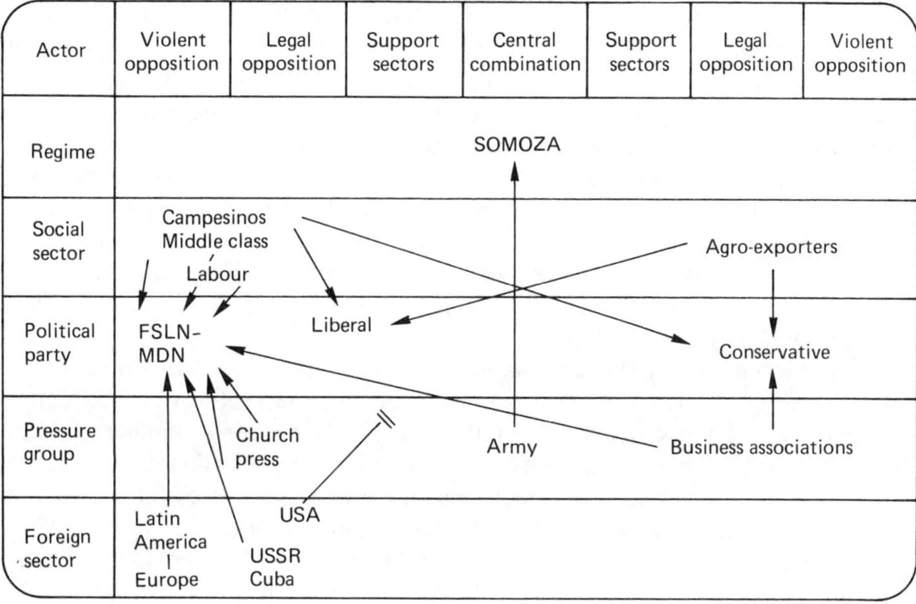

Figure 10.1 Nicaragua's political map, March 1979

and support mechanisms present in the political scene. For this we construct the political map shown in Figure 10.1. During this activity disagreements become even more heated as people usually see what they would like to see, and thus when it comes to evaluate who supports whom, discussions become quite strong.

For Nicaragua in 1979 our political associates estimated the political map shown in Figure 10.1; there we indicate the direction of political support with arrows, and as can be seen Somoza's regime was isolated. Its only support was through violent means, the army's guns.

Under these conditions country managers following the political and economic scene concluded that a devaluation of the cordoba with respect to the dollar was imminent and inevitable, and that an export tax of some sort would have to be created to finance the deficit. The following reasoning was commonly accepted:

1 Foreign aid with which to finance the deficit was unlikely. Neither the Americans nor Europeans were fans of Somoza's regime.
2 More taxes would not produce the desired money but just increased depression and unemployment. Politically, all employees and business people would resent this measure and Somoza's support base would deteriorate even further.
3 Central Bank financing would hurt all cash crop exporters because of increased inflation. This would be a sure recipe for 1979's economic demise, because agro-exporters would not plant if losses were foreseen.
4 Doing nothing was also eliminated because there was a war to fight and the army had to be paid.

Since the regime needed the economic activity of the cash crop exporters, it had to arrange its financing in a way that assured the activity of this important sector. So, a system was conceived that permitted financing the fiscal deficit while simultaneously maintaining economic incentives for cash croppers. The idea was to implement multiple foreign exchange rates.

Nicaragua's economic structure did not leave many degrees of freedom to the economic decision-makers. The country lived from its cash crops, five crops made up two-thirds of all exports, and crop decisions were taken before the rainy season started in April or May of each year. So, if the incentives were not there, these business people might forgo planting for a year or two. Thus, the political decision was expected to go in this direction.

But the amount of the devaluation and the multiple exchange rates could also have been forecast. Consider a group of business people who had known Roberto Incer, President of Nicaragua's Central Bank, for a number of years. They would have known that Roberto was an honest professional, who participated in the design and implementation of Nicaragua's successful export programmes: cotton, cattle, shellfish, coffee, export zones and so on. These business people guessed that Roberto would look after the economic viability of the country's export sector, with special protection of the cash crops.

The technical problem was to find financing for 800 million cordobas. This financing would come from a differential exchange rate between the dollars bought by the Central Bank and those sold to importers.

In Central America and Nicaragua, 70 per cent of all cash crop exports happened between December and April, and in 1979, there were still US$370 million to be exported from Nicaragua. So the economic advisors reasoned that if R is the new exchange rate, then the difference between the old exchange rate is (R – 7); this, multiplied by the amount of dollars still due, US$370 million, should give the total amount of cordobas that could be used for financing the deficit and distributing an incentive to cash croppers. This simple reasoning was expressed with the straight line equation 10.1, which we call the *political line*.

$$(R-7) \times 370{,}000 = 80{,}000 + I \qquad (10.1)$$

where I is the incentive transferred to cash croppers.

From this equation we note that the minimal devaluation was from 7 cordobas per dollar to 9 cordobas per dollar, this is, without passing incentives to agro-exporters. As the incentives transferred to the agro-exporters increased, the devaluation needed to finance the deficit increased as well. So, for an incentive of about 400 million cordobas, the required new rate of exchange was around 10 cordobas per dollar. The trick was to guess the size of the incentives.

For this, our economic advisors reasoned the same way that the Central Bankers did. They estimated the profit and loss statements of average cotton and coffee growers and reviewed how the inflationary forces had deteriorated their bottom line. Then, they simply multiplied the country's planted areas in these two cash crops, and decided that to restore profitability, the total size of the subsidy would be about 350 million cordobas. This was in fact the way in which the Central Bankers reasoned, and the cordoba was devaluated to an exchange rate of ten to a dollar.

10.5 Conclusions

Instead of representing country risks with a single number – an incremental discount rate – our fundamentalist approach provides a better understanding of what is happening in the environment of the host country. For this, we make use of political and economic analysis in a way that seeks to understand the risks in the country.

We propose to first understand the political and economic actors, their objectives, resources and alliances. Next, we propose to understand the economic decisions and public policy formulation, so that likely scenarios are identified. Then, we believe that, with our understanding of the pressures applied to the decision-makers we can guess what the major policy decisions will be. In this way, inflation, devaluations, economic incentives, etc. can be understood. Of course, there will be many times when we don't get it right but we may be close enough to the real events to guide the business unit through that environmental ocean.

The longer a set of decision-makers remains in power, the easier it becomes to predict the direction of their decisions. This is why when an old dictator is thrown out of power, some corporations may worry; they lose their understanding of how the flow of resources is distributed in that country.

Assignment questions

1 What are an investor's aversions under political risk?
2 How can we understand a political system?
3 Why was Nicaragua's cordoba devaluated in 1979?
4 Explain Uphoff-Ilchmann's political mapping technique.
5 Why did the Sandinistas win in Nicaragua in 1979?

Appendix B
Understanding an economy

B.1 Balance of trade and finance

Executives usually understand a country's economy as a gigantic firm; buying and selling products and services to and from other economies. For them countries also have debt capacity with private and development banks, as well as with other governments. In a market economy, smaller, private companies, buy and sell products and services in world markets. In this way, a country's balance of trade reveals how much these companies export and import from other countries. Both exporting and non-exporting companies are free to contract debt with local and foreign banks, attract foreign investments or to invest in other economies.

An economy has five sources of foreign exchange: exports, grants and loans, interest, dividends and capital movements or investments. Similarly, foreign exchange is lost in five ways: imports, grants and loans, interest, dividends, and capital movements or investments. There are no other ways to produce or consume foreign exchange: subvaluation of exports, technical assistance or fake accounts receivables, they all fall into one of the five mentioned categories. Therefore, in the face of trade deficits, an economy either has to produce the missing foreign exchange from the other four sources, or deplete any savings from previous years, e.g. financing imports with the economy's international reserves.

An economy's balance of payments (Table B.1) reflects the deficit or superavit resulting from international trade as well as the way this trade is being financed. Amortizations and interest payments, new loans and capital movements are reflected in the balance of payments of an economy.

The balance of payments is composed of the trade balance, the service balance, all capital movements, mistakes and omissions and changes in international reserves. Net reserves result from subtracting short-term payments (interest and amortizations due in a year) from the gross international reserves. In the absence of capital flight, a country's reserves increase if both trade and financial balance are favourable.

A country's political and economical stability can be assessed by the direction of the investment dollar's flow. When the balance of payments shows capital flight, the local investor's opinion on the country's political and economical stability is unfavourable, otherwise it is favourable. Capital flight shows up in private capital movements, subvaluation of exports, overvaluation of imports and errors and omissions.

People, private and state companies, make up a country's market; Every year they generate the country's Gross National Product (GNP). Private business competes in that market by buying, selling, employing people, making loans, importing, exporting and using the country's physical and social infrastructure.

Table B.1 Nicaragua's balance of payments

Component	1976	$000,000s 1977	1978
Exports FOB	541.8	636.2	646.0
Imports FOB	(485.0)	(704.2)	(553.3)
Trade balance	56.8	(68.0)	92.7
Service income	91.8	105.4	131.5
Other	(119.5)	(152.6)	(157.3)
Interest and profits	(78.0)	(78.0)	(101.2)
Service balance	(105.7)	(125.2)	(127.1)
Net donations	10.2	11.2	9.4
Direct investments	12.9	10.0	7.0
Loan income	15.0	16.0	13.9
Amortisations	(6.0)	(9.0)	(16.9)
Commercial credit	4.9	(84.1)	(286.6)
Private capital movement	26.8	(67.1)	(282.5)
Loan income	74.7	245.3	101.5
Amortizations	(40.5)	(50.2)	(52.2)
Other	31.1	1.3	(6.1)
Official capital movement	65.3	196.4	43.2
Mistakes and omissions	(13.9)	(3.9)	(10.0)
Total	39.7	(56.6)	(274.3)
Net change in reserves	39.7	(56.6)	(274.3)

The government in turn, sees to it that the social and physical infrastructure needed for economic prosperity is put in place, i.e. transport (roads, railroads, ships and planes), services (health, water, power, mail, phones, etc.), and social support (police, justice, schools, universities, etc.). This infrastructure is financed by taxes or the sale of goods and services through government enterprises. Both the state and government enterprises have debt capacity which is also used to finance investment projects.

B.2 Macroeconomic variables

A manager interested in understanding a country's economy has to obtain the following information:

1 National accounts.
2 Public finances.

3 Monetary status.
4 Balance of trade.
5 Balance of payments.
6 Inflation and rate of exchange.

With this information an educated guess as to where a country's economy is headed can be made. For example, central bank financing of fiscal deficits may or may not generate severe inflation in the economy; this inflation may or may not trigger a devaluation of the local currency; and political forces may create economic disturbances. It all depends upon the specific social conditions.

The public finances can be divided into three main parts: first, income that is generated through the sale of goods and services and taxes, which are regulated by the country's fiscal policy; second, the national operating budget; and third, the national investment budget. Now, whenever the operating and investment budgets are bigger than the generated income, a fiscal deficit is created. These deficits are sometimes created on purpose to finance the country's development by inflating the investment budget; or to finance government employment, by inflating the operating budget.

Basically, there are only two ways to close the fiscal deficit: with internal resources obtained from bonds or monetary emission or with resources external to the economy. Financing through monetary emission may or may not be backed by international reserves, and may or may not generate inflation. When external resources are used to finance the fiscal deficit, the implicit assumption is that in the future the country will produce enough to pay for the loans. Foreign investments also make this assumption, but not so foreign donations.

There are, of course, different ways to avoid fiscal deficits: on the income side by generating more taxes, first, through an encouraged economic activity; second, through increased tax rates; and third through more efficient and effective tax collection systems. On the expense side, the deficit can decrease if the operating budget is reduced; and on the investment side, by postponing the country's development. Either of these alternatives carries its political and economic costs that occur in the short, medium and long run. So, when considering a country's economic outlook, country managers must also develop an acute feel for the political scene.

A country's currency is attractive if its international reserves back up its purchasing power in relation to important currencies like the dollar or Deutschmark. In the long run, this is possible if the currency is backed by productive power that is competitive in world markets; that is, production that can generate a positive trade balance. A country's currency is attractive if investors can freely move their profits, fees and other monies, in and out of the country. However, it is possible to have an economically stable country, where it isn't possible to take any money out.

The state can influence economic activity through minimum, wages, fiscal and monetary policies. Fiscal policies are used to create investment incentives, protect industries, and so on; and monetary policies are used to create export inventives, channel funds into priority industries, cool the economy, etc. Regulated by the central bank, a country's financial organization constitutes its nervous and circulatory systems. The central bank's credit policies signal the incentive systems to the economy and determine the credit given to public and private sectors.

B.3 Imported inflation

Inflation originates in countries supplying goods and services (imported inflation), or in the country itself (internal inflation). Imported inflation originates in financial disequilibria in the economies of the supplier countries, i.e. USA, Germany, Japan, etc.; whereas internal inflation originates in disequilibria in the country's economy.

An economy is inflationary if the prices of goods and services increase without corresponding increases in the saisfactors created by these goods and services. For example, when the price of a small car increases without improvements in the product, inflation is said to exist in these small cars. Moreover, inflation occurs whenever the quantities of paper money chasing a fixed amount of goods and services increases.

Imports from the USA include American inflation in their prices. All countries import inflation through their international trade, but the impact of this inflation is more important in small and open economies than in large and closed economies.

The impact of imported inflation on a country's financial stability can be estimated by the percentage of the country's inflation caused by the imports. The percentage of imports originating in each country is first found, i.e. USA, RFA; next, the inflation in each of these countries is obtained; then, all currencies are transformed to a base currency (say the dollar); and finally a weighted average for the imported inflation (in local currency) is obtained.

The importance of imports in the GNP can then be taken as an indicator of the importance of the imported inflation. For example, the division of imports by GNP is taken as the percentage of the imported inflation that is transmitted to the internal economy, So,

$$\text{Impact of imported inflation} = \frac{\text{Imports}}{\text{GNP}} \times \text{imported inflation}$$

For example, if the inflation of imported goods and services is 12 per cent, and the country's inflation is 20 per cent, one can estimate how much of this 20 per cent inflation is imported. Assume that Imports/GNP is 50 per cent, then 6% (0.5 × 12%) is imported inflation, caused by financial disequilibria in foreign countries whereas 14% (20% – 6/%) is caused by financial disequilibria in the country.

B.4 Internal inflation

Basically, financial disequilibria occur because governments spend more than they earn. When this happens, the central bank uses its international reserves to finance the deficit. If this situation continues, the reserves are depleted and loans are then needed to finance the deficit. If this happens a process of internally generated inflation may be established.

Generally, paper money, printed to finance the deficit, will first chase the international reserves, and then create inflation. Of course, if the citizens of foreign countries take this paper money, as is the case with the US dollar and the Deutschmark, inflationary pressures are dampened. However, under normal conditions, the excess monetary mass chases foreign exchange as well as goods and services available in the country. Clearly, if the quantity and quality of goods and services increases in proportion to the increments in paper money, there would be no inflation, because the real production of goods and services would back up the increments in monetary mass. Internal inflation occurs when the demand is bigger than the supply, that is, when there are too many bills, not demanded by foreigners, chasing a few goods and services in the internal market.

Financial disequilibria can also be caused by capital flight or excessive financing, which may also deplete the international reserves and cause internal inflation.

Variations in inflationary pressures are estimated from the index deficit/GNP. If the index is relatively stable, inflationary forces are more or less stable, otherwise they increase or decrease.

Some business people assess inflationary forces from the way fiscal deficits are financed. When the deficit is financed with internal resources inflationary forces increase because no fresh foreign exchange is available to back up the imports of goods and services. When these internal resources are backed by international reserves or loans or donations, inflationary pressures are lower. When foreign exchange does not back printing money, the central bank can only reduce its credit to the private sector (cool the economy) or print the money anyway, creating inflation.

Inflationary pressures are also measured by estimating a liquid ratio with the quotient of an economy's liquid assets (money and quasi-money) over GNP. The liquid assets in an economy are cash, deposits, bonds, long-term deposits and other financial instruments. Liquid assets are created by the economic activity and the way it is financed. If the liquid assets don't grow in relation to the GNP, then enough real production is said to have happened to satisfy the additional demand created by the monetary growth; otherwise, there is more paper money chasing goods and services than before. Whereas in the first case the monetary growth is caused by an increase in real productive growth, in the latter it is caused by financial disequilibria. It has been shown that the nominal credit should grow as fast as the GNP and not faster to avoid inflation.

Part Four

Doing Business in Turbulent Environments[1]

'This Palace's congress, comrades, has never heard such discussions as ours; and we are not far from the truth, I think, when we say that, in the last sixty years, nothing like this has occurred in this country' said Mikhail Gorbachov, General Secretary of the Soviet communist party, on 1 July, 1988, in his closing speech of the XIX Federal Conference where he had proclaimed 'there is no alternative to perestroika' (UPI, AP, AFP, EFE, Moscow).

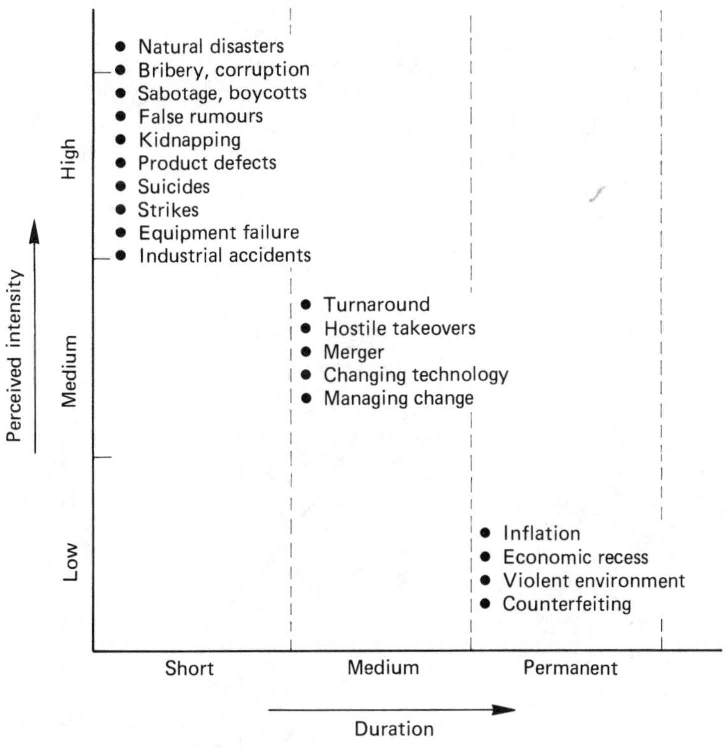

Environmental Disruptions

[1] Based on Ketelhöhn, Werner, 'Doing business in turbulent environments', *IMEDE Perspectives for Managers*, No. 4. June 1989.

The collapse of the Soviet Union at the beginning of the 1990s, and other internationally famous disruptions like the Arab oil embargo in 1973, the Iranian and Central American revolutions, the Yugoslavian civil war, nuclear plant accidents, natural disasters; and many other turbulent situations like corporate theft, hostile takeovers, boycotts, strikes and inflation make up a wide range of unusual disruptions to the 'normal' ways of doing business. These environmental disruptions which are classified in the environmental disruptions illustration above using two empirical dimensions, must and can be managed, but how does one do business under these conditions?

To manage in turbulent environments, corporations have to change from 'business as usual' to managing extraordinary events. Rather than improvise organizational responses, both corporations and government must proactively identify management processes with which to respond to extraordinary disruptions of the 'normal' ways of doing business. This can be done using frameworks that first classify turbulent situations into families of problems, which submit management teams to similar pressures; and then create generic management processes with which executives can respond to situations belonging to a family of disruptions, as illustrated in the generic management approaches illustration below.

Turbulence varies in duration and intensity

First we recognize that the duration of the abnormality calls for different management responses. Short intense disruptions, like the 3 February 1975 suicide of Eli Black, CEO of United Brands, are best handled by crisis management teams.[2] Permanent turbulence, on the other extreme, like the Soviet democratic revolution or the Yugoslavian civil war, demands longer lasting changes in a corporation's operating policies in those markets.

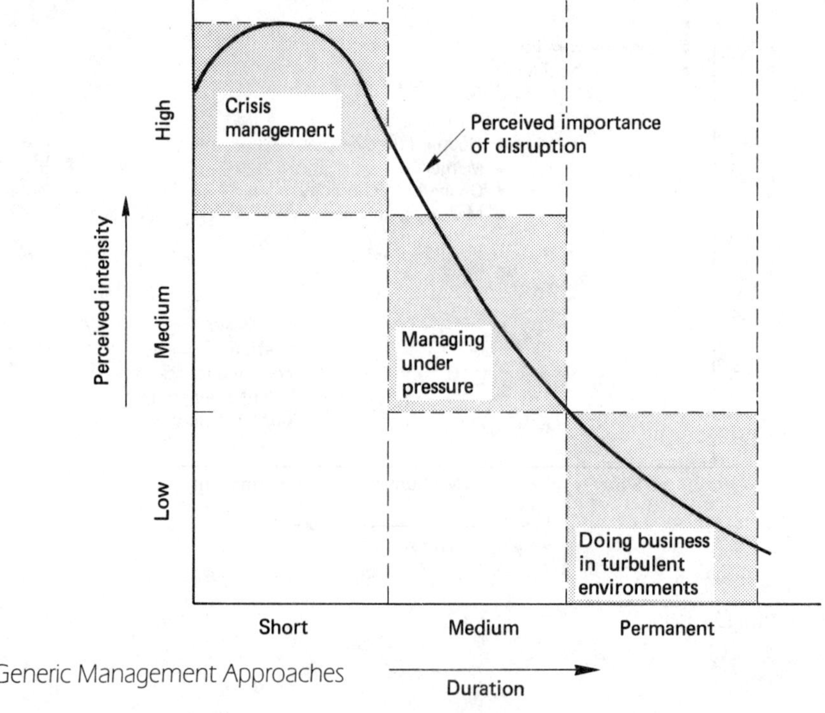

Generic Management Approaches

[2] Eli Black jumped out of a window of the 44th floor in the Panam building in New York, when it was uncovered that United Brands supposedly bribed Economics minister

A second distinction is to recognize that disruptions vary in the intensity with which managers perceive their impact on the corporation. For example, the Bhopal industrial accident in India provoked a short and intense disruption of the normal ways of doing business at Union Carbide; it also triggered a more sustained change process in the company. Mastering emergent technologies, managing change, launching a turnaround, facing a hostile takeover and implementing a merger, are medium duration disruptions which last between one and three years; they are recognized as special forms of managing under pressure. Thus a second genre of management processes are those concerned with medium duration and medium intensity disruptions of the 'normal' ways of doing business. These disruptions may also originate in the competitive environment of the firm, such as the 1988 hostile takeover attempt made by Ticino financier Tito Tettamanti on Sulzer Brothers Ltd.

Corrupt public administration, counterfeiting, inflation, devaluations, civil war and revolutionary governments create long-term disruptions to the 'normal' ways of doing business. We call managing under sustained environmental turbulence, doing *business in turbulent environments*.

The main theme of this fourth and last part is concerned with the processes that adapt a corporation's strategic posture to cope with ongoing disruptions of the social, political and economic environment. Managing in turbulent environments is the third genre of management processes that needs to be studied to be able to respond to ongoing disruptions in the business environment.

In summary, the intensity with which a disruption is perceived by management depends upon the duration of the turbulence. Since managers eventually learn to cope with sustained long-run turbulence, its perceived intensity tends to decline over time. Thus perceived intensity and duration correlate as illustrated in the generic management approaches diagram.

The Central American experience

We asked a sample of 87 Nicaraguan, 144 Salvadorean and 18 Guatemalan managers, to report on their perception of the most important problems during 5 years of the Central American social revolt (1977–82). Their answers reveal three major findings:

1. Disruptions originating in social revolts belong to one of three generic management problems: short duration with high intensity; medium duration with medium intensity; and sustained duration with lower intensity.
2. As illustrated in the generic management approaches diagram, executives respond with different management approaches to each family of disruptions: crisis management for short intense disruptions; management under pressure for disruptions with medium intensity and duration; and managing in turbulent environments for disruptions with long duration.
3. Managing in turbulent environments also includes short-term crises and medium-term turbulent disruptions.

Doing business in turbulent environments requires flexible management and adaptable business policies. Headquarters must include local managers' perceptions in its strategic decision process. Likewise, country managers' knowledge of local economic and political conditions must be tapped if the corporation decides to compete in a

Abraham Bennaton Ramos and President Oswaldo Lopez Arellano, in exchange for lower export taxes on bananas from Honduras.

turbulent business environment. The global implications of changing corporate business policies in response to local conditions, i.e. the message that this sends to other countries, must be evaluated at headquarters in a logical and objective manner; put in place, it forms a part of the market-to-market learning processes.

In this part we discuss the lessons learned from many Central American company case studies and interviews. Useful generalizations can be drawn for use in other markets subjected to the same generic disruptions.

11

Crisis management

11.1 Crises under social revolts

How did it happen?, we asked.

> '– It was around 18:30, my usual time to walk back to my room in El Conquistador, when a black limousine pulled over in front of me and three armed men jumped out of the car and forced me into the back seat. As I struggled to free myself someone fired a Magnum 45 and a girl, in the driver's seat, knocked me out. I awoke to find myself lying on a hammock in a small but clean room, with bandages on my head and a terrible headache.'

It was late June 1988 when Georg Heuer,[1] then regional manager of Allfood, told us about the ordeal he had gone through in the previous two months as hostage to a guerrilla movement in Central America. Curious about the dangers experienced by this regional manager, we continued to talk about his odyssey. At the time Allfood was facing demands for security guards and other protective systems from all Central American managers, sometimes three layers down from the country manager, and the regional office was wondering what to do. Later we learned that Wilhelm Rueda, a close friend of Georg Heuer and a colonel in the Salvadorean army, turned out to be the mastermind behind a wave of Central American kidnapping; his front was a well-known security company in El Salvador.

Then, we found out that Jacques Mermy, country manager in El Salvador, had his family living in San Jose, Costa Rica, where he officially spent one week per month. In fact he travelled every weekend to San Jose – on company business – arriving Thursday night in San Jose and leaving Mondary morning for El Salvador. As a consequence, managers of several subsidiaries in El Salvador were asking Costa Rican staff for help with operating problems that should have been solved by Mermy. What should these managers do?

Next, out of the blue, Fernando Siles, country manager in Panama, began to receive increased public exposure in Panamanian politics by challenging the election of Manuel Palma Solis (fictitious name) as President of Panama. Fernando was arguing publicly that Palma Solis had not won the elections but rather, had been installed by General Noriega's army. Although Fernando had political potential, his present controversial position could harm Allfood's image in Panama. What should the regional manager do?

The disruptions above form a sample of the pressures to which executives are subjected when they manage in countries undergoing violent social revolts. These experiences, documented in the Central American social revolt, could

[1] All names are fictitious including this regional manager of a fictitious corporation, but the situations are based on documented real-life case studies.

serve as case studies from which lessons can be drawn for operations in other markets.

11.2 Central American social revolts

By 1988 we had seen social revolts in many Third World countries, and by 1992, we had to include revolutions in Eastern Europe as well. Even the mighty former Soviet Union is being subjected to drastic economic, political and legal changes. In summary, the rate of social change in some of these countries requires that managers learn to adapt the strategic posture of their business unit to expected and unexpected disruptions in the environment. But there are many questions that require answers. The managers need to know which disruptions or changes are significant; which ones will have an impact on the strategic posture; which are most important and what adaptation processes could be succesful? Undoubtedly, several of these countries merit the question 'time to stay or go?', and looking at the other side of the coin, 'time to invest?'

As mentioned before, 87 Nicaraguan, 44 Salvadorean, and 18 Guatemalan managers answered a survey that covered 5 years of the Central American social revolt (1977–82). The results of this survey (see Table 11.1) show that in

Table 11.1 Ratings assigned to the disruptions created by the Central American social revolt during 1977–1982

I Perceptions of Nicaraguan managers[2]

			Period:		
Disruption	*Normal* (%)	*Civil war* (%)	*Civil War* (%)	*Revolutionary infantilism* (%)	*Coexistence* (%)
A Personal crisis					
Threats, kidnapping	10	17	13	4	4
Focusing	5	4	9	7	4
Family's security	4	8	10	2	2
Attract workers	2	2	2	3	1
Sub-total	21	30	34	16	12
B Corporate crisis					
Protect fixed assets	4	9	13	6	5
Protect liquid assets	14	15	12	11	5
More operating risk	10	8	8	7	6
More equity risk	4	9	5	7	8
Sub-total	33	41	37	30	23
C Permanent impact in the corporation					
Other[3]	46	29	29	54	55
Total	100	100	100	100	100

[2] Rounded off percentages.
[3] Discussed below in Chapter 12.

II Perceptions of Salvadorean managers

Disruption	*Normal* (%)	*Period:* *Civil war* (%)	*Revolutionary infantilism* (%)	*Coexistence* (%)
A Personal crisis				
Threats, kidnapping	16	17	11	8
Focusing	4	4	5	5
Family's security	1	6	5	4
Attract workers	0	1	0	1
Sub-total	21	28	21	18
B Corporate crisis				
Protect fixed assets	14	14	7	5
Protect liquid assets	8	8	8	7
More operating risk	7	4	8	8
More equity risk	12	9	8	8
Sub-total	40	35	31	28
C Permanent impact in the corporation				
Other	39	37	29	54
Total	100	100	100	100

III Perceptions of Guatemalan managers

Disruption	*Normal*	*Period:* *Social Revolt*	*Coexistence*
Personal crisis			
Threats, kidnapping	16	17	13
Focusing	6	3	3
Family's security	5	3	7
Attract workers	0	3	1
Sub-total	27	25	24
B Corporate crisis			
Protect fixed assets	7	4	8
Protect liquid assets	8	7	8
More operating risk	2	1	7
More equity risk	8	6	8
Sub-total	25	17	30
C Permanent impact in the corporation			
Other	48	58	46
Total	100	100	100

order to do business under crises created by violent social revolts it is useful to make a distinction between pressure to managers and workers as individuals, and pressure to the corporation and its systems.

11.3 Crisis management

Crisis[4] management is a well-studied field that includes such elements as managing the media, managing interviews, managing crisis teams and managing liabilities. The short but intense effect of turbulence upon the operations of the firm were best handled by crisis management teams. A systematic and orderly set of responses to crises allowed corporations to continue with their normal operations while the crisis was being handled by specially trained teams. British American Tobacco's fixed assets in Nicaragua, for example, were defended from angry looters by a crisis management team during the June–July 1979 civil war, while operations were handled by normal management. Under the same circumstances, Dietrich Zimmermann, Bayer de Centroamerica's country manager in Nicaragua, had to assume crisis management tasks on top of his normal duties, because the size of his operations did not allow for the creation of a special team.

Crisis management starts with the appointment of a crisis manager who is responsible for the selection of a crisis management team selected from functional executives. After the team has agreed how to work together, they classify all possible crises into generic crisis situations in which the corporation may be involved. Which crises are generated by violent social revolts? In Table 11.1 answers are found to this question and eight generic crises situations were identified:

Personal crises
1 Threats and kidnapping.
2 Family security.
3 Focusing managerial energy.
4 Keeping the work force.

Corporate crises
5 Threats to fixed assets.
6 Threats to liquid assets.
7 Increased operating risk.
8 Increased risk to owners.

It is for these crises that a corporation's crisis management team must prepare action plans. In Nicaragua, for example, a 5-year period of social revolt was divided into five sub-periods of differing duration: the foundation, corresponding to the period before the September 1977 insurrection; the social revolt, between October 1977 and April 1979; the civil war, between May and July of 1979; revolutionary infantilism or decrees period, between August and December of 1979; and coexistence, between January of 1980 and June 1982.

Since there was no time to learn during these crises, corporations had to

[4] A crisis is provoked by any event that directly threatens the attainment of corporate objectives in a market by causing the normal working procedures and personnel to become inadequate in handling the disruption. It is a relative and subjective concept best understood through the corporation's needs in the market.

respond with existing people, systems and working procedures. This meant that crisis teams had to be recruited from among the executives already working in the market; these teams changed most normal working procedures and created emergency systems with which to respond to each generic crisis.

11.4 People crises

The crisis management team proceeded to classify all possible crises into *generic crises*, e.g. events dealing with personal security, in which the subsidiary could get involved. Then, they usually prepared a 'plan' to handle one crisis from each crisis scenario. 'People crises' included the following:

1 Threats, kidnapping, and family security: personal security at work, the streets and home.
2 Focusing managerial energy: political involvement and absenteeism of unreliable managers, and remuneration and conservation of good managers.
3 Keeping the work force: desertion of workers and public transportation problems.

At Exxon, for instance, all top executives went through a special security course, including driving lessons, and were trained on what to do in case of kidnapping or terrorist attack. This way, since all crises in a genre were related, the subsidiary was ready to handle a specific crisis genre.

Intense crisis affected peoples' personal lives: first, in the form of threats and actual kidnappings, mainly before and during the civil war; second, with respect to family security during the civil war; and finally, during the civil war and revolutionary infantilism. In these periods, different people fell victims to these crises. Before and during Nicaragua's civil war, for instance, peak pressure was felt by managers, but afterwards people problems shifted to workers and employees.

For example, Don Francisco De Sola, partner of Unisola of El Salvador, was kidnapped before the widespread Salvadorean civil war; his release was negotiated by a crisis team that included English experts. During the same period, however, Eduardo Poma, heir of the Poma business group and a promising politician, was kidnapped and murdered in cold blood. The Poma family chose to organize their business so that it could be run out of Miami. Our Central American survey shows that managers get used to unusual danger levels with time, but that owners always offer attractive targets.

Personal and family security was indeed perceived as one of the most important problems that a management team and its workers faced during a civil war and the collapse of an old regime. Executive and worker requests for special services, concessions, incentives or protection were well founded.

Regional managers solved protection issues on an *ad hoc* basis. As not all countries had the same danger level, different protection measures were used and accepted in each country. Moreover, people seemed to adapt to abnormal danger levels to the point of coexisting with danger as a normal thing. Even in the spring of 1979, Danilo Lacayo, Exxon's country manager in Nicaragua said: 'I don't know why people in Europe and the USA make such a big deal about the risks we are running. Sure, going to the war zones is dangerous, but there is no danger if one stays out of trouble spots.'

Although danger levels were high, top management's presence in countries subjected to civil war proved to be a crucial factor for company survival. Managers biting the bullet were more effective in defending the corporation's assets than those leaving the country. The latter were not fully able to understand the different and dangerous changes created by the revolution. Top management needs to bring about the appropriate behaviour with which to face the danger levels in which executives and workers live.

During peak danger periods, for example, some managers would disappear either to Miami, in search of peace, or to join the guerrilla movements. Management by telex, telephone or any other remote control device is out of the question, as it increases the risks that company assets are running. A manager must harness his fears, encourage all members of the organization to face the problems and lead the way out of the dangerous crisis situation.

Despite all corporate efforts, some executives took sides in these conflicts, not only rooting for but also helping, one of the warring factions, sometimes with corporate resources. This behaviour increased company risk, because one side perceived the corporation as an ally of their enemy.

Focusing managerial efforts on the job became a problem if executives involved themselves in revolutionary or government activities and neglected their normal duties. This was observed and documented both in Central America's and Malagasy's revolutions. Alfonso Robelo, CEO of a cotton oil complex in Nicaragua, for example, invested his time, and that of several of his executives, in overthrowing the Somoza regime; executives in many other companies were also deeply involved in revolutionary activities. After Somoza's downfall most 'consequent'[5] executives were absorbed into government jobs, while many of their colleagues were not. In small countries, scarce executive talent can not only be lured away with ideological arguments but also can be distracted from their duties by the explosive social environment.

What seems clear is that a country manager's presence in a market subjected to a violent social revolt is necessary to increase the chances of corporate survival in that market. The manager must discharge his responsibilities at the scene of the events, rather than by remote control. The right attitude is not to delegate, but rather, to lead the people in the organization to face crises created by civil war.

Organized labour pressures reached a peak immediately before civil war only to disappear during it. An accepted explanation is that labour leaders abandoned civil pressure mechanisms, such as strikes and union negotiations, and, in frustration, joined violent movements for social reform. Right wing terrorism also forced labour leaders underground, while left wing terrorists remained immune in their hideaways.

11.5 Company crises

'Move back! Don't come closer!', yelled the security chief at Tabacalera Nicaraguense, a subsidiary of British American Tobacco, as he fired into the

[5] A nickname for executives following the revolutionary organizations.

air in front of an angry mob of a thousand looters who were trying to invade the well-guarded premises of the company. Even during maximum threats from civil war, security companies were able to protect the fixed assets of their clients, specially when top management was leading the decision-making process.

Protection of fixed assets by conventional crisis management teams worked best when managerial leadership was provided. When we reviewed the characteristics of destroyed and surviving companies in the Nicaraguan revolution we found the following policy and executive behaviour patterns (see Table 11.2):

Table 11.2 Characteristics of destroyed and surviving companies

Characteristic	*Destroyed*	*Surviving Co.*
Country manager	absent	present:leading
Practising corruption	yes	no
Governmental partners	yes	no
Located in battle zones	yes	no
Taking sides in the conflict	yes	no
Labour relations	bad	good

Insurance companies refused to buy the risks occurring under violent conditions, pushing all risks to equity shareholders. However, in the long run, all Central American governments, regardless of their ideology, were interested in protecting the assets of private business. Therefore, those threats to assets that originate in civil wars, disappear once revolutionaries take political power.

The Central American revolts created four main types of crises within the operations of a firm:

1 *Threats to fixed assets.* Protection of fixed assets because of invasion of plants, sabotage, boycotts and attacks on the corporation's assets, occurred mainly during the civil war.
2 *Threats to liquid assets.* Special cash expenses due to war wages and downtime, accounts receivables lost; and/or extortion and assaults, occurred mainly during the foundation and social revolt.
3 *Increased risk to owners.* Unexpected liabilities because of environmental uncertainty and failing to get insurance, or risks created by government partners, especially during social revolt and the civil war.
4 *Increased operating risk.* Executive time spent in unproductive activities, political strikes; as well as demand contraction, loss of supplies, and difficulties in loan restructuring, occurred mainly during social revolt and coexistence.

Another decision in which managers needed help, was on the amount of inventory to carry under civil war. The rules of rational economic behaviour cease to be 'rational' under violent social revolts; and any inventory is 'too much' when war breaks out near your warehouses, specially if it is not insured.

11.6 Perceived importance of crises

Although these crises may also occur in countries not subjected to violent social revolts, the ratings assigned to them by the interviewed managers show that their importance increased by about 50 per cent under civil war conditions; that is, in a civil war these crisis situations received 75 rating points out of a total of 100 points; the other 25 points being assigned to permanent disruptions; under 'normal' conditions these same crises received a rating of about 50 from the same managers.

Similarly, under 'normal' conditions, people crises received a rating of 20, whereas in a civil war the rating rose to 37, almost double the perceived importance. Not surprisingly, disruptions having an impact on people increased more in importance than those impacting on the corporation.

In Nicaragua and El Salvador, initial attempts to impart social justice made business operations impossible; an avalanche of decrees distributing liquid assets to workers hit the paralysed companies. Regulations demanding pay increases, extra salaries, new taxes, increased employee benefits and the like, made labour negotiations an everyday activity for the first 3 months of the new regimes. Tentative agreements and flexible policies proved to be the best answers to these pressures. It was only when internal government negotiations were settled that more stable rules emerged.

The Central American experience suggests that, since there is no time to learn in crisis situations, the crisis management team must not only understand the enterprise system in a specific market, but also be trained to handle crises, and have the ability to:

1 Identify and prepare for most crises.
2 Differentiate immediately between a temporary crisis and a permanent, sustained disruption.
3 Set the basic goals for company survival.
4 Construct scenarios and diagnose possible future events.
5 Understand the risks involved in each alternative action.
6 Set priorities for action; have the courage to implement and not panic, i.e. an adequate risk taking attitude.
7 Identify when to do things differently.

Assignment questions

1 How do we understand crisis management?
2 What generic crises were identified?
3 Describe the nature of people rises,
4 Describe the nature of corporate crises,
5 What were the characteristics of surviving companies?

12
Turnaround management is not Rambo management[1]

12.1 Managing under pressure

Techniques for managing under pressure are usually found in management responses to special problem areas such as: mergers, emergent technologies, managing change, turnarounds and hostile takeovers. These are probably the most studied of the three generic management approaches, and typically consume between 2 and 3 years of intensive management time and attention. Responses to technological changes in the competitive environment, for example, are found with industry analyses appropriate to the country/market in which the corporation operates.

It took, for example, well over a year to mount a defensive strategy against the takeover attempt launched by Ticino financier, Tito Tettamanti on Sulzer Brothers. Management had first to uncover his intentions; second, recognize that some Swiss investors were trying to take over the company; third, launch a search for possible solutions; fourth, decide on an appropriate defence, and finally, implement it.

Given the confidential and important nature of this type of problem, it is extremely difficult to delegate 'management under pressure' to crisis management teams, and it generally has to be discharged by existing management in addition to their normal business responsibilities. As an example of typical managerial responses in this category, we discuss below, turnaround management.

12.2 Stop the bleeding!

'Stop the bleeding!' is, for many people, the first requirement of turnaround management. This can often mean that positions are slashed and only then is the question asked: 'By the way, what were these people doing for us?' All too often, the answer has been, 'quite a lot'.

Conventional wisdom has it that, after an early phase of swift cost cutting, the company can stabilize so that, once survival seems assured and resources start to flow back in, new patterns of growth can be developed. Another argument is that businesses with a high market share should stress innovations, whereas businesses with a low market share should not. Businesses with high-

[1] Taken from Ketelhöhn, Werner, Jarillo, J. Carlos and Kubes, Jan, 'Turnaround management is not Rambo management', *European Management Journal*, Vol. 9. No. 2, June 1991

capacity utilization should stress cost reduction, while those with low-capacity utilization should stress asset reduction.

But things are never so simple and certainly not so linear. Our research has shown that what successful turnaround managers did first was develop a clear, long-term vision of the organization, its products and its markets. This vision was an essential up-front part of the company's ultimate success, enabling turnaround managers to develop ways of doing new and different things (innovation) and ways of doing things differently (efficiency improvements).

We examined management approaches to turnarounds in some of IMD's one hundred MBA consulting projects, as well as in the many case studies researched and written at IMEDE-IMI on European companies in the 1980s. A turnaround was considered to be successful if, after the period of losses, management could sustain at least two consecutive years of profit. Therefore a turnaround period lasted for at least 4 years:

1 A first year of losses (when major turnaround decisions are made).
2 The break-even year (testing what works).
3 The first year of profits (confirming improvements).
4 A year for consolidation of profits, proving that the turnaround decisions produced sustainable, profitable performance.

12.3 Vision

Vision is essential from the start, as the decisions taken early in the turnaround (usually, in the first 6 months) will determine the long term viability of the enterprise.

> When Chresten Reeves was interviewed in early 1982 by the chairman of the Danish 'Berlingske Publishing House' for the position of CEO of the newspaper and magazine conglomerate, he was asked for his vision of what business the conglomerate should be in, and how it could be turned around. Although operating at full capacity, the Berlingske House had five consecutive years of losses behind it and about another DKr 50 million loss forecast for 1982. Said Reeves, 'Berlingske must concentrate on its core business, newspapers, sell all satellite businesses, and take a giant technological leap forward.

Without this type of vision for the future of the company, management runs two risks: believing that a clearer picture will emerge they may delay taking the necessary action when the situation continues to deteriorate, consequently a possible turnaround becomes more and more difficult; and in other cases, rash action may seriously hamper the company's future.

A visionary strategy communicated to the organization at the start of a turnaround may be more easily accepted. Mere cost-cutting may be interpreted as further proof that top management does not know how to manage the firm. In a turnaround situation, rallying the deepest commitment from everybody in the company is essential. And the only way to engender this support is by showing clear, visionary leadership. Without this vision, the organization may feel, with some justification, that the short term cost-cutting approach may well be jeopardizing any chances of future profitability.

Of course, having a clear and articulate vision from the start presupposes an intimate knowledge of the industry. Although there will surely be exceptions to this rule, we have found no instance of a long-term turnaround achieved by a 'turnaround specialist', as opposed to an 'industry specialist'. Successful turnarounds were led by people with a thorough understanding of the industry in which their company operated. They gave top priority to developing a clear vision of what business their company should be in, and the way this vision should be implemented. These characteristics, combined with business acumen and a personal style emphasising hard work and persevering hands-on management, were shared by such successful European turnaround managers as Jean-Marie Descarpenteries at Carnaud, Jan Carlzon at SAS and Chresten Reeves at the Berlingske House.

12.4 Innovating: doing things differently

This is where conventional wisdom fails the most. It is often believed that in the early phases of a turnaround it is enough to be 'getting things right' and we shouldn't even think of playing around with innovation. However, innovation seems to be the way to save a company with a severely threatened future. All the successful turnarounds we saw introduced elements of innovation right from the beginning, without 'waiting to restructure'. Some of them even started their turnaround drive by emphasizing innovation, not efficiency.

When Jan Carlzon was appointed president of Scandinavian Airline Systems (SAS) in 1981, he adopted an entrepreneurial strategy emphasizing his SAS's Euroclass, a 'new' version of business class. Carlzon concentrated the company's products on the niche market of the business traveller, and reorganized SAS to provide 'service' to this specialized customer. Conventional wisdom calls for productivity drives in low market share, high capacity utilization companies. Carlzon, however, turned SAS around with a major product-service innovation drive which affected the organizational structure of the airline and the interactions and relations between line workers, ticket agents, cabin attendants and middle management. The company's culture evolved towards one in which management kept out of the way of employee creativity and innovation in customer service. Strategic decisions like aeroplane acquisition, corporate diversification and European and world-wide alliances with other airlines were guided by the new Euroclass (service) vision.

12.5 Efficiency improvements

Consider the approach taken by Jean-Marie Descarpenteries, who in May 1982 was made president of Carnaud Emballage, a French producer of metal and plastic containers that had lost $25 million in 1981. A market leader in metal packaging in France and Spain, Carnaud operated well below capacity. Instead of simply going for a reduction in assets, which would have seemed an appropriate turnaround strategy given Carnaud's excess capacity, Descarpenteries reorganized the company into nine profit centres, taking great care to create a process that motivated management. A productivity improvement programme was put into place consisting of the decentralization of both social and economic responsibilities. It included creating market regions for business units; establishing a unified production system; assuring optimal use of human resources and standardizing products and management systems. As a result, sales grew 9 per cent per year from 1981 to 1985, and major improvements in productivity per employee were achieved; a 16 per cent yearly increment in revenues per person was attained in these 3 years.

Productivity improvements are, of course, the basic 'meat and potatoes' of turnarounds. But, as we have argued, cost-cutting without a clear sense of where the company is going, and without innovation, cannot save a company. Companies do not go bankrupt from lack of efficiency. But lack of efficiency tends to be a symptom of a deeper malaise: usually lack of industry understanding and a bureaucratic inability to innovate.

Chresten Reeves' actions at Berlingske illustrate how efficiency improvements are a consequence of an innovative vision and not the driving force behind it. Reeves implemented skilfully his turnaround by:

1 Changing the design and layout of Berlingske's main morning paper. The motto 'first fix what is clearly broken' guided staff changes and the concentration on 'Det Berlingske Tidende'.
2 When the effects of staff changes and the new design and layout had impacted on the circulation (one month into the turnaround), Reeves proceeded to review advertising and increase space sales; changing concepts and using new staff where appropriate.
3 About 3 months into the turnaround, Reeves reorganized the conglomerate, creating different profit centres and trimming down the staff. This not only increased the productivity of the new units, but also clarified which businesses were good candidates for divestment. Reliable trends were visible about 6 months later. This productivity drive was the first turning point in management emphasis in Reeve's efforts to improve the bottom line.
4 Then, six months into the turnaround, Reeves continued to stress cost cutting and began to negotiate the lay-off of 250 typographers, which was necessary because of the introduction and implementation of new printing technology. Training programmes for the remaining typographers were also discussed.
5 Lastly, 18 months into the turnaround, the newspaper's design and lay-out were reviewed again in the company's third innovative drive.

Berlingske's turnaround was triggered first by innovation and then fuelled by productivity improvements. Long-term sustainable profitability was pursued with investments in new printing technology and divestments of satellite businesses. Both the divestment decisions and investments in new technology were considered very early (in the first 3 months of the turnaround), which required a very clear idea of where the company should be in the longer term.

Cost-cutting or, perhaps even worse, additional rounds of investment, with the basic problems still in place, will not produce long-term results. Waiting for these results may be fatal. A company that has gone bankrupt because of lack of innovation, cannot pretend to survive by postponing innovation another year or two while 'the bleeding is stopped'.

12.6 Starting the turnaround

Instead of engaging an eager, 'Rambo-like' turnaround specialist, the board of directors is responsible for recruiting an experienced manager, seasoned in the business.

Like Chresten Reeves, most CEOs will be alone. Below them, managers may fear the tough decisions which may take place. Above them, the board of directors may want to see immediate action. Taking the lead in a turnaround effort can be like agreeing to be the jam in a sandwich.

Furthermore, at the first hint that the company may be in trouble, internal and external interest groups are set in motion. Internally, scarce talent may decide to join the competition if a clear vision of how the company will survive does not emerge. Afraid of losing their jobs, leading union members may strike or try to negotiate binding clauses with management. Externally, the banks may refuse to renew credit lines, increasing the likelihood of bankruptcy.

To calm external stakeholders, it may be useful to seek the protection of the law. In most countries, the law offers protection from creditors so that the troubled company can get its act together. This creates time to fix things, but external pressures will arise as customers wonder about deliveries, and suppliers about their accounts receivables. Too many companies postpone the decision to seek legal protection, only to see their situation deteriorate beyond solution.

Therefore, the CEO should establish a task force that will help him with some of these problems, and start by recruiting an experienced lawyer and a financial advisor. In addition, a few promising managers should be selected from inside. It is extremely important that middle managers be involved in defining the vision, as they will have to implement it, in a difficult environment.

12.7 Selling the vision

Once the task force is in place, the company's stakeholders must be given a reason to commit their energy to the turnaround effort. Internal and external stakeholders must be motivated by a vision of the company's future that inspires them to believe in its viability. Creating this shared vision inside and outside the company is vital if support from the work-force, as well as from customers, suppliers, bankers and the government is to be gained.

An information and communication campaign is necessary to reassure suppliers, clients and the world at large. The CEO cannot depend on unmotivated personnel, sceptical customers and suppliers and bankers who are ready to pull the plug. He must get the company's management involved, allay their fears and motivate them to support the turnaround efforts. Communication with labour representatives will help clarify the company's new goals and the procedures to be followed. Next, the banks have to be reassured that the situation is under control. Last, the help of local and central government agencies may be enlisted.

An effective vision is ambitious; it stretches management's imagination and creates the desire to accomplish the selected goals. If it is tangible and perceived as achievable, a vision will guide and inspire. Such a vision will include long overdue strategic investments that were ignored by the ousted management.

12.8 'Rambo-like' measures that may need to be taken

Eventually, however, tough decisions will have to be made, and they will probably include some divestments. For example, non-performing assets, overstretched operations, and wrong diversification moves all tend to be features of bankrupt companies accompanied by an acute shortage of cash. Divesting, however, takes time and meanwhile the cash drain continues. Therefore, closing some facilities often becomes unavoidable.

Personnel may have to be reduced since overheads (Parkinson's law), are the most common cause of company problems. If so, this must be done in a planned and orderly manner, and if possible only once, as repeated layoffs only serve to worsen the unpleasant situation.

Clearly, management must set an example, as Iacocca did when he started the Chrysler turnaround. It is very demoralizing for workers to be told that plant closings and pay-cuts are necessary, and then realize that top management is keeping (or increasing) its remuneration and perks. Top-class managers have to be well paid or nobody would accept a turnaround assignment, but that pay has to be linked to the success of the turnaround. No one will complain about a large compensation package for a management team that has saved a company, but demanding high remuneration before the turnaround succeeds smacks of insensitivity or, worse, of taking advantage of a sinking ship.

12.9 Conclusions

Turnaround management does not result from the use of simplistic formulae. It is not 'Rambo' management. It is extremely dangerous to oversimplify and attribute successful turnarounds to single causes such as productivity or innovation. Effective turnaround managers first develop a clear vision of both long-term and short-term adaptation of the business to their environment, and then launch an action plan that starts with either a product/market innovation or productivity management. However, during the turnaround, management emphasis must be skilfully alternated between innovation and productivity.

Simple turnaround Rambo formulas don't work, managers must be ready to think their way out of the crisis by relying on business sense and a thorough understanding of the industry in which the company operates.

Assignment questions

1 What situations can be understood as managing under pressure?
2 What is the first thing to do in a turnaround?
3 How long does it take to declare success with a turnaround?
4 What is the role of vision in a turnaround?
5 What is more effective – innovation or productivity?
6 What Rambo measures may need to be taken?

13
Managing in turbulent environments

13.1 Typical management issues

'Christ!' he exclaimed 'over the last two years our partner paid himself US$320,000 in advance'. We were reviewing Allfood,[1] a recently bought (1987) controlling interest in Plasticos Centroamericanos (Plateca), a Salvadorean producer of plastic materials for industrial and household uses. Georg Heuer, Allfood's regional manager, explained that, as desired, Plateca's general manager and co-owner Rodrigo Perez, had been disinvesting[2] under cover from Salvadorean authorities, mainly by increasing accounts receivables of wholly owned wholesalers in other Central American countries. A quick and dirty analysis of the sources and uses of funds revealed, however, that Rodrigo had not only increased Plateca's accounts receivables by US$2,400,000, but had also paid himself US$320,000 in advance. US$2,100,000, of this money, originated in short-term debt, and US$520,000 in inventories. How should Allfood handle this situation?

Then, one day, a request for approval of a special 'consulting assignment' was submitted by Erick Handel, country manager in Mexigua.[3] Company profits of US$3 million commanded a 40 per cent income tax, but a tax consultancy company, owned by several employees of the Ministry of Finance, had reduced, in previous years, corporate income taxes to 20 per cent of profits. The consultant's fee for halving the tax rate had traditionally been 15 per cent of the savings, which in 1987 would have amounted to US$90,000 but this time they were asking for 20 per cent of the savings, because several new government officials, they claimed, now needed to be involved in the consultation. What should he do?

These two disruptions, originating in the social environment, show how country-specific forces call for the adaptation of 'normal' corporate strategic postures. Managers of corporations operating in these markets must understand the processes that adapt corporate strategic postures to sustained disruptions originating in social revolts. What frameworks can help when adapting strategic postures to violent social revolts?

[1] A fictitious European multinational food company with operations in Central America. Names are disguised, but all characters are based on documented real life case-studies.

[2] The term 'disinvestment' refes to the act of closing, selling or withdrawing physical assets, in countries subjected to violent social revolts. The term 'divestment' refers to the act of selling the stock of corporations doing business in countries subjected to violent social revolts.

[3] Disguised Central American country.

13.2 Doing business in turbulent environments

Forces creating a permanent impact on the strategic posture of a corporation are different from those creating peak crises. The information provided by Central American managers suggests that one distinction to recognize is that the turbulence may affect different components of the strategic posture: first, an impact on the strategic decisions of the corporation; second, an impact on corporate business policies in those markets; and third, an impact on the corporation's mission in those markets. These distinctions help to identify two different generic adaptation approaches to permanent disruptions in the environment: one consists of adapting strategic decisions and the other of adapting business policies. Country managers did not see adapting the mission of the corporation to turbulent environments as 'their' responsibility; central coordination was expected for such decisions.

Consider the reactions of two American corporations to identical permanent disruptions in the environment. When the Sandinistas' ideological preferences were first understood in late 1979, Sears and Roebuck's Nicaraguan subsidiary was closed in a matter of days. A team of two Rambo executives flew down and liquidated the subsidiary in less than a week: they found no mission for Sears and Roebuck in Nicaragua. Compare this with IBM who proceeded to invest its local currency in a new Managua building for the subsidiary. Two years later, in reaction to an 800 per cent devaluation of the local currency in the politically stable Costa Rica of 1981, Sears & Roebuck again decided to close operations, while IBM again decided to stay in that, now prosperous, market.

Both corporations responded consistently to permanent changes in two different environments: a 'permanent' change in the political environment, from capitalist to communist ideology in Nicaragua; and a 'permanent' change in Costa Rica's economic environment. However, IBM has not always stayed in a market to manage through turbulence; in India, for example, IBM decided to pull out rather than adapt its subsidiary's operating policies to new tough government regulations. Put simply, IBM found a mission in Nicaragua and Costa Rica, but not in India.

The environment in which a permanent disruption originates suggests different corporate response processes. For example, Central America's social revolt was accompanied by sustained inflation and devaluations, which, although intensified by the social revolts, would have occurred anyway because of failing economic development strategies.

The distinction between having an impact on business policies and strategic decisions, was useful for selecting between centrally taken corporate decisions and local adaptation processes. In Central America, for instance, strategic decisions concerning the following issues were affected: scarcity of foreign exchange, market diversification, strategic audits, nationalization or expropriation threats, and disinvestment, hibernation or adaptation questions. These decisions were more suited for central coordination. Our research also revealed that business policies dealing with the following issues were affected: dealing with scarcity of inputs, scarce financing, taxes, strikes, labour negotiations, devaluations, inflation, corruption, information problems, communication problems and constantly changing business rules. These were best dealt with by local adaptation processes of global corporate policies.

Permanent disruptions to the 'normal' ways of conducting business in a market may originate in environments other than the economic and political. Our research of Central American managers identified the importance of these issues and events, as shown in Table 13.1

Table 13.1 Ratings assigned to permanent disruptions created by the Central American social revolt during 1977–82

I Perceptions of Nicaraguan managers[7]

			Period:		
Disruption	Normal (%)	Civil war (%)	Civil war (%)	Revolutionary infantilism (%)	Coexistence (%)
A Permanent impact of the economy on business policies					
Inflation, devaluation	3	6	2	3	6
Scarcity of materials	1	1	3	3	8
Strikes, negotiations	2	2	3	8	5
Financial scarcity	2	3	2	3	3
New taxes	4	1	1	4	5
Sub-total	12	13	10	22	28
B Permanent impact of the social revolt on business policies					
Lack of information	2	1	1	2	2
Bribery, corruption	13	3	1	0	0
New legislation	10	4	5	14	14
Sub-total	25	8	7	16	16
C Impact of the economy on strategic decisions					
Scarce foreign exchange	0	1	1	1	7
Strategic reviews	1	1	1	1	0
Search new markets	2	0	0	0	0
Sub-total	3	2	2	2	8
D Impact of the social revolt on strategic decisions					
Invest?	4	3	3	3	3
Disinvest?	0	0	0	1	2
Adapt? reactivate?	2	1	2	1	2
Hibernate?	0	1	0	1	0
Nationalization	0	0	2	5	3
Sub-total	7	5	7	10	11
Total	100	100	100	100	100

II Perceptions of Salvadorean managers

	Normal (%)	Civil war (%)	Revolutionary infantilism (%)	Coexistence (%)
A Permanent impact of the economy on business policies				
Inflation, devaluation	2	3	3	2
Scarcity of materials	2	1	3	9
Strikes, negotiations	14	8	1	0
Financial scarcity	3	4	4	4
New taxes	0	1	0	1
Sub-total	20	17	11	16

Disruption	Normal (%)	Civil war (%)	Civil war (%)	Period: Revolutionary infantilism (%)	Coexistence (%)
B Permanent impact of the social revolt on business policies					
Lack of information	0		1	1	1
Bribery, corruption	3		2	2	2
New legislation	2		3	13	13
Sub-total	5		6	16	16
C Impact of the economy on strategic decisions					
Scarce foreign exchange	1		1	3	6
Strategic reviews	1		1	1	3
Search new markets	0		0	1	1
Sub-total	2		3	5	10
D Impact of the social revolt on strategic decisions					
Invest?	2		2	2	3
Disinvest?	2		2	2	3
Adapt? reactivate?	0		1	1	1
Hibernate?	1		1	1	2
Nationalization	2		3	9	3
Sub-total	8		9	14	11
Total		100	100	100	100

III Perceptions of Guatemalan managers

	Normal (%)	Social revolt (%)	Coexistence (%)
A Permanent impact of the economy on business policies			
Inflation, devaluation	7	8	1
Scarcity of materials	1	2	1
Strikes, negotiations	4	8	0
Financial scarcity	5	8	7
New taxes	1	0	0
Sub-total	17	25	10
B Permanent impact of the social revolt on business policies			
Lack of information	1	2	2
Bribery, corruption	11	6	9
New legislation	5	7	3
Sub-total	17	14	14
C Impact of the economy on strategic decisions			
Scarce foreign exchange	2	0	5
Strategic reviews	2	1	2
Search new markets	1	5	1
Sub-total	5	6	9
D Impact of the social revolt on strategic decisions			
Invest?	7	11	10
Disinvest?	0	0	0
Adapt? reactivate?	0	1	2
Hibernate?	0	0	1
Nationalization	0	0	1
Sub-total	7	12	14
Total	100	100	100

13.3 Adapting strategic decisions

In Nicaragua and El Salvador certain industries and businesses, for instance, commerce, exports, and banking, were immediately expropriated or nationalized. This was more often in some industries than in others. Two complementary reasons explained this revolutionary behaviour.

First, ideology played an important guiding role. In the communist religion anything resembling a mine, even the salt taken from the oceans, was considered to be something so sacred only governments were allowed to exploit it. They also believed that charging interest for the use of money is evil, so revolutionaries nationalized all banks. Commerce, an equally 'dirty' activity, was also eliminated or controlled by revolutionary governments. Somehow, the communist religion does not recognize the value added by services in general, and wholesalers, retailers and bankers in particular.

But, when a corporation added value that revolutionaries had difficulty replacing, they opted for tolerating these corporations. Revolutionaries had difficulty in replacing the value added by changing technology (computers), management know-how, successful working methods imported from other parts of the world, and the ability to export and wholesale bananas in the triad countries. Sandinista Minister Jaime Wheelock, recalled and reimbursed the Standard Fruit Company for its expropriation because the Nicaraguans could not wholesale bananas in the USA.[4]

Instead, investments in fixed assets, money, slowly changing technology, or ownership of land and cash crops, proved to add little non-replaceable value to the revolution and were subjected to expropriation. In both Nicaragua and El Salvador, nationalization and expropriation were important events that shaped corporate legal strategies.

Taking advantage of a low-cost country is attractive if earnings can be increased through exports. This not only helps the foreign exchange earnings of the host country but also provides opportunities for profit repatriation. However, lack of foreign exchange in an economy demands a revision of the investment decisions of the corporation in that market. The decision to invest in a market where profits cannot be freely converted to foreign exchange must be examined and reviewed by both country and corporate management.

Structural economic conditions cause chronic inflation in Central America; one may forecast yearly inflations ranging between 15 per cent and 25 per cent for the early 1990s. In order to respond to changes in the economic environment, managers must acquire influence and build effective information and communication networks beyond the organization so that they can negotiate proactively with governmental authorities.

In an economic environment in which there is no repatriation of profits, no access to foreign exchange, chronic devaluations and hyper-inflation, many corporations reconsider their mission and decide to pull out. Consider American

[4] The Sandinista government nationalized Nicaragua's banana industry only to find out that they could neither export nor service the nationalized plantations. They had to pay Standard Fruit Company several million dollars for their technological, logistic and marketing know-how.

Standards, an American ceramics corporation with operations in most Central American countries. Corporate managers decided to freeze the operations (hibernate) of their Nicaraguan subsidiary because of the above mentioned economic circumstances. A centrally-taken and implemented decision, the subsidiary closed operations after negotiating with the Nicaraguan government and the labour force.

However, hibernating during a few lean years could have been a dangerous decision in revolutionary Nicaragua. Corporations ran the risk of expropriation or nationalization if the decision was not carried out properly. But, when the book value of relatively new industrial equipment drops to around 4 per cent of replacement value, most corporations will review the viability of the business in that country, and consider selling or hibernating through the bad years. Under such circumstances assets were totally owned by stockholders, because inflation and devaluations wiped out leverage (in dollar terms). As a consequence, taxes were unfairly high, and a company could literally cancel its liabilities with a fistful of dollars, but had difficulties in using this debt capacity to increase leverage.

13.4 Adapting business policies

In some countries corruption was so bad that some government jobs were up for auction and as they were valuable possessions for the holder, they could be sold. Since corruption was widespread, complaining to the higher authorities proved sometimes to be useless. Demands for consulting fees from organized teams of government officials were a typical complaint of CEOs in Central American corporations. However, only a few could 'throw the first stone'.

Corrupt practices are a serious problem for market heads. On the one hand, tax problems could get worse if these 'consulting fees' were not paid. On the otherhand, corporations don't go to jail, CEOs do. At United Brands, for instance, Eli Black committed suicide when it was discovered that his company had allegedly participated in bribing the Honduran Minister of Economics.

Bribing public officials because it is a 'common business practice' in a country, does not protect CEOs from law, nor does it improve their ethical behaviour. Two difficult questions need to be answered. First, how can we tell that bribing is 'common business practice' in a country; and second, who decides that bribery is indeed 'common business practice'? Adherence to such policy justifies corrupt business practices in any country, particularly in the triad countries.

In the final analysis, we can't see how this excuse can protect a corporation from either the law or the moral consequences. If bribery has been accepted as a corporate policy, how do we know that the money doesn't end up in the hands of some of our own executives? For executives practising bribery, the question is not whether they are prostitutes, but with whom do they sleep?

In the long run, corrupt practices don't pay. In Central America, for instance, companies associated with corrupt government officials suffered the most damage during the civil uprisings. Thus short-term gains through association or *entente* with the officials of corrupt regimes should be kept in a proper perspective.

As revolutionaries consolidated their power, the rules of the economic game were constantly changing. The flow of economic benefits was directed to the supporters of the new regime. And, since corporate information, communication and other operating systems were created to interact with the supporters of the old regime, managers profoundly disliked the series of changes implemented by the new authorities.

To manage a subsidiary effectively under these changing conditions, executives must interpret the new legislation correctly, understand how corporate policies have to be changed and maintain a clear perspective of the laws and events in the pipeline. In Nicaragua, however, the rules of the game zigzagged from left to right because legislators had first to develop a consistent approach to the way the benefits were going to be distributed. Therefore, legislation was sometimes extremely left wing, as in the total price controls in Nicaragua; only to swing back to the other extreme, total price freedom. Eventually, legislative and economic experience accumulated, contradictions were smoothed out and the direction of the flow of economic benefits was consolidated.

Economic negotiation processes with, for example, central bankers, dealt more with rational business principles and related arguments than ideology; whereas negotiations with political actors, like unions, the military or kidnappers, dealt more with emotions and ideology than business principles. In the former, principled negotiations were feasible, whereas in the latter, negotiations on positions were more likely.

The economic environment intensified the need to review export strategies of Nicaraguan and Salvadorean business units. Managers had to cope with a new and permanent scarcity of raw materials and financial resources, including difficulty in obtaining new bank financing and lack of supplier credit. Economic information and communication channels with Central Bank authorities were crucial for the adaptation of financial policies. Communication skills were also needed to understand the behaviour of the Minister of Labour and related government officials. In Nicaragua and El Salvador, government interests swung from populist measures during the revolutionary takeover, to production oriented measures later on.

Necessary inputs for operations became increasingly scarce and difficult to obtain as the economic crisis deepened and was accelerated by civil war. In Nicaragua, for example, Allfood owned Cerveceria Suprema, a beer company that had problems obtaining parts and raw materials for its operations. By 1988, Nicaragua's economy was destroyed; there was no foreign exchange with which to pay for imports. On the other hand, La Suprema's bank accounts were bulging with 500 million cordobas, the Nicaraguan currency. The problem was that in 1988 inflation was estimated to be around 1000 per cent, that is, these cordobas were shrinking at an amazing rate per month. What should they do with the money?

When cash levels rise abnormally because they cannot be converted into goods, services, or foreign exchange, several sub-problems arise:

1 The corporation presents a fat target for extortion or nationalization.

2 Inflation and/or devaluation may wipe out the purchasing power in a couple of months.
3 Without foreign exchange, supplier credit may be lost because of lack of payments.

Some corporations were able to convert their excess cash into export products and pay their debts with barter. This was possible when the value added by a multinational to the local economy was viewed as a positive contribution.

Consider, Prolacsa, Nestlé's subsidiary in Nicaragua, which exported powdered milk to Central America until, under the Sandinista government, Nicaragua's milk farms dried up. Then, Prolacsa's role was changed to reconstituting Dutch dried milk and eventually, Nestlé was also subjected to the scarcity of foreign exchange. This way our familiar strategic dilemma also appeared in Nestlé: either stop operations for lack of foreign exchange or inject 'fresh' corporate resources to keep Prolacsa going. Nestlé solved the dilemma by engaging in a clever barter trade of Dutch powder milk for Nicaraguan coffee beans; the company changed an old and rigid policy of 'we don't do barter trade' to accommodate 'permanent' changes in Nicaragua's economic environment.

Operating without access to foreign exchange, the money to import raw materials and a scarcity of essential inputs is a permanent distortion of the economic environment that can only be solved through economic negotiations. Corporate strategic decision makers have to decide whether or not to provide 'fresh' foreign exchange to keep the subsidiary going.

Nestlé has not always solved this strategic dilemma with barter trade; consider the Malagasy (African) case in which the company decided to pull out of the country to show that it was not ready to pay any price (barter trade) to do business there. What remains to be understood is when to do a Malagasy and when a Prolacsa.

Our position on the matter may be a bit disappointing. We believe that Nestlé, IBM, Sears, American Standard and other corporations do not function as a single rational decision-maker. Management is composed of a number of small and large decision-makers who differ in beliefs, values and attitudes. These differences occur among country managers and over time. There is no Nestlé or IBM 'way' of taking decisions because they depend heavily upon the people in charge at the time and place that the problems are uncovered. The existence of a Nestlé or IBM 'way' depends on how widespread their corporate cultures are and how much the hundreds of dispersed decision-makers share the same corporate perspective, i.e. beliefs, values and attitudes about the business and its systems.

Rather than stick to 'normal' operating policies in the management of inventories, liabilities, accounts receivables and personnel policies under these bizarre environmental conditions, effective managers adapted policies with the following decision process:

1 Evaluation criteria were: reversibility, fast pay back and implementability of alternatives.
2 Partial solutions were common because government policy changes were never considered final.
3 Sophisticated approaches were avoided.

This means that policies were adapted slowly and flexibly to new permanent changes in the economic environment; slowly because the direction of the changes was not evident, and flexibly because the adaptation could rapidly become obsolete as different trends emerged. Under conditions of sustained turbulence, permanent changes to the policies of the corporation in a market were obtained by working via the managers in the market, for this it was necessary to:

1 Introduce a change in attitudes: making managers crisis conscious.
2 Identify managers effective at working under pressure.
3 Get their support and involvement in diagnosis, decision making and implementation.
4 Introduce changes in systems and working procedures.

13.5 The CEO and corporate culture

Since no one knows enough to forecast all environmental pressures in advance, excellent European companies tend to adapt their business practice to specific country conditions in a series of small steps rather than relying on centrally conceived sweeping strategies. As expressed by Mr Helmuth Maucher's address on management practice to an attentive audience of IMEDE professors in spring 1988, his efforts to simplify corporate reporting practices included reducing country reports to one page of reliable figures; he added, 'this forces country managers to think about what is really important and eliminates the need for further analysis at headquarters'.

The role of the CEO is to transmit his perspective about the business across the corporation, so that this perspective influences the way in which far away country managers handle difficult situations. Responsibility and authority for these decisions must be articulated by top management so that country managers, who are in touch with local realities, can react with flexibility, while keeping HQ informed. They should also open communication channels with economic and political authorities to maintain the flows of information.

At Nestlé[5] it is normal to find a minimal number of standardized policies; but when they exist, management insist that they be strictly observed unless there is a good argument to the contrary. To obtain results they set a few but well-defined objectives for their country managers. On this Mr Maucher wrote:[6]

> we prefer maximum standardisation in terms of systems and methods. But the contrary is true when it is a question of personnel management, marketing, product quality and questions linked to the consumer and local competition; then we opt for as much decentralisation as possible. Our general policy is to adapt ourselves as much as possible to regional circumstances, outlooks and situations. When we are in other countries, we want to be insiders, not outsiders.

[5] Maucher Helmuth, 'Future aspects of Nestlé's global business strategies', 9 Apr., 1988, Tokyo, Japan.
[6] Ibid.

Tetrapak's 'small is beautiful' organizational structure is also a step in this direction because it makes country managers the top strategic decision-makers in their markets.

Contradiction between local and global policies reflects differences in the perspective of a subsidiary's mission; but this is also a pleasant reality: no matter how centralized a CEO wants to make his business, local management, if of any value, will act according to local needs, whether or not it violates global policies. The job of local management is to defend the best interests of their subsidiary; and the job of the CEO is to provide a guiding business perspective.

Assignment questions

1 What do we mean by turbulent environment?
2 How do you handle requests for bribery?
3 How do we adapt strategic decisions?
4 How do we adapt business policies?
5 Is there anything wrong with barter trade?
6 What was the decision process under turbulent times?
7 What is the role of the CEO?

14 Inflation's impact on financial policies

14.1 Impact on financial statements

One permanent turbulence of extreme importance is created by relatively small but sustained inflation. Inflation has a direct impact on financial policies, and in this chapter we point to some of the concepts that need to be revisited. To understand a business operating in an inflationary environment, the 'normal' frameworks are of little help; an inflationary mentality is required. We will deal here with concepts useful when inflation is below 25 per cent per year; this capability may prove crucial for managing in the Eastern Europe of the 1990s. For inflations higher than that, our frameworks may not help as a barter mentality prevails when money loses its value in very short time periods.

Consider Santa Rosa, a disguised non-exporting Latin American company, operating in a country with a permanent inflation of 15 per cent per year. The company pays 5 per cent sales tax, and 50 per cent income tax. Although short-term interest rates go as high as 25 per cent, the company enjoys an advantageous average of 12.5 per cent interest on its liabilities. The operating policies of the business include maintaining its sales in units, but they adjust prices to follow the average inflation rate; maintain 70 per cent as cost of sales; distribute 50 per cent of its profits as dividends; maintain an asset to equity ratio of 1.8; and use average yearly cost, to cost its inventories. The company's last revaluation of assets and depreciation was made in 1988.

The first thing to review is our understanding of financial statements. What do they tell us? Inflation makes today's numbers different from last year's. How can we compare apples with pears? Santa Rosa's financial statements are presented in Table 14.1.

These financial statements report the value of fixed assets, debt, inventories and receivables, registered using the currency's value in different years. Thus the financial statements in Table 14.1 confuse the company's picture. We need to know how to read these statements and understand the financial ratios. We need to be able to know what our growth and dividend policy should be. And what about our long-term debt policy? In what follows we discuss distortions in financial statements caused by yearly inflations below 25 per cent.

Table 14.2 seems to indicate that inflation has a favourable impact on the business. Both the profit margin and the turnover improve, despite the lower leverage. Does this mean that financial results improve while financial risk diminishes? Business people operating under such conditions often argue that these financial interpretations are biased by monetary illusions.

Business people prefer to separate inventory profits, being those generated by items bought without inflation but sold at inflated prices, from profits generated by the business; a 15 per cent inflation, for instance, apparently diminishes

Table 14.1 Santa Rosa: raw-financial statements

Concept	*Variables*	*1988*	*1989*	*1990*
A Income statement ($000s)				
Inflation	15.0%			
Sales		50.00	57.500	66.125
Cost of sales	70.0%	35.000	37.950	43.643
Overhead expenses		3.000	3.450	3.968
Depreciation		3.500	3.500	3.500
Sales tax	5.0%	2.500	2.875	3.306
Interest expense	12.5%	1.669	1.763	1.909
Total costs		45.669	49.538	56.325
Profit before tax		4.331	7.963	9.800
Taxes (50% profit)	50.0%	2.166	3.981	4.900
Profit after tax (PAT)		2.166	3.981	4.900
Dividends % of PAT	50.0%	1.083	1.991	2.450
B Balance sheet ($000s)				
Cash		500	575	661
Accounts receivables		7.500	8.625	9.919
Inventories		12.000	12.900	13.868
Total liquid assets		20.000	22.100	24.448
Total fixed assets		10.000	10.000	10.000
Total assets		30.000	32.100	34.448
Short-term liabilities		5.000	6.017	6.374
Working capital		15.000	16.083	18.073
Equity		16.650	17.733	19.723
Long-term debt		8.350	8.350	8.350
Total liabilities		30.000	32.100	34.448

Table 14.2 Key raw-financial ratios

Concept	*1988*	*1989*	*1990*
Margin (PAT/sales)	4.3%	6.9%	7.4%
Turnover (sales/assets)	1.67	1.79	1.92
Leverage (assets/equity)	1.80	1.81	1.75
Return on equity	13.0%	22.5%	24.8%

relative inventory costs. These profits have nothing to do with the nature of the business operations, and disappear as soon as inventories are replaced.

On the other hand, as the profits of the company are inflated the income tax paid also increases, and business people argue that it increases more than it should, causing the government to drain the company's working capital.

As we pointed out before, the cause of these distortions is the indiscriminate mixture of currencies registered in the company's books in different years. For instance, assets and depreciation expenses that were valued in 1988 are added, subtracted and divided by sales, costs of sales and overheads registered in later years. To eliminate these distortions, all components of the financial statements must be expressed in the same year's currency, as shown in Table 14.3, with Santa Rosa's adjusted financial statements. The ratios generated by these adjusted statements, see Table 14.4, show that the profitability of Santa Rosa has not improved; it remains about the same. Is there any reason to worry?

Tables 14.5 and 14.6 show the comparison between the adjusted and raw financial statements for 1990. The monetary illusion is revealed by these comparisons. Most importantly, these tables reveal the need for revisiting the

Table 14.3 Santa Rosa: adjusted financial statements

Concept	*Variables*	*1988*	*1989*	*1990*
A Adjusted income statement ($000s)				
Sales		50.000	57.500	66.125
Cost of sales		35.000	40.250	46.288
Overhead expenses		3.000	3.450	3.968
Depreciation		3.500	4.025	4.629
Sales tax		2.500	2.875	3.306
Interest expense		1.669	1.763	1.986
Total costs		45.669	52.363	60.176
Profits before taxes		4.331	5.138	5.949
Taxes (50% of profit)		2.166	2.569	2.975
Profit after tax (PAT)		2.166	2.569	2.975
Dividends % of PAT		1.083	1.284	1.487
B Adjusted balance sheet ($000s)				
Cash		500	575	661
Accounts receivables		7.500	8.625	9.919
Inventories		12.000	13.800	15.870
Total liquid assets		20.000	23.000	26.450
Total fixed assets		10.000	11.500	13.225
Total assets		30.000	34.500	39.675
Short-term liabilities		5.000	5.463	5.985
Working capital		15.000	17.537	20.465
Equity		16.650	19.434	22.647
Long-term debt		8.350	9.603	11.043
Total liabilities		30.000	34.500	39.675

Table 14.4 Key adjusted-financial ratios

Concept	*1988*	*1989*	*1990*
Margin (PAT/sales)	4.3%	4.5%	4.5%
Turnover (sales/assets)	1.67	1.67	1.67
Leverage (assets/equity)	1.80	1.78	1.75
Return on equity	13.0%	13.2%	13.1%

financial policies of a company operating under permanent inflation. For instance, inventory costing methods should be changed to LIFO,[1] instead of average cost; and the private sector's organized pressure groups must lobby the tax authorities to adopt accounting procedures that adjust the company's assets and depreciation expenses according to the year's inflation.

If such policy changes are not implemented, Table 14.5 shows that the cost of goods sold is underestimated, profits overestimated, and unfortunately, the company overtaxed; this is especially so when the tax rate grows proportionately with the profits. Distorted profits may also increase dividends. So, if nothing is done about these policies, both the tax authorities and the shareholders may be involuntarily draining the company's working capital.

It follows that both dividend and leverage policies must be revisited in inflationary environments. The dividend policy must be adjusted to avoid distributing equity instead of profits, and the leverage policy must be reviewed because undervalued assets impact upon asset to equity ratios in unexpected ways.

Table 14.5 also shows that inflation provides the business unit with increased debt capacity because its assets are undervalued. However, because of the uncertainty surrounding the inflation rate, it is our experience that banks make it easier to increase short-term debt than long-term debt. This probably increases interest expenses because short-term loans include an adjusted discount factor for inflation. Furthermore, with undervalued assets the business unit's debt capacity is under-utilized.

14.2 Impact on financial ratios

Table 14.6 shows that the financial ratios also change, and that inflation affects the company's profitability. Since sales, receivables, inventory and operating costs increase under inflation, the company's working capital also increases. An estimate of inflation's impact on working capital needs can be obtained by multiplying the working capital needs of the base year (1988) by (1+g) every year where g is the year's inflation rate. These larger working capital needs may reduce the profitability of the company.

[1] LIFO: Last In First Out; that is, inventories cost equal the cost of the last unit bought.

Table 14.5 Santa Rosa: comparative financial statements

Concept	*1988*	*1990 (Raw)*	*1990 (Adj.)*	*Difference*
A Comparative income statement ($000s)				
Sales	50.000	66.125	66.125	0
Cost of sales	35.000	43.643	46.288	(2.645)
Overhead	3.000	3.968	3.968	0
Depreciation	3.500	3.500	4.629	(1.129)
Sales tax	2.500	3.306	3.306	0
Interests	1.669	1.909	1.986	(77)
Total costs	45.669	56.325	60.176	(3.851)
Profit before tax	4.331	9.800	5.949	3.851
Taxes (50%)	2.166	4.900	2.975	1.925
Profit after tax	2.166	4.900	2.975	1.925
Dividends % PAT	1.083	2.450	1.487	963
B Comparative balance sheet ($000s)				
Cash	500	661	661	0
Receivables	7.500	9.919	9.919	0
Inventories	12.000	13.868	15.870	(2.003)
Total liquid assets	20.000	24.448	26.450	(2.003)
Total fixed assets	10.000	10.000	13.225	(3.225)
Total assets	30.000	34.448	39.675	(5.228)
Short-term liabilities	5.000	6.374	5.985	389
Working capital	15.000	18.073	20.465	(2.391)
Equity	16.650	19.723	22.647	(2.923)
Long-term debt	8.350	8.350	11.043	(2.693)
Total liabilities	30.000	34.448	39.675	(5.228)

Table 14.6 also shows that inflation causes an overestimation of profit margins, turnover and return on equity. Thus, the efficient use of assets is overestimated, and in general, the business's profitability is exaggerated. These monetary illusions may create a dangerous euphoria and an equally distorted dividend policy. It is clear that adjusting these reports to show the real statements and ratios is the only way to understand what is really going on.

The ratios estimated in Table 14.2 have no meaning; they represent apparent ratios and diffuse financial issues. However, these ratios are commonly used in the absence of revaluations to examine businesses operating in inflationary environments; hence many financial policies are based on incorrect interpretations of financial health. The financial statements of Table 14.5 and corresponding ratios of Table 14.6, were estimated by converting all currencies to the corresponding year. That is, the statements of 1988 are expressed in the currency of 1988, whereas the statements of 1990 are expressed in the currency of 1990.

Table 14.6 Comparative key financial ratios

Concept	*1988*	*1990(1)*	*1990(2)*
Margin (PAT/sales)	4.3%	7.4%	4.5%
Turnover (sales/assets)	1.67	1.92	1.67
Leverage (assets/equity)	1.80	1.75	1.75
Return on equity	13.0%	24.8%	13.1%

With these revised ratios we can compare such elements as the current profit margin, 4.5 per cent in the base year, with its equivalent 2 years later, also 4.5 per cent. They tell us that for every \$100 sold in 1990, we really get \$4.5, just as we did in 1988. Things seem to be all right, except that in 1988 we got back 1988 dollars, whereas in 1990 we got 1990 dollars; these profit margins are expressed in current terms. Thus, some business people claim to lose margin to inflation. Are they right?

These demands originate in the notion of purchasing power. Given that there is inflation, some business people would like to see their current profit margins grow with inflation; they claim to be losing purchasing power. The basic business proposition is that a 15 per cent return with 4 per cent inflation is more than a 15 per cent return with 12 per cent inflation. What should be the adjusted rate of return? The answer to this question depends on what target return we shoot for. For instance, if we choose to maintain 11 per cent – our pre-inflation rate of return – we could adjust our estimates with 11 per cent – (15 – 12 per cent) = 8 per cent. Clearly, if a different target return is chosen, the adjustment changes. This raw reasoning must be adjusted by the mathematics of compound interest. Exaggerated price corrections may however, turn into a source of real inflation, because the goods sold could command a greater 'real' profit margin than necessary to recover lost purchasing power. In what follows we examine the problem of acceptable rates of return under inflation.

14.3 Impact on acceptable rates of return

The internal rate of return (IRR) of a strategic investment depends upon how inflation affects the income and costs flows in the project. Thus we start by recognizing the different approaches that incorporate inflationary forces into the project's flows. In what follows we assume that investors would like to maintain a required internal rate of return (k).

The basic assumption is that inflation varies each year, and furthermore it varies among cash flow components. Thus, it affects the components of the yearly cash flows differently. Let the returns be represented by:

R_t, t = 1 to n,
f_t represents price inflation

h_t represents cost inflation, and
g_t[2] represents the country's inflation.

The first two inflationary factors depend more on management's actions than the last one. Business people try to keep costs as low as perceived quality permits, thus managers have a say in the inflation in their operating costs. With their competition, they also have a say in price inflation. Competition has a moderating influence on inflation, but the forces creating it are controlled by fiscal policies and government budgets.

Under these conditions, we adjust the cash flows of our strategic investments to the corresponding inflation rates. So, project cash flows, inflated with the year's inflation, will be called current cash flows and expressed in current[3] currency and not in real[4] currency. So, to estimate the net present value (NPV) in real terms, we must deflate the project's returns with the economy's average inflation, g, and the corporation's 'real' discount rate.

The following equation summarizes the arguments presented for the estimation of a project's cash flow in year t in current terms.

$$R_t = I_t \, \pi_j(1+f_j) - E_t \, p_j \, (1 + h_j), \; j = 1,t \tag{14.1}$$

where I_t revenues of year t, and
E_t costs and expenses of year t; j = 1,t.

In real life it is extremely difficult to estimate what the inflationary forces will be in the different years and the components of the stream of cash flows. Thus, business people usually make a realistic simplification by assuming a single inflation rate for the duration of the project. Thus we obtain the following equation.

$$R_t = I_t \, (1+f)^t - E_t \, p_j \, (1 + h)^t \tag{14.2}$$

where f = average inflation on revenues, and
h = average inflation on costs and expenses.

In some situations business people prefer to simplify further, and use a single inflation rate – the economy's inflation g – as the rate to apply across the board. In these cases the NPV of an investment project can be expressed with:

$$NPV = -I_o + \Sigma R_t/(1+k)^t(1+g)^t \text{ for } t = 1 \text{ a } n \tag{14.3}$$

where k is the discount rate,
g is the economy's inflation and
$1/(1+k)^t(1+g)^t$ is the discount factor for year t; t=1 to n.

This way the original cash flow, expressed in current currency, is deflated and expressed in real currency, before being discounted.

[2] Measured with the general price index or implicit GNP deflator.
[3] Expressed in the year's purchasing power.
[4] Expressed in the base year's purchasing power.

Consider the following investment with a NPV of 18,920 for a required 15 per cent rate of return.

$$NPV = -80{,}000 + \frac{40{,}000}{(1.15)} + \frac{50{,}000}{(1.15)^2} + \frac{40{,}000}{(1.15)^3}$$

$$NPV = 18{,}920 > 0$$

This positive NPV reveals that the project returns more than 15 per cent per year. However, if the yearly inflation rate for the next 5 years is 12 per cent the 'real' NPV is a negative 17.

$$NPV = -80{,}000 + \frac{40{,}000}{(1.15)(1.12)} + \frac{50{,}000}{(1.15)^2(1.12)^2} + \frac{40{,}000}{(1.15)^3(1.12)^3}$$

$$NPV = (17) < 0$$

This shows that the project does not return 15 per cent on investment once the inflationary forces are taken into account. But these detailed calculations are not necessary. We can show that the 'real' IRR, i.e. the apparent IRR adjusted by inflation, can be estimated as follows:

$$r = \frac{r' - g}{1 + g} \qquad (14.4)$$

where: r = 'real' rate of return,
r' = apparent rate of return, and
g = average inflation rate.

For instance, the 'real' rate of return of a project apparently returning 32 per cent, in an inflationary environment of 12 per cent per year, is 18 per cent per year. This 18 per cent should be compared with the inflation-free minimum acceptable rate of return.

$$r = \frac{0.32 - 0.12}{1 + 0.12} = 18\%$$

Some investors prefer to adjust the inflation-free discount rate, and use it on the project's current cash flows. They argue that the modified discount factor equals the inflation-free factor multiplied by the inflation factor.

$$(1 + k_a) = (1 + k)(1 + g), \text{ or}$$
$$1 + k_a = 1 + k + kg + g, \text{ and}$$
$$k_a = k + kg + g = k(1+g) + g \qquad (14.5)$$

where: k = inflation free discount rate, and
ka = adjusted discount rate.

In conclusion, if we enjoyed a 15 per cent rate of return with inflation of 8 per cent and we wish to maintain an equivalent rate of return under inflation of 20 per cent, the required adjusted rate should be 27.8 per cent per year.[5] The adjusted discount rate k_a is applied to cash flows expressed in current currency.

14.4 Revaluing assets and depreciation expenses

To express the currencies reported in the financial statements in a common currency, both assets and depreciation expenses need to be adjusted for inflation. The idea is to understand the financial reports so that financial policies can be discussed without draining the corporation's equity or ability to carry on with its business. In accounting terminology, a business does not generate profits until the reserves necessary to maintain the productive capacity of its assets have been made.

This means that, in principle, assets should be valued at replacement cost, as should costs and expenses.[6] The way to go about this is to adjust the book value of all assets each year with an estimate of its replacement value. In the absence of a known market value, a price index is usually used to make these adjustments.

For instance, we can use as base index the country's general inflation index. Each asset is associated to the index corresponding to the year it was registered in the books or corresponding to the last year in which the asset was revaluated. Then, an adjustment index can be constructed for each asset by estimating the percent increment of the inflation index from the date in which the asset was last valued to the date in which the asset is being revalued. This index is then applied for revaluation and a typical change in financial statements is shown in Table 14.7.

14.5 Impact on investment decisions[7]

In this section we extend the concepts presented above to include cash flows in investment projects. In general, the impact of inflation on these cash flows is greater on income than on costs and expenses; this is so because the income is greater than the costs and expenses. Therefore, as we saw above, the apparent rate of return is greater under inflation than without it.

To estimate the 'real' rate of return we use equation 14.4; this states that inflation lowers the apparent rates of return. To understand a little bit better how this happens, consider Santa Marta, a project in an inflation-free environment with a 60 per cent income tax, shown in Table 14.8. What is the impact of a yearly 10 per cent inflation. To answer this question we estimated cash

[5] The deflated rate of return is (15–8)/1.08 = 6.5% per year; thus the adjusted minimum acceptable rate of return is (1.065 × 1.20 = 1.278).

[6] Rappaport, Alfred, 'Como Medir la Capacidad de Crecimiento de una Compañía durante la Inflación', *Harvard Business Review*, 1978.

Table 14.7 Industrias Unidas S.A.: financial statements

Concept	*1985*	*1985 (Adjusted)*
A Income statement ($000s)		
Sales	500.000	500.000
Cost of sales	300.000	300.000
Overhead	95.000	95.000
Depreciation	8.455	28.164
Sales tax (5%)	25.000	25.000
Interest (12.5%)	23.879	23.879
Total costs	452.335	472.043
Profit before tax	47.665	27.957
Taxes (50% profits)	23.833	13.979
Profit after tax (PAT)	23.833	13.979
Dividends (50% PAT)	11.916	6.989
B Balance sheet ($000s)		
Cash	50.000	50.000
Accounts receivables	75.000	75.000
Inventories	120.000	120.000
Liquid assets	245.000	245.000
Fixed assets	96.032	466.318
Total assets	341.032	711.318
Current liabilities	11.032	11.032
Working capital	233.968	233.968
Equity	150.000	520.285
Long-term debt	180.000	180.000
Total liabilities	341.032	711.318

Table 14.8 Santa Marta: strategic investment (000s)

Concepts	*0*	*1*	*2*	*3*	*4*
Investment	1000				
Sales		750	750	750	750
Operating costs		250	250	250	250
Depreciation		250	250	250	250
Profit before taxes		250	250	250	250
Income tax		150	150	150	150
Profit after tax		100	100	100	100
Depreciation		250	250	250	250
Cash flow		350	350	350	350

Table 14.9 Santa Marta: strategic investment (000s)

Concepts	*0*	*1*	*2*	*3*	*4*
Investment	1000				
Sales		825	908	998	
1,098					
Operating costs		275	303	333	366
Depreciation		250	250	250	250
Profit before taxes		300	355	416	482
Income tax		180	213	249	289
Profit after tax		120	142	166	193
Depreciation		250	250	250	250
Cash flow		370	392	416	443

flows (shown in Table 14.9) which include the impact of inflation on income and costs.

The impact of inflation on the cash flows of Santa Marta are presented in Table 4.10. First, we estimated the extra taxes paid because depreciation expenses were not revalued; and secondly, we also see the impact on net cash flows. Although the latter increase with inflation, the former increase even more. This is because, without revaluation, all depreciation expenses keep their original book value, causing lower 'real' tax shields in the inflated profits before taxes. Thus, the 'real' income tax also increases.[8]

The 'real' impact of inflation on income tax can be estimated (see Table

Table 14.10 Inflation's impact on Santa Marta (000s)

Income tax	*1*	*2*	*3*	*4*
With inflation	180	213	249	289
Without inflation	150	150	150	150
Difference	30	63	99	139
Cash flows				
With inflation	370	392	416	443
Without inflation	350	350	350	350
Difference	20	42	66	93

14.11) by comparing deflated income taxes with inflation-free profits before taxes. Clearly, 'real' income tax increases in inflationary environments if depreciation expenses are not adjusted periodically.

But, amortizations, long-term interest expenses and other inflation-free expenses, also create 'imaginary' profits which distort our profits. Therefore,

[7] Based on, Allen, Brandt, 'Evaluación de Desembolsos de Capital bajo Inflación: Compendio', *Business Horizons*, Vol. 19, No. 6, 1978, pp. 30–9.

[8] An asset's replacement value increases with inflation, whereas its depreciation expense – if we don't re-evaluate – remains constant.

Table 14.11 Santa Marta 'real' income tax (000s)

Current cash flow	*1*	*2*	*3*	*4*
Profit before taxes	300	355	416	482
Inflated income tax	180	213	249	289
'Apparent' income tax rate	60%	60%	60%	60%
Deflated cash flows				
Profit before taxes	250	250	250	250
Deflated income tax	164	176	187	198
'Real' income tax rate	65%	70%	75%	79%

revaluation of amortization and interest expenses should be included in our assessment of project and company profitability. The bottom line is that the 'real' rate of return may diminish under inflation.

Finally, inflation may also have an unpleasant effect on capital gains taxes created by sales of salvaged assets. The 'real' salvage value may be reduced because of higher capital gains tax rates.

14.6 Reviewing other policies[9]

Just as we worry about the maximum-feasible growth rate under normal conditions, under inflation, this concept must be revisited. The reason is that inflation imposes additional working capital requirements, as explained before, and a business may be subjected to capital drainage both by fiscal authorities and shareholders. So one objective is to estimate a revised maximum-feasible growth rate under inflation. Other financial policies that need to be explored should provide answers to the following questions: What should our dividend policy and financial leverage be? How much working capital is needed? How fast can the business grow?

These worries originate in the desire to maintain the company's productive[10] and business capabilities[11] under inflation. For instance, an accelerated growth in sales, due to inflation, creates greater working capital needs. A company's dividend policy under inflation should be adjusted so that the remaining equity is big enough to maintain its business capability. Thus, we have to estimate, by using a funds flow statement, the company's maximum disposable cash

[9] Based on, Brandt, Allen, 'Evaluación de Desembolsos de Capital bajo Inflación: Compendio, *Business Horizons*, Vol. 19, No. 6, 1978, pp. 30–9.

[10] A business does not generate profits until reserves have been made to maintain the productive capability of its assets. The productive capacity eroded by inflation must be replaced, as well as that eroded normally through economic life.

[11] The business capability of a company depends on its assets, their productive capacity, its working capital needs, its dividend, leverage, growth policies and its operating costs.

flow,[12] and the remaining minimum required cash flow for operations. These two concepts indicate the constraints within which the dividend policy must be created to avoid damaging the company's business capability.

A company's disposable funds are limited by four financial objectives: first, we would like to replace the real productive capability of its assets;[13] second, we would like to maintain the company's debt capability,[14] recover a desired 'real' leverage; third, we would like to achieve a 'real' target growth rate; and fourth, we would like to maintain the working capital[15] needed to achieve the above objectives without damaging the company's business capability.

14.7 Conclusions

The details of these analyses can be found in consultation with financial specialists. We limit our chapter to point out the most important policies to be revised when the economic environment presents permanent inflations below 25 per cent per year. For higher inflation, we don't believe traditional financial approaches are helpful.

When the value of goods and services changes on a daily basis, say by 3 per cent to 10 per cent per day, the distortions imposed on the economy are of such magnitude that any analysis of end of year financial statements sheds little light on the business' productive capability, working capital needs and other policies. Under such bizarre conditions we have seen two complementary approaches in use: first, some business people simply work in dollars, a currency relatively stable to theirs; but when the economy's distortions are also reflected in the country's dollar prices of goods and services, they switch to a barter business, which is a difficult trade to learn.

Assignment questions

1 What happens to financial ratios under inflation?
2 Are margins inflated? So what?
3 What is inflation's impact on income taxes?
4 How are inventory profits discovered?
5 How are rates of return affected?
6 How should we analyse investment projects?
7 How is the maximum feasible growth affected?
8 Did you spot any mistakes in Santa Rosa's adjusted financial statements?

[12] Disposable funds are the maximum cash flows that can be distributed without harming the company's business capability.

[13] This reflects the mission of the business unit in the market.

[14] This could differ from the present leverage policy.

[15] This, so far, may have been determined at random.

15
Devaluation's impact on the strategic posture

15.1 Origin of devaluations

The currencies of the triad countries are linked practically twenty-four hours a day through the New York, Tokyo, Frankfurt, London and other stock exchanges. Like everything else being traded in these exchanges, very little can be predicted about the future relative prices of the world's main currencies. In the long run, however, the market cannot avoid reflecting the macroeconomic forces in action within the American, Japanese, German and other European economies. In the absence of market mechanisms to evaluate the relative positions of a country's currency, some developing countries have adopted a fixed rate of exchange with respect to the dollar, sometimes coupled with periodic devaluations.

Drawing on our business experience, we consider the macroeconomic changes that occurred in Central America during the 1980s. Until 1979 these countries had maintained a fixed exchange rate with respect to the dollar for about 20 years. This was sustainable because the Central Banks had enough foreign exchange to back the imports generated by the monetary mass. They had access to resources to finance imports, service foreign debt and even to accumulate international reserves.

Central American governments did not have large fiscal deficits to begin with, and when they did, they were able to finance them with international reserves or foreign loans. So the region's currencies were so called 'hard currencies'; internal inflation equalled imported inflation, the region was, indeed, a net capital importer and it also had access to foreign loans. In addition, the growth of the countries' internal credit was proportional to the growth of the GNP, so Central Bank financing was not inflationary.[1]

At the end of 1970s, the deficit of most Central American countries grew out of control and their reserves of foreign exchange were drastically drained by a ten-fold inflation in the price of crude oil. Thus, their commercial balance had to be financed, first, with the international reserves, and then with foreign loans.

Furthermore, between 1978 and 1981 we saw the explosion of Nicaragua's, El Salvador's and Guatemala's violent social revolts, discussed before, which introduced a shift in the direction of investment funds into the economic picture; within just one year, the region turned from being a net importer of investment funds into a net exporter: put simply, business people were disinvesting. Furthermore, the external credit also dropped and Central America had foreign exchange deficits.

[1] Because the economy's liquid coefficient – liquid assets/GNP – was constant.

So, some of these countries started to finance their fiscal deficits with monetary emission not backed by foreign exchange. This triggered the Central American inflationary spiral, which in Nicaragua reached hyper-inflation levels of between 1000 per cent and 10,000 per cent per year and in the other countries it ranged from 10 per cent to 30 per cent per year during the decade of the 1980s. This occurred because the monetary mass chased the international reserves in order to import goods and services, and then chased the goods and services within the frontiers of these countries.

A consequence of such inflation is that local manufacturers and cash crop exporters lose competitiveness in world markets. As inflation grows, alternative imported products and services also gain competitiveness in the local market. Under these conditions everybody loses: employees lose their salary to inflation, exporters lose their competitiveness and the central bank loses foreign exchange.

A vicious circle may take hold of the economy: lower exports produce lower export taxes and a lower generation of foreign exchange; this produces a larger fiscal deficit and smaller reserves from which to finance it, thus more inflationary financing may be necessary. To break this circle, the Central Bank devalues the local currency to restore the competitiveness of the export sector. Of course, if foreign resources become available to finance the deficit, through loans or grants, devaluation may be postponed.

15.2 Aluminum S.A.

To illustrate the impact of inflation and a devaluation on an export industry, consider our business experience with Aluminum S.A. This company manufactured aluminium pots and pans for local consumption and exports to Central American markets. By 1978, the economics of the situation looked as shown in Table 15.1.

Under these financial conditions and low inflation, Aluminum S.A. enjoyed, during 1977/1978, the unitary profit and loss statement shown in Table 15.2. With these operating policies and results we pursued our break-even in Nicaragua and tried to harvest our profits in the Central American common market. Our idea was to chase marginal contributions (C$4.05 per unit) in our export markets, and our break-even money (C$17.10 per unit) in Nicaragua.

Table 15.3 shows the inflation factors as well as the cordoba's devaluation that hit the company during 1978/1979. The new unitary profit and loss statements for under these conditions are shown in Table 15.4.

Table 15.4 shows how Aluminum lost competitiveness under the country's inflationary environment as the contribution of the exported units dropped from C$4.05 to (1.90). This created an incentive to minimize our exports, because with a negative contribution the more we did so, the less money we lost. Unless we wanted to maintain market share by investing the negative contribution, we were forced to abandon export markets. In this way inflation has a direct impact on the export policies of a business unit. These policy changes are best handled by managers close to the problem, because they are closer to the country's economic decision makers.

Table 15.1 Aluminum's basic economic conditions

A Standard production volume: 40,000 units

B Sales policy:

	Price (cords/unit)	*Volume* (units)
Nicaragua:	C$105,0	20,000
Exports:	C$90,0	20,000

C Variable costs as % of sales price:

Component:	*Factory*	*Nicaragua*	*Exports*
Commissions		3	4
Labour	5		
Raw materials	44		
Suppliers	4		
Financial		8	6
Other inputs		2	3
Energy	2		
Contribution	45	87	87

D Fixed costs and expenses:

Salaries	C$580.000
Other inputs	C$90.000
Depreciation	C$80.000
Rent	C$75.000

Table 15.2 Unitary profit and loss statement (C$; low inflation)

	Nicaragua	*Exports*
Sales price	105.00	90.00
Variable sales costs	13.65	11.70
Contribution to standard costs	91.35	78.30
Variable cost	53.62	53.62
Contribution to fixed costs	37.73	24.68
Standard fixed costs	20.63	20.63
Standard costs	74.25	74.25
Profit or loss	17.10	4.05

To restore the competitiveness of the exporting sector, Nicaragua's Central Bank devalued the currency from 7 cordobas per dollar to 10 cordobas per dollar in early 1979. This produced the results shown in Table 15.4, where our contribution per exported unit increased to C$13.45, and affected our export policies again. What this shows is that exporters have to weigh up their export

Table 15.3 The impact of inflation on Aluminum's costs and expenses

Component	*Inflation without devaluation (%)*	*Inflation with devaluation (%)*
Export prices	0	43
Domestic price	7	16
Raw materials	8	43
Labour	12	25
Suppliers	10	30
Energy	8	30
Salaries	8	15
Other inputs	10	30
Average inflation	8.4	39.9

Table 15.4 Unitary profit and loss statement (C$; with inflation)

	Without devaluation		*With devaluation*	
	Nicaragua	*Exports*	*Nicaragua*	*Exports*
Sales price	112.35	90.00	121.80	128.70
Variable sales costs	14.61	11.70	15.83	16.73
Contr. to standard costs	97.74	78.30	105.97	111.97
Variable cost	58.19	58.19	75.05	75.05
Contr. to fixed costs	39.56	20.11	30.92	36.92
Standard fixed cost	22.01	22.01	23.48	23.48
Standard cost	80.20	80.20	98.52	98.52
Profit or loss	17.55	(1.90)	7.45	13.45
Salaries	626.400	667.000		
Other inputs	99.500		117.000	
Depreciation	80.000		80.000	
Rent	75.000		75.000	
Fixed costs	880.900	939.000		

policies in an environment where there is chronic inflation coupled with devaluations, very carefully. It may not be wise to abandon an export market because of a temporary loss of competitiveness only to see it return after devaluation. Country managers must have a clear idea of whether they expect to generate profits in export markets or in the local market as this is important for the business unit's delivery strategies, activities and policies.

But there is another consequence of devaluation: it is the sudden inflation in operating costs. Companies like Aluminum S.A. that work in export markets have a chance to recoup these sudden increases in operating costs through their automatic increase in competitiveness; but companies working only in the local market have to increase their prices to face the sudden inflation. The latter do however, benefit from the price umbrella provided by the immediate increase in the price of competing imports; which is contrary to their pre-devaluation competitive position.

In the following section we discuss the exposure of the different economic players to the problem of inflation and devaluation. We would like to remind the reader that the Central Bank can, and does, transfer some of the benefits of the devaluation to other sectors in the economy, such as financing the fiscal deficit of the central government with an export tax. This actually happened to us in Nicaragua in April of 1979, when the devaluation of 10 cordobas for a dollar was valid for imports, but for exports we only received 9 cordobas per dollar.

15.3 Exposure to devaluation risk

The impact of a devaluation on the different economic sectors depends upon the nature of their business. Let us propose a classification scheme for the various exposures to devaluation risk, by recognizing three variables that determine this risk:

1 The percentage (p) of the goods or services exported.
2 The percentage (q) of imported raw materials.
3 The percentage (r) of financing in hard currency.

Clearly, these percentages may vary from zero to 100 per cent according too the economic activity. Thus, an actor's exposure to devaluation risk falls into one of the eight categories presented in Table 15.5, where an x represents a percentage different from zero. The fifth actor, for instance, represents those non-exporting companies that import a percentage of their raw materials and carry loans in foreign currency. A devaluation impacts upon these actors differently, and we give here a general idea of what happens.

Table 15.5 Exposure to devaluation risk

Actor	*Exports*	*(p%)*	*Imports*	*(q%)*	*Loans*	*(r%)*
1	Exports	x		0		0
2	Exports	x	Imports	x		0
3	Exports	x		0	Debt	x
4	Exports	x	Imports	x	Debt	x
4	Public Sector	x	Imports	x	Debt	x
5		0	Imports	x	Debt	x
6		0	Imports	x		0
7		0		0	Debt	x
8		0		0		0
8	Wage earners	0		0		0

Notice that a currency tied to the dollar can be devalued with respect to it; or with respect to the yen and Deutschmark, as the dollar devalues against them. In the first case it is a decision controlled by the country's Central Bank, in the latter case it is decided by capital markets. It is interesting to notice that our three factors (p, q, y & r) have a different impact when the devaluation is direct or indirect; it all depends upon where our imports come from, where our exports go, and where our foreign loans are held. Thus we consider four situations:

1 Exports to countries with strong currency.
2 Exports to countries with weak currency.
3 Imports from countries with strong currency.
4 Imports from countries with weak currency.

The economic actors presented in Table 15.5 can be separated into two types: the exporters, who are at the core of the country's competitiveness, and the rest. These can be categorized into three types: the non-exporting productive sector, the public sector, and wage earners. These four sectors determine the political-economic game in a country; and accordingly, the benefits of public policy flow in one or another direction.

For instance, a devaluation improves the competitiveness of exporting companies, as shown with our Aluminum S.A. example, whereas non-exporting companies don't benefit from higher competitiveness in other markets. Instead they benefit from the fact that they depend less on imported raw materials, and that the government does not transfer the devaluation benefits to wage earners. In addition, both types of companies benefit from increases in local prices, for as long as the government does not impose price freezes.

Wage earners generally chase behind the effects of a devaluation, as salary increases follow negotiations. Only when salary increases are imposed by decree do they get something immediately, but then, governments do try to keep the economy's competitiveness, and these decrees are designed to be non-inflationary. In conclusion, wage earners end up paying most of a devaluation's costs, whereas the public sector – our original villain – finances its fiscal deficit with special taxes.

This is why it is important to follow the political scene in foreign markets, so that country managers understand the likelihood of devaluations, their size and their connection with the flow of benefits to the different actors depicted in Table 15.5. These decisions involve complex multi-party negotiations.

In summary, when a company exports, a devaluation increases its profitability; but if the devaluation is with respect to the yen, its competitiveness will only be relative to Japanese exports. A devaluation increases the costs of imports, affecting the raw material costs of all importing companies. As usual, the company that best controls the increases in their other costs is best positioned to face a devaluation. A devaluation also affects a company's import policies, which may affect quality of inputs. The biggest exposure to devaluation risk is taken by those companies that don't export, import from the country whose currency was revalued and also have loans in the revalued currency. Such companies have a tough problem on their hands and have to review their operating and financial policies.

15.4 Impact on effective interest rates[2]

The reason it becomes so attractive to take loans in a foreign currency is because the differential in interest rate between the local currency and the selected foreign currency is so high that business people take the risk of a devaluation of their national currency with respect to the hard currency. In these situations it is interesting to examine the impact of a devaluation on such financing decisions.

Consider a loan for Sfr.3,000,000 (three million Swiss francs) obtained at a 9 per cent interest rate. The loan is equivalent to C$280,000,000 at a 93.33 Colones per Swiss franc exchange rate. If a year later this exchange rate remains unchanged, then the company saves the difference between the interest expenses it would have paid in Costa Rica and those it actually paid to a foreign bank. However, if a devaluation of the local currency occurs with respect to the Swiss franc these savings may not only disappear but also turn into a loss.

Let us now assume that in a year, the Colon devalues 20 per cent with respect to the Swiss franc. What effective interest rate would have been paid? This problem can be generalized as seen below. Let:

r = contracted interest rate,
d = devaluation rate with respect to the currency in which the loan was made,
i = effective interest rate,
P = amount of the loan, and
A = accumulated debt.

then,

$$A = P(1 + r) \text{ is the pre-devaluation debt.}$$

A devaluation increases the cost of each foreign currency unit by d%, thus there will be an increment in local currency to:

$$A = P(1 + r)(1 + d)$$
$$\text{or} \quad A = P\{1 + [r(1 + d) + d]\}$$
$$\text{or} \quad A = P(1 + i).$$

where the effective interest rate is,

$$i = r(1 + d) + d. \tag{15.1}$$

Applying this principle to our example we obtain:

$$d = 20\% \text{ and } r = 9\%$$

[2] Based on: Marín José, N. y Werner Ketelhöhn; Inversiones Estratégicas: Un Enfoque Multidimensional; San José, Costa Rica: Asociación Libro Libre, 1986.

$$i = 0.09(1 + 0.20) + 0.20,$$
$$i = 30.8\%.$$

In a country where there are yearly devaluations we must adjust the beginning of year interest rate with equality 15.1. For instance, assume three consecutive yearly devaluations of 20, 17, and 22 per cent of Costa Rica's Colon with respect to the Swiss franc, then our loan contracted at 9 per cent per year would be costing:

$$i = 0.09(1.20) + 0.20 \quad = \quad 30.8\% \text{ the first year,}$$
$$i = 0.30.8(1.17) + 0.17 \quad = \quad 53.04\% \text{ the second year, and}$$
$$i = 0.53(1.22) + 0.22 \quad = \quad 86.7\% \text{ the third year.}$$

But how can anybody make money with such interest rates? In countries where inflation runs at 25 per cent or more, these interest payments can be made in local currency, but the company assuming such financial risks rarely gets ahead unless it exports to the countries in which they contracted these loans, or similarly hard currency markets. Thus, financial exposure to devaluation risk must be carefully evaluated before accepting these loans.

In some foreign markets it is customary to devalue the local currency with respect to the dollar by a series of mini-devaluations. In such cases, we can estimate an average yearly devaluation through the life of an investment project and proceed to estimate expected rates of return which include the impact of these devaluations.

$$r = \frac{r' - d}{1 + d} \tag{15.2}$$

where:

r' is the apparent IRR in local currency,
r is the effective IRR, and
d is the average yearly devaluation rate.

Equation 15.2 shows that a periodic devaluation reduces the real internal rate of return just as inflation does. This means that the impact of the devaluation is expressed in the flows of the project, and the apparent IRR is then adjusted (reduced) to its 'real' effective value.

15.5 Periodic devaluations

In our experience, when the financial disequilibria in small and open economies are not corrected by a devaluation, price distortions will eventually appear in the economy because the official rate of exchange differs from the parallel – black – market rate. Under such conditions, currency exchange businesses flourish and the prices of goods and services may also suffer unimaginable distortions. Amazing transactions may take place, as in one case where a colleague bought in local currency, a US$150,000 villa in exchange for a US$20,000 used car.

When these disequilibria are maintained for too long, the economy is awakened by a shocking quantum devaluation, which impacts violently upon the economy. This is why some countries, like Costa Rica, have adopted the policy of monthly devaluations that serve several purposes. Starting in 1983, Costa Rica has followed a policy of mini-devaluations which by 1991 were made each week. In 1991 the Colon was devalued by about 30 per cent with respect to the dollar, and the economy was able to absorb this gradual devaluation over one year without too much disruption to the businesses operating within the country.

This policy allows the country to finance the fiscal deficit with internal resources, without having access to fresh external resources. Internal inflation, of course, is higher than imported inflation because there is a disequilibrium between the real internal production of goods and services and the demand created by this monetary mass.

However, with a known policy of mini-devaluations business people are able to estimate the cost of imports with some accuracy, whereas exporters are assured that their competitiveness will be periodically restored by these mini-devaluations. This creates some certainty in business, and country managers are able to operate with both some degree of certainty in their decision-making, and some understanding of their 'real' competitive position in international markets.

What is really happening is that the Central Bank rotates the problem of financing the fiscal deficit between the four economic actors described in section 15.3. For instance, for a while the Central Bank finances the deficit with inflation, which hurts wage earners and exporters, but the public sector solves its financing problem; then a mini-devaluation restores the competitiveness of exporters; and finally salaries get adjusted. Next, the inflationary cycle begins again.

A devaluation recognizes that the local currency has diminished its purchasing power with respect to the countries from which we import; and this is reflected in the amount of the devaluation. This decrease in purchasing power can be seen in the level of inflation within the country as compared with the imported inflation. It is the difference between the internal and imported inflation which creates the need for devaluation.

For instance, with 25 per cent inflation in Costa Rica and 5 per cent inflation in the USA, the devaluation necessary to maintain the purchasing power of Costa Rica's currency is roughly 20 per cent. Otherwise, the excess monetary mass would affect the competitiveness of the exporting sector; this is why rotating the problem of financing the fiscal deficit is a viable way out, as summarized in Table 15.6.

Table 15.6 Impact of inflation and devaluation

Economic sectors	*Inflation*	*Devaluation*
Exporters	Lose export competitiveness	Recover competitiveness
Other companies	Lose internal competitiveness	Raise prices
Salaried People	Lose purchasing power Social pressures	Salary adjustments Social pressures
Public Sector	Finances deficit Social problems	Export taxes

But a mini-devaluation policy does not cure the original problem: the Central Government's fiscal deficit. What it does is to rotate the financing problem among the four sectors. However, it does create the political space to work at the problem of reducing the size of the public sector. This cannot be done immediately. Time is needed for well-meaning politicians to reduce the number of public employees and programmes gradually. It is a matter of minimizing the political costs, and providing time for job creation in the private sector.

15.6 Conclusions

What we have learned from these experiences is that country managers operating in inflationary markets have to adjust their policies to permanent disruptions of the economic environment. Specifically, long-term financing has to be examined for its exposure to inflationary and devaluation risks. But on the other hand, there may be some benefits and planned financial profits if long-term debt is acquired in local currency at pre-inflation fixed interest rates. A whole new game of monetary caution and speculation may open new opportunities and risks and distract the management team from its fundamental business.

For instance, consider a loan of C$5,000,000 (Colones) for 5 years at a fixed 35 per cent yearly interest rate. Suppose that we foresee an average 25 per cent inflation rate for the next 5 years and yearly devaluations of 20 per cent. Should we take this loan? The answer to this question is yes. Consider that the effective interest rate is:

$$(35\text{–}25)/1.25 \text{ or } 8\% \text{ per year in local currency.}$$

What appeared to be a terribly high interest rate is reduced to something affordable in local currency, once inflation is taken into account. So, there are opportunities available under inflation and devaluation; even when these interest rates are indexed, the principal of the loan may not be.

Assignment questions

1 What is the origin of inflation?
2 Why do countries devalue their currency?
3 What is dumping?
4 How can a business be exposed to devaluation risk?
5 How can we make money with devaluations and loans?
6 What happens to the effective interest rate?

Conclusive remarks

The purpose of this book is to provide a set of ideas and organizing concepts for use when thinking about the strategic posture of business units operating in international markets. It is hoped that these will be useful to practising managers, strategy consultants and business schools professors in the solution of strategic adjustment problems.

They key message is that there is no such thing as a purely deliberate – nor randomly generated – strategic posture[1] in corporations engaged in global competition: a business unit's strategic posture results from adapting corporate strategic postures to a market's environmental pressures. In short, global corporate strategic postures are sensitive to market-specific environmental events, human resources, leadership style and subsidiary culture.

Since no one knows enough to work out every detail of a stategic posture in a market in advance, nor how correctly to forecast all environmental pressures, business unit managers must constantly adjust the strategic posture of their firm to the pressures of the environment in which they operate. Business unit managers must construct a strategic posture that incorporates all market-specific demands and pressures while maintaining those key elements of the corporate, strategic posture that characterize their firm. This process of strategic adaptation is essentially a synthetic proposition: the business unit manager identifies key events, trends and pressures in his environment and examines their impact on the strategic posture and operations of his company.

This book reflects the fact that international business cannot be reduced to foreign trade, currency speculation, accounting or politics, but that at some point in an international manager's career he has to live, work and successfully lead a business unit within a foreign environment, where economics, politics and other events interact with the strategic posture and operations of the firm. Therefore, this book not only offers the missing unified framework for the country manager's job but also complements publications in all other categories, particularly those dealing with managing subsidiaries in foreign markets.

This book is based upon the value of learning from real businesses. The business ideology presented in Part One was derived from ideas formed through the observation of Benetton, IMS, NWZ and SEMCO. This approach to learning also contributed to Part Two in the form of the search for similarities and differences between ABB Robotics, IBM and Uponor Oy.

[1] The strategic posture of a corporation is composed of its shared vision, specific objectives, strategic decisions and business policies.

Part One: Competitive and Cooperative Business Strategy

Presents our easy-to-use framework for strategic analysis. It originated in the theoretical frameworks developed by both researchers and consultants in triad countries.

In summary, answers to the question 'How do we add value in this business unit?' are found in two steps. First, we investigate the systemic question, how are the different businesses participating in this industry linked? This leads us to understand the structure and dynamics in the industry as well as the alternative coordination mechanism found in the management of the flows of people, information, goods and money. The *enterprise system* emphasizes the understanding of the links between the raw material suppliers, the intermediate businesses and the final consumer. An industry's definition depends on the businesses included in the enterprise system, clearly a personal decision. The enterprise system is industry related, it defines the industry and describes how the different businesses are linked.

Second, we investigate the integration strategies followed by the most successful competitors and the activities they chose to perform themselves in their search for profits. This defines the *business system* used by the different competitors. Understanding their business system permits us to also understand the way these companies have chosen to add value – *their value adding activities*; the technology used in these activities – *the technological chain*; and the cost incurred with these activities – *their cost structure*. The business system is company specific, it describes how specific competitors have chosen to deliver their products–services to the final consumer.

To compete in today's demanding environment, companies must make sure that the business system that they choose to manage can deliver the desired goods/services with the high perceived quality and low delivered cost of world class competitors. This can be achieved if the whole system is coordinated. But coordination really means strategic management. Therefore, the company must make sure it is choosing the right integration strategy in the enterprise system; and the way to do that is to recognize and adopt – over time – those generic strategies that yield the most profitable system in the long run.

In this sense, vertical integration decisions are at the centre of a company's strategy: they not only determine the shape of its activity chain but they also determine the long-run overall efficiency of the business system that the company adopted and the coordination mechanisms required to manage the company's strategic posture.

The process of strategic analysis is straightforward. It begins by understanding the possible integration strategies as well as the possible sourcing, processing, delivery, and support activities in an industry. That is, it identifies the generic ways of competing within the industry and the corresponding key success factors (KSFs).

A company that chooses to compete with one set of generic strategies must be well able to identify the KSFs. By matching the strengths of the company with the KSFs of each generic strategy we can determine which of the many strategies may be followed by the company. Clearly, for each different set of strategies, there may be some KSFs in which the company is weak.

Strategic investment projects are generated in the following way: they are projects conceived to increase company capabilities in key success factors that are precisely defined for use in the chosen generic strategy.

In summary, to understand the strategy of a company, consulting teams start with a set of hypotheses about the generic strategies in the industry and the key success factors for each strategy. Then they check their understanding of the industry by comparing their hypotheses with documented facts. Once they are satisfied with their understanding of the industry, they compare the company's capabilities with the KSFs of the generic strategies. By identifying the strategy that best fits the company's capabilities, consultants are able to select and recommend investment projects necessary to build strengths in those KSFs in which the company is weak.

Part Two: International Business Strategy

The essential forces affecting the international corporation and alternative organizational forms were discussed in this part.

We found that an internally negotiated strategy allows a company's management and work force to concentrate on the value adding activities in their organization, while avoiding unnecessary overhead costs and diluted energy in political fights. As at IMS, employees in companies following internally negotiated strategies concentrate on adding value.

An externally negotiated strategy allows a company to concentrate on its distinctive competence while benefiting from efficiencies in other firms which, in turn, concentrate on their distinctive competencies. The specialization choice is based on a complicated blend of motivation, participation, information and technology. Benetton is able to invest in big warehouses and telecommunication technology while its subcontractors do so in labour intensive activities; the *NWZ* is able to concentrate on national news editing, printing and advertising while the local partners concentrate on what they do best, local news editing and newspaper distribution; and IMS' machinists are able to concentrate on improving their skill base and manufacturing processes while management gets the space to pursue a bigger client base.

Building a negotiated strategy is based on Kupia Kumi[2] – the attitude of letting others prosper while we prosper – in fact, successful growth in cooperative networks can only be achieved if all members of the partnership can grow and prosper simultaneously. The reason for this is that the core company has chosen not to compete with them, but rather to concentrate its efforts on specific and complementary economic activities: managing the flows of people, information, goods and money.

The network organization also seems to be an effective answer to the question of how to inject entrepreneurialism into mammoth corporations. We have seen how Lithonia and General Electric are in the process of creating external

[2] 'Kupia Kumi' a Nicaraguan Misquito Indian expression for 'eat and let all eat'.

networks and internally negotiated strategies respectively. We believe that after careful study of a company's industrial environment, some type of network partnership can be developed in its industry. The advice we offer is: go out and look for potential partnerships that have not yet been created.

For instance, marketing solutions to customer problems does not provide a fundamental answer to competing against low-cost hardware manufacturers. Adding new service layers to the core hardware product brings high margins. However, the high risk nature of the business and the new market in which the corporation gets involved, changes the basis for profitability. We can't pretend that the exploitation of this additional value added costs nothing. In fact, if exploited to perfection, none of the additional profits generated should go to the hardware vendors; they should all belong to the partners of the service organizations. Thus, if a corporation wants a share of these additional profits, without degenerating into a simple distribution channel of value-adding service subcontractors, a new form of industrial organization needs to be created: the Hammock Organisation.

Thus, to remain competitive in the marketing of solutions in the 1990s, a corporation needs to implement a dual market strategy: first, exploit the top of the pyramid by offering solutions that really add value; and second, face the lowest-cost hardware competitor with low-cost, high-quality, commodity hardware, and compete with them in exploiting the price umbrella created by proprietary top-of-the-range models.

Moreover, corporate competitiveness is gained by cultivating core businesses. Strategic management must identify which core competencies and supporting technologies are to be cultivated. Corporate management should then spend time nourishing, building and protecting the people that carry the corporation's distinctive competencies. Furthermore, these people should be placed in core businesses so that synergy can take place, protected from organizational politics.

Part Three: Understanding Environmental Pressures

Here, simple models demonstrating how to understand the economy and political forces in a country were presented. The identification of environmental events, trends and pressures – with their significance to the strategic posture of a company – were discussed.

We found that for Nestlé, Tetrapak and other corporations, there was more to the world than Western Europe, Japan and the USA; and many more environments than the competitive one. For corporations with major operations in Russia, Ukraine, India, mainland China, Brazil, Mexico, Indonesia, Philippines, Nigeria and the like, we recommend looking at a few of the alternative environments before deciding on a global strategic posture.

In adapting a corporation's strategic posture to the different country environments, dilemmas over technological adaptation; new product introduction; political and economic situations; and operational policies, appear for each country. In all of these situations the basic dilemma between central coordination and local adaptation holds, but the solutions adopted are not always the same; instead, they are country specific.

For example, a technology is appropriate to a country, only if it is economically more productive than the challenging technology. So, how much of the technology used in each country should be decided at headquarters? Products marketed in countries with young populations are usually different from those marketed in countries with ageing populations; which products should have a global standard? The political processes of certain countries demand different strategic postures from developed western countries; what should be the global ethical posture? And obviously, financial policies and accounting practices in high inflation countries should differ from those used by the same corporations in low inflation countries.

The process of strategic adaptation is essentially a synthetic proposition: the management team identifies key events, trends and pressures in its environment so that it can examine their impact on the strategic posture and operations of its business unit. It is a bottom-up process in which all executives in a market participate in the adaptation of the strategic posture of the corporation to specific environmental pressures in that market. The philosophy of this approach is to push strategic decision-making closer to the people with market knowledge; closer to the country/customer.

By specifying the events, trends and pressures we can evaluate whether or not these phenomena have a positive or negative impact on the strategic posture of the corporation. Once all events, trends and pressures have been specified, a strategic agenda for the participants in the industrial sector has been created. Then, business people can act either as an association or as individuals in their efforts to influence changes in the environment through lobbying. Each industrial sector builds its own strategic agenda, as the events, trends and pressures affect them differently. A corporation's strategic agenda is a simple list of events, trends and pressures and their impact on the corporations' operations in the country. This agenda must generate action plans for different scenarios constructed by the agenda. If the pressures are too strong, the strategic posture of the corporation may be modified.

The strategic agenda defines the events, trends and pressures occurring in the environment, whose impact on the strategic posture of a corporation must be evaluated.

Experienced business people try to understand the country's culture, politics and economy by appealing to frameworks originating in these disciplines. They ask: why oversimplify a country's complexity when we have disciplines offering useful frameworks to understand it? This fundamentalist approach to country analysis starts with macroeconomics.

In our experience, country managers have a rudimentary understanding of how economies work – they are doers, not economists – and use their views to raise questions with experienced economic consultants. We strongly recommend using such expert advice. In Appendix B we presented a simplistic framework for understanding an economy. In Part Four of this book we showed how country managers cooperating with macroeconomists were able to understand the economic turning points in Nicaragua in 1979. The reasoning presented, however, does not apply to all environmental conditions; country specialists should and must be recruited to construct a fundamental understanding of an economy.

Thus, instead of representing country risks with a single number – measuring country risk – our fundamentalist approach provides a broader understanding of what is happening in the environment of the host country. We propose first to understand the political and economical actors, their objectives, resources and alliances. Next, we propose to understand the economic decisions and public policy formulation, so that likely scenarios are identified. Then, we believe that, with our understanding of the pressures applied to the decision-makers, we can guess what the major policy decisions will be. In this way, inflation, devaluations, economic incentives, social pressures and so on, can be monitored close enough to the real events, so that we can guide the business unit through that environmental ocean.

Part Four: Doing Business in Turbulent Environments

Here we discussed the adaptation of a strategic posture to countries subjected to violent social revolts. We called this managing in turbulent environments. Among others, we discussed changes originating in inflationary forces and violently changing environments.

The main theme of this fourth and last section is concerned with the processes that adapt a corporation's strategic posture to cope with ongoing disruptions of the social, political and economic environment. In summary, the intensity with which a disruption is perceived by management depends upon the duration of the turbulence. Since managers eventually learn to cope with sustained long-run turbulence, its perceived intensity tends to decline over time.

Doing business in turbulent environments requires flexible management and adaptable business policies. Headquarters must include local managers' perceptions in its strategic decision process. Likewise, country managers' knowledge of local economic and political conditions must be tapped if the corporation decides to compete in a turbulent business environment. The global implications of changing corporate business policies in response to local conditions, i.e. the message that this sends to other countries, must be evaluated at headquarters in a logical and objective manner; put in place, it forms a part of the market-to-market learning processes.

These crises may also occur in developed countries like USA (Los Angeles in 1992), Russia (Moscow in 1992) and Germany (Berlin in 1992), not permanently subjected to violent social revolts. The Central American experience suggests that, since there is no time to learn in crisis situations, crisis management teams must not only understand the enterprise system in a specific market but also be trained to handle crises.

However, since no one knows enough to forecast all environmental pressures in advance, excellent European companies tend to adapt their business practice to specific country conditions in a series of small steps rather than relying on centrally conceived sweeping strategies. As expressed by Mr Helmuth

Maucher's address on management practice to an attentive audience of IMEDE professors in spring 1988, his efforts to simplify corporate reporting practices included reducing country reports to one page of reliable figures; he added, 'this forces country managers to think about what is really important and eliminates the need for further analysis at headquarters'.

The role of the CEO is to transmit his perspective about the business across the corporation, so that this perspective influences the way in which far away country managers handle difficult situations. Responsibility and authority for these decisions must be articulated by top management so that country managers, who are in touch with local realities, can react with flexibility, while keeping HQ informed. They should also open communication channels with economic and political authorities to maintain the flows of information.

Contradiction between local and global policies reflects differences in the perspective of a subsidiary's mission; but this is also a pleasant reality: no matter how centralized a CEO wants to make his business, local management, if of any value, will act according to local needs, whether or not it violates global policies. The job of local management is to defend the best interests of their subsidiary; and the job of the CEO is to provide a guiding business perspective.

Finally we point out the most important financial policies to be revised when the economic environment presents permanent inflations below 25 per cent per year. For higher inflation, we don't believe traditional financial approaches are helpful. The details of these analyses can be found in consultation with financial specialists.

When the value of goods and services changes on a daily basis, say by to 10 per cent per day, the distortions imposed on the economy are of such magnitude that any analysis of end of year financial statements sheds little light on productive capability of the business, working capital needs and other policies. Under such bizarre conditions we have seen two complementary approaches in use: first, some business people simply work in dollars, a currency relatively stable to theirs; but when the economy's distortions are also reflected in the country's dollar prices of goods and services, they switch to a barter business, which is a difficult trade to learn.

What we have learned from these experiences is that country managers operating in inflationary markets have to adjust their policies to permanent disruptions of the economic environment. Specifically, long-term financing has to be examined for its exposure to inflationary and devaluation risks. But on the other hand, there may be some benefits and planned financial profits if long-term debt is acquired in local currency at pre-inflation fixed interest rates. A whole new game of monetary caution and speculation may open new opportunities and risks and distract the management team from its fundamental business.

In essence, this book takes the international business strategy debate a step further: it deals with those strategic problems that every business unit manager, business school educator, and business consultant confronts in his international, executive, teaching and consulting career.

Strategic thinking demands a proactive attitude and a deeply held conviction that the future is built with managerial decisions based on appropriate business ideologies and not with mysterious meta-economic myths.

Bibliography

A Cases

Distribución de Alimentos: Decisiones bajo Emergencia.
Case: Emergencia Nacional en Naduras.
Case: Societé de Banques Suisse (A).
Case: Kay-Maha (A), (B), (C).
Case: Promoviendo Exportaciones.
Case: Profusa.
Case: Agrosusa.
Case: Hercasa 1986.
Case: Transeguros de El Salvador.
Case: Pinturas Estilo S.A.
Case: Gusa (A) (B).
Case: Turrialba Mining Company (A), (B).
Case: Delipan (A) & (B).
Case: Aluminum S.A. (A), (B).
Case: Paccasa-Lombard (A), (B), (C).
Case: Cemsa (A), (B).
Case: Pedrera, S.A. (A), (B), (C).
Case: Algosa.
Case: Panda.
Case: Vistalona S.A.
Case: La Favorita (A), (B), (C), (D), (F).
Case: Sembrando Algodón con la Revolución.
Case: Cerámicas POAS S.A. (A), (B), (C), (D), (F).
Case: Un Problema de Etica.
Case: Cerveza Suprema S.A.
Case: Multiban S.A.
Case: Santorino Industrial.
Case: Banco de Comercio S.A.
Case: Finca 'La Montaña'.
Case: Standard Fruit Company in Nicaragua (A).
Case: Joyería La Perla (A), (B), (C).
Case: Una Tonelada de Ladrillos.
Case: Indunic (A).
Case: Ideology Exercise.
Case: Agenda Estratégica de las Universidades Centroamericanas.
Case: Nestlé–Rowntree (A), (B), (C).
Case: Berlingske Tidende (A), (B), (C).
Case: The Fashion Success Story of the 1980s.
Case: Edizione Holding SpA. (A), (B), (C), (D), (E).
Case: The European Newspaper Industry in 1988.

Case: The European Women's Outerware Industry in 1987.
Case: Honda (B) a Harvard Business School case number 9–384–030.
Case: The *Nordwest Zeitung*. Copyright by IMD in March of 1988.
Case: Edizione Holding Sp.A. case series Copyright by IMD in 1991.
Case: Building The Benetton System. GM 437, Copyright by IMD in 1990.
Case: Aldo Palmeri: Taking Charge (A) and (B). IMD cases GM 463 and GM 464 Copyright by IMD in 1991.
Case: Palmeri, Aldo, 'Managing Growth', IMD case GM 467 Copyright by IMD in 1991.

B Books and articles

Abell, Derek F., *Defining the Business*, Prentice-Hall Inc., 1980.
Abegleen, C. James and Stalk, George Jr., *Kaisha: the Japanese Corporation*, Basic Books Inc., 1985.
Ackoff, Russell, *Redesigning the Future*, John Wiley & Sons, 1974.
Andrews, Kenneth R., *The Concept of Corporate Strategy*, Dow Jones-Irwin, 1971.
Bartlett, Christopher and Ghosal, Sumantra., *Managing Across Borders: the Transnational Solution*, Harvard Business School Press, 1989.
Brandt, Allen, "Evaluación de Desebolsos de Capital bajo Inflación: Compendio', *Business Horizons*, Vol. 19, No. 6, 1978, pp. 30–9.
Bilas, Richard A., *Microeconomic Theory: a Graphical Analysis*, MacGraw-Hill Company, 1967.
Bower, Joseph L., *Simple Economic Tools for Strategic Analysis*, 9–373–094, Publishing division, Harvard Business School, 1972, Boston, MA 02163.
Bright, J.R., *A Brief Introduction to Technology Forecasting*, Permaquid Press, 1972.
'Cadbury Schweppes: more than chocolate and tonic', Sir Adrian Cadbury interviewed by Timothy B. Blodgett, *Harvard Business Review*, Jan.–Feb. 1983.
Conference Board, The, *This Business of Issues: Coping with the Company's Environments*, 1979.
Corey, Raymond E., *Marketing Strategy – an Overview*, 579–054, Publishing division, Harvard Business School, 1978, Boston, MA 02163.
Chapman, Peter F., 'Un Método para Explorar el Futuro', *Long Range Planning*, Feb. 1987.
Davis, John H. and Goldberg, Ray A., *A Concept of Agribusiness*, Division of Research, Harvard Graduate School of Business Administration, Boston, Mass, 1957.
DeNero, Henry, 'Creating the "hyphenated" corporation', *The McKinsey Quarterly*, 1990. No. 4.
Delbeke, Jos, research assistant at the Centrum voor Economische Studien, Katholieke Universiteit Leuven, Van Evenstraat 2b, B–3000 Leuven, Belgium, 'Recent long–wave theories: a critical survey', *Futures*, Aug. 1961.
Economist, The, Lighting The Way, an article in the Management Focus section of 6 Oct. 1990.

Eisenhardt, Kathleen M., 'Speed and strategic choice: how managers accelerate decision making', *California Management Review*, spring 1990.

Ekman, Jan, 'The scrapping of forecasts', *Euromoney*, Oct. 1981.

Fahey Liam, King, William R. and Narayanan, Vadake K., 'Environmental scanning and forecasting in strategic planning – the state of the art', *Long Range Planning*, Vol. 14, Feb. 1981.

Ferguson, Charles, 'Computers and the coming of the U.S. Keiretsu', *Harvard Business Review*, July–Aug. 1990.

Gilbert, Xavier and Strebel, Paul, 'Developing competitive advantage' in Guth, William (Ed.), *The Handbook of Business Strategy*, 1986–1987 Year Book.

Gilbert, Xavier and Strebel, Paul, 'Taking advantage of industry shifts', *European Management Journal*, Vol. 7, No. 4, 1989.

Hamel, Gary and Prahalad, C.K., 'Strategic intent', *Harvard Business Review*, May–June 1989.

Hanna, Alistair M. and Lundquist, Jerrold T., 'Creative strategies', *The McKinsey Quarterly*, No. 3, 1990.

Henderson, John, 'Plugging into strategic partnership: the critical IS connection', *Sloan Management Review*, spring 1990.

Iacocca, Lee with Novak, William, *An Autobiography*, Bantam Books, July 1986.

Informe Anual, Banco Central de Nicaragua, años 1976, 1977 y 1978.

Instituto Nacional de Vivienda y Urbanismo, *1984: Encuesta de Demanda Efectiva*, Costa Rica.

Instituto Nacion de Vivienda y Urbanismo, *1985: Encuesta de Demanda Efectiva*, Costa Rica.

Instituto Nacion de Vivienda y Urbanismo, *Boletín Estadístico de 1984*, Costa Rica.

Johnston, Russell and Lawrence, Paul, 'Beyond vertical integration – the rise of the value-adding partnership', *Harvard Business Review*, July–Aug. 1988.

Ketelhöhn Werner, Boscheck Ralph, *et al.* Compaq Computer Corporation. IMD Case Copyright 1991 by International Institute for Management Development, Lausanne, Switzerland.

Ketelhöhn, Werner, 'Foreign investment risks: operating problems under violent social change', Imede note.

Ketelhöhn, Werner, 'Crisis-management teams will ease the turbulence', *The Wall Street Journal/Europe Tuesday*, 22 Aug. 1989.

Ketelhöhn, Werner, 'Managerial problems in violent social revolts: the Central American experience', Imede working paper, Apr. 1983.

Ketelhöhn, Werner R. and Marin, Jose N., *Inversiones Estrategicas: Un Enfoque Multidimensional*, San José, Costa Rica, Asociación Libro Libre, 1986.

Ketelhöhn, Werner, 'Doing business in turbulent environments', *IMEDE Perspectives for Managers*, No. 4, June 1989.

Ketelhöhn, Werner, Jarilla, J. Carlos and Kubes, Jan, 'Turnaround management is not Rambo management', *European Management Journal*, Vol. 9, No. 2, June 1991.

Ketelhöhn, Werner, 'The missing link in the solutions business: managing flows through business systems', *European Management Journal*, Vol. 10, No. 1, March 1992.

Killing, Peter y and Fry, Joseph N., 'Managing change: pace, targets and tactics', *Perspectives for Managers*, No. 4, IMEDE, Jan. 1986.

Kotter, John, *The General Managers*, The Free Press, 1982.

Kotter, John, *A Force for Change: How Leadership Differs from Management*, The Free Press, 1990.

Lindenberg, Marc and Crosby, Benjamin, *Managing Development: the Political Dimension*, The Kumarian Press, 1982.

Loomis, Carol J., 'State farm is of the charts', *Fortune*, 8 Apr. 1991.

Lovelock, Christopher and Vendermerwe, Sandra,

Magizaner, Ira and Patinkin, Mark, *The Silent War: Inside the Global Business Battles Shaping America's Future*, Random House, New York, 1989.

Maucher, Helmuth, 'Future aspects of Nestlé's global business strategies', 9 Apr. 1988, Tokyo, Japan.

McMillan, John, 'Managing suppliers: incentive systems in Japanese and U.S. industry', *California Management Review*, Summer 1990.

Montgomery, Cynthia A. and Porter, Michael E., 'Strategy: seeking and securing competitive advantage', *Harvard Business Review*, 1991.

Myers, Stewart C., 'Finance theory and financial strategy', *Interfaces*, 14, Jan–Feb. 1984, pp. 127–37.

Neubauer, Friedriech and Solomon, Norman B., 'A managerial view of environmental analysis', *Long Range Planning*, vol. 10, Apr. 1977.

Ohmae, Kenichi, 'The global logic of strategic alliances', *Harvard Business Review*, Mar.–Apr. 1989.

Ohmae, Kenichi, *The Mind of the Strategist*, McGraw-Hill, 1982.

Ohmae, Kenichi, *Triad Power: the Coming Shape of Global Competition*, The Free Press, 1985.

Peters, Thomas J. and Waterman, Robert Jr., *In Search of Excellence*, Harper and Row, 1982.

Porter, Michael E., *Competitive Strategy*, The Free Press, 1980.

Porter, Michael E., *Competitive Advantage*, The Free Press, 1985.

Porter, Michael E., 'From competitive advantage to corporate strategy', *Harvard Business Review*, May–June 1987.

Porter, Michael E., 'On competitive strategy', *Harvard Business School*, Video Series, 1988.

Prahalad, C.K. and Hamel, Gary, 'The core competence of the corporation', *Harvard Business Review*, May–June 1990.

Ramirez, Noel E., 'Las Causas de la Inflación en Economías Pequeñas en Vías de Desarrollo con Tasas Fijas de Cambio: Un Análisis Comparativo de Costa Rica y Nicaragua', disertación doctoral, Universidad de Yale, 1982.

Rappaport, Alfred, 'Como Medir la Capacidad de Crecimiento de una Compañía durante la Inflación', *Harvard Business Review*, 1978.

Rappaport, Andrews and Halevi, Shmuel, 'The computerless computer company, *Harvard Business Review*, July–Aug. 1991.

Rumelt, Richard P., Strategy, Structure and Economic Performance, and 'Diversity and Profitability', UCLA Working Paper, 1977.

Salter S. Malcolm and Porter, Michael E., *Note on Diversification as a Strategy*, 9–382–192, publishing division Harvard Business School, 1982–Rev 6–86, Boston, MA 02163.

Sakai, Kuniyasu, 'The feudal world of Japanese manufacturing', *Harvard Business Review*, Nov.–Dec. 1990.

Saxenian, Anna Lee, 'Regional networks and the resurgence of Silicon Valley', *California Management Review*, autumn 1990.

Schumacher, E.F., *Small is Beautiful: Economics as if People Mattered*, Perennial Library, Harper & Row, 1973.

Schroeder, Dean and Robinson, Alan, 'America's most successful export to Japan: continuous improvement programs', *Sloan Management Review*, spring 1991.

Selnick, Philip. *Leadership in Administration: a Sociological Interpretation*, Harper and Row, 1957.

Senge, Peter M., 'The leader's new work: building learning organizations', *Sloan Management Review*, autumn 1990.

Smothers, Norman, 'Patterns of Japanese strategy: strategic combination of strategies', *Strategic Management Journal*, Vol. 11, 1990, pp. 521–33.

Stewart, Thomas A., 'GE keeps those ideas coming', *Fortune*, 12 Aug. 1991.

Stryker, Perrin, 'Can you analyze this problem?: a management exercise', *Harvard Business Review*, May–June 1965.

Stryker, Perrin, 'How to analyze that problem: Part II of a management exercise', *Harvard Business Review*, July–Aug. 1965.

Turpin V., Dominique, Gambare, '"Never Say Die!" Why Japanese Companies Won't Give Up', *IMD Perspective for Managers*, No. 3, 1991.

Ulshak, L. Francis, *Finishing Unfinished Business: Creative Problem Solving, The 1979 Annual Handbook for Group Facilitators*, University Associates.

US Government Printing Office 1980. *The Global 2000 Report to the President–Entering the Twenty-First Century*, Vol. One.

Von Braun, Christoph-Friedrich, 'The acceleration trap', *Sloan Management Review*, autumn 1990.

Webber, Alan, 'Concensus, continuity, and common sense: an interview with Compaq's Rod Canion', *Harvard Business Review*, July–Aug. 1990.

Index